THIS WILL ONLY HURT A LITTLE

· · · · · · · · ·

BUSY PHILIPPS

TOUCHSTONE

New York   London   Toronto   Sydney   New Delhi

Touchstone
An Imprint of Simon & Schuster, Inc.
1230 Avenue of the Americas
New York, NY 10020

Many names and identifying details have been changed.

First Touchstone hardcover edition October 2018

TOUCHSTONE and colophon are registered
trademarks of Simon & Schuster, Inc.

For information about special discounts for bulk purchases,
please contact Simon & Schuster Special Sales at
1-866-506-1949 or business@simonandschuster.com.

The Simon & Schuster Speakers Bureau can bring authors to your
live event. For more information or to book an event contact the
Simon & Schuster Speakers Bureau at 1-866-248-3049 or visit our
website at www.simonspeakers.com.

Interior design by Jill Putorti
Endpaper and interior illustrations by Geoff McFetridge

Manufactured in the United States of America

10   9   8   7   6   5   4   3   2

Library of Congress Cataloging-in-Publication Data

Names: Philipps, Busy, 1979- author.
Title: This will only hurt a little / Busy Philipps.
Description: First Touchstone hardcover edition. | New York : Touchstone, 2018.
Identifiers: LCCN 2018036731 | ISBN 9781501184710 (hardcover)
Subjects: LCSH: Philipps, Busy, 1979- | Actors—United States—Biography.
Classification: LCC PN2287.P465 A3 2018 | DDC 791.4502/8092 [B] —dc23
   LC record available at https://lccn.loc.gov/2018036731

ISBN: 978-1-5011-8471-0
ISBN: 978-1-5011-8473-4 (ebook)

This book is for my mother.

"When there's nothing left to burn,
you have to set yourself on fire."
YOUR EX-LOVER IS DEAD
(STARS)

ALL OF THE LIGHTS
(Kanye West)

Once, a (former) guy friend of mine, who happens to be gorgeous and famous and all of the things, said this to me: "You know, I think people would consider you really beautiful, if only you didn't talk so much. Your personality is *just a lot*. Don't get me wrong, I love you, but I think people get distracted by that."

My clear reaction should have been, "Ewww. Go fuck yourself."

But for so long, even with my *strong personality*, telling a man to fuck off wasn't easy for me to do. Instead, I would just nod and laugh and agree, "Hahaha. *Yeah*," and then swallow whatever insult and seethe later.

During my twenty years working as an actress, there were times I even went along with being mildly bullied on set, not wanting to make a big deal out of something. I was a girl who could work within the incredibly sexist system that was set up, a girl who could take it. Men love a woman who laughs at the joke, especially if the joke is at her expense.

"She's so cool. She just *gets it*."

As outspoken and sure of myself as I've always imagined myself to be, it was hard to find my voice in Hollywood. Or it seemed pointless. That no matter what, I was working in a boys' club and that's just the way things were. *Don't you want to work?*

There was the on-set painter on a show who casually told me he'd found sexy pictures of me online and that they'd really kept him company the night before.

"Hahaha. Okay!"

I'm not gonna get that guy fired, right? Also, this seems insane (or maybe it doesn't), but there have been *more than a few* dudes on sets who've told me they jacked off to me. *Thank you?*

Or the actor who loudly proclaimed, "I'm gonna get them to write us a sex scene so I can really *get in there* and see what it's like."

"Hahahaha. *Whatever.*"

Or the head of casting who told me the only way I was ever going to get movie roles was if I did a *Maxim* shoot.

So I did. It didn't help.

Or listening to Harvey Weinstein tell me what model he was currently having a relationship with, obviously not knowing the full extent of his depravity and horribleness. (I have the odd distinction of him *not* trying anything with me, I think weirdly because he met me and my husband, Marc, together and really liked Marc and thought we were *friends* or something?! Who fucking knows how a psychopath's brain works.) As he would casually objectify whatever woman it was, tell me that he fucked her, I would nod and mumble, "Oh. Cool. She's beautiful."

And then I would try to lose him as fast as I could.

Here's the thing: It's not easy to be a woman in this business. There will always be jokes about your body. There will always be guys who steal your best ideas and pass them off as their own. There will always be actors who push you to the ground. There will always be networks that ask you to lose weight. There will always be jobs you will not get based on your looks.

And the men will continue to support one another and show up for one another and hire one another, but if *you* want to stick around, girl, you'd better be *damn* sure you smile when they ask and wear a low-cut top to your network test and lose the fucking weight and let them take credit for your words, because *you* are expendable.

At some point, I started not to care if I was expendable. It was beginning to wear on me, the things I watched some of my friends go through in order to get where they wanted to be in their careers, the things I'd put up with and witnessed myself. But also life. Life is exhausting and it never gets easier. For anyone.

Two years ago, I was working on a web series for Jenny Mollen. Her friend Tom Lenk was showing me Instagram stories, which had just launched. I had done Snapchat a little, because my friend Kelly Oxford was into it and I liked the filters, but honestly, Instagram stories seemed kind of lame to me.

"I don't get it. Why would they do this if Snapchat exists? Is anyone even gonna watch this shit?"

"I don't know," said Tom. "But look, you have way more followers on Insta than on Snapchat, so *probably* more people will watch these. You can also just do both?"

"Tom. Who has the fucking time?"

Turns out . . . me. I did. I had the fucking time. I wasn't really working as an actress. After *Vice Principals*, I sold a show to HBO with Danny McBride's Rough House Pictures producing. We were in the middle of developing that, so I was sort of holding off on other TV jobs until we could see where it was going.

Other than that, I was working with some friends, thinking maybe I would finally try to write another movie script. But mostly, I was just hanging out. I was meeting people for lunch. I started working out every day as a way to handle my anxiety. I was doing some surrogate stuff for Hillary Clinton, and also volunteering at one of my favorite charities, working with under-served kids who were struggling with mental illness. And then I was a mom. I am a mom.

At night, after the kids were asleep, I would go downstairs and turn on the TV and wait until Marc came down, so we could watch some show and go to bed. Routine marriage stuff. But then Tom introduced me to this thing. Instagram stories. And there was something appealing about it. I could talk about my day. Or what was going on in my house. Or the episode of *Friends* that was on. Or my life. Were people watching? I didn't really care. It was like a diary. Or a confessional on a reality show. Me, starring me.

But then people *did* start watching, in a way that was truly unexpected. And they were responding to my honesty and open-ness, which I completely hadn't anticipated. I just didn't know how to be any other way at this point in my life. I was done trying to put on a face, done trying to be something that I thought someone else wanted me to be. I was too tired.

Besides, I've always liked telling stories, real or imaginary.

And there are things that happen to me that *only* happen to me. Like almost getting murdered in an Uber that may actually have not been an Uber. Or going to the Golden Globes as Michelle Williams's date and then getting locked out of my house in the rain at three in the morning, drunk and increasingly panicked. Or witnessing raccoons having insane, horrible-sounding raccoon sex on my balcony. Or having a front-row seat to the craziest Oscars mix-up in history. And that's only been in the last two years of Instagram stories!

And in between all that, I work out every morning, I make mac and cheese for my kids, I forget their favorite stuffed animals in Hawaii and start a transpacific search party, I cry when my TV pilot doesn't get picked up by NBC, I go see bands play, I hang out with my best friends, I have anxiety attacks and eat nachos and drink margaritas and go on vacation and live my life and live my life and live my life and live my life. For me. For you. To entertain you. To be seen. It's the only thing I've ever wanted.

FANTASTIC VOYAGE
(Lakeside)

My therapist, Bethany Rosenblum, says that everyone has one defining story. The story that basically sums up who they are and why they are the way they are.

I mean, personally, I feel like I have half a dozen of these defining stories. But if I go all the way back, back to when I was preverbal, there's a story that sums up how I've always seen myself. The fact that I don't actually remember it might seem problematic. But I think it's the perfect story *because* I don't remember it.

Look, I'll be the first to admit I can be a terrible witness to my own history. I think most of us probably are. I mean, certainly there are facts that exist. Like if you were in a particular city at a particular time in your life. Or if you went to college. Or if you were on that TV show. But other bits and pieces are totally dependent on what you choose to focus on. Remember when James Frey wrote that book and then everyone was so fucking mad that he made up parts of it? And then he had to go on *Oprah* and *look her in the eye* and admit that *maybe* some things had been exaggerated for dramatic purposes? That is literally my worst nightmare—to be judged by Oprah.

But see, I *am* a dramatic human. I always have been. And I come from a fairly long line of dramatic humans and storytellers. And part of being a good storyteller is knowing which parts need to be embellished a bit, and which details need to be lost completely. I was recently recounting a story (which you will read later in the book, hopefully. Unless you give up on me. Don't, though. I'm worth it, I promise. I mean, I think I am.) Anyway, I was recounting a story to my husband, Marc, and as I was telling it—or retelling it, as the case may be, since this is one of "my stories"—I revealed something new. Marc has heard this particular story at least a million times over the course of our twelve-year relationship, and somehow I had never included these new details. Details that maybe change some of the intention.

All this is to say, I'm telling you these stories, my stories, as I remember them. As I see them. As they have affected me. But that's not to say it's the whole truth or even what the full story would be if you were to track down the star witnesses to my life and line them up and ask their impressions of said stories.

Here's something: Occasionally in my life, it's possible I may have been a bit more of a glass-half-empty kind of girl. That might seem incongruous to the persona I've cultivated via social media and interviews—I understand and recognize that. But even though I can sometimes be a bit of a Debbie Downer, I *am* a performer. I live to make sure everyone is happy and having a good time. Sometimes that means pushing my own feelings and anxieties to the side and putting on a good show. And sometimes it means that the way I remember things happening isn't exactly the way other people remember the same events. Look, I'm going to try to be as honest with you as I can be. But it's obviously *my* truth. Not my mom's or my sister's or my friends' or my ex-boyfriends' or my husband's truth. Mine.

So anyway. This defining story. The one I can't possibly remember because I was two. It's the story my mother *also* chooses as the defining story to explain who I am. Except her takeaway and mine are a bit different. To Barbara Philipps, the story has been used over the years to illustrate just how headstrong and willful I was as a child. "Oh, that Busy! There was just *no controlling her*! Have you ever heard about the time she decided to take a walk around the block??! *No?! Well. Let me tell you!*"

So! From my birth to age six, my family lived in Oak Park, Illinois, a suburb of Chicago. Both my parents grew up there. In fact, they had met as high school students at Oak Park High and began dating when they were just sixteen. They didn't go to prom together, because, as my mother puts it, "your dad wanted to go with a big-boobed cheerleader." My mom went with her theater friend Steve. Anyway, I don't remember much from that time, but I've seen pictures and Oak Park is beautiful. It all looks super Americana, and from my mother's various stories I know it was the kind of place where there were block parties in the summer and sledding in the winter and all the kids walked to school together and knew the crossing guard's name.

So, the story!

Apparently, when I was two or three, there were a bunch of

neighborhood kids playing on our block, and at some point, my mom noticed I was missing.

"Wait, Mom," I always say at this point. "How did you notice I was missing?"

"I don't know," she says. "Just, at some point, you weren't there."

"So how long was I gone for?"

"I'm not sure, Busy. But that's what you were like. This was before we installed the high locks on our doors. It was a different time. If you were in the house playing somewhere, I wasn't always watching you. I was doing dishes or laundry. And if you decided you wanted to do something, you would do it. There was no stopping you."

"Even at two?"

"Even at two! Even at one! *Still! It's who you are!*"

"Okay. So then what?"

"Well, I gathered all the neighborhood kids and said, 'Busy is missing,' and they all got on their bikes and Big Wheels and went up and down the street calling your name, and I was apoplectic! I called the police! There was no sign of you."

"That's crazy."

"It *was* crazy! But that's just what you were like. It's like the time I took you shopping to Carson's, and you know I didn't like that mall where Carson's was—"

(I don't even know what Carson's is, by the way. I'm assuming it's some sort of department store from the early '80s.)

"—and one second you were with me and then you were

just *gone* and I couldn't find you and we called mall security. My heart was racing and then this very nice saleswoman said sweetly, 'I think I've found her.' And there you were! In the middle of a rack of clothes, sitting alone, happy as can be, looking up at all the clothes around you! But I just about had a heart attack!"

"Oh. I actually think I remember looking up at the clothes. But I must have been really little."

"You *were*!!"

"Wait. So my walk around the block?"

"Yes! I was also terrified because there was a construction site on the street behind us and I was afraid you had fallen in—"

(This is also fucking crazy to me. I mean, can you imagine? Like, there's some construction site on the street behind ours and there I was, just inches away from falling into a ditch and becoming the next Baby Jessica!)

"—but just as the police van pulls up we could see you coming around the corner in your diaper. And there was a woman on a bike behind you."

"Who was this woman?!?"

"Oh. A nice lady. Well, I guess she lived on the corner of the street you had turned down and she was on her porch having her tea and saw this little thing toddling by and thought, 'This doesn't look right.' So she got her bike out and just slowly followed behind you to see where you were going and make sure you didn't hurt yourself."

"That's weird. If *I* saw a toddler walking down the street alone in a diaper I'd probably do more than just quietly follow behind on my bike, you know?"

"She was just trying to make sure you were okay, Busy. But that's how you've always been. You and Jessie from across the street used to plan out how to run away to the park on your Etch A Sketch. And you always had some sort of black eye or bruise. There was just no stopping you!"

"It's a theme."

"Well, it *is* a theme, Elizabeth."

(Sometimes, my mom calls me Elizabeth, which is my given name. But she only uses it in order to emphasize a point. Or when I'm annoying her. Or both.)

"You just aced out in your nudes and there was no stopping you!"

I need you to take a moment to truly appreciate how insane a phrase like "aced out in your nudes" is. It never occurred to me that other people's parents didn't talk the way mine did. My parents one hundred percent made up weird phrases like "aced out in her nudes" and sold them to me and my older sister like they were things normal people said and generally understood. There are other misunderstandings from my childhood that I'm not sure were actually my parents' fault. Like, until about seven years ago, I was convinced fl. oz. (as in fluid ounces) stood for "floor ounces"—which I weirdly thought was a unit of measurement?? I still don't have any idea where I got that.

Anyway, I was recently telling my friend Piera the walk-around-the-block story and we decided maybe that should be the thing I get tattooed on myself, if I ever get a tattoo. "Aced out in her nudes" is totally my "Nevertheless, she persisted."

So that's the story, more or less. The police left. The lady on the bike rode home. My parents installed high locks on the door. And I continued getting lost or injuring myself until I figured out not to do it. But to my parents, and probably my older sister, Leigh Ann, that's just *who I was*. And the story became a humorous anecdote to illustrate my personality.

Unstoppable. Headstrong. Defiant.

And I probably *am* all of those things. But when I look at who I was then and who I've become, I think it might be a little deeper.

Look, I'm a mom now and I get it. It's fucking hard to parent two little girls. We have a full-time nanny and it's still not easy for me. When I was a kid, my dad worked and my mom didn't have any help. I know it was a different time; especially in a neighborhood like that, where everyone kind of looked out for each other. But when I think about two-year-old me, walking around the block in a diaper, a toddler who had been left alone long enough to "ace out in my nudes" and make it all the way around the corner before anyone noticed I was missing . . . well, it just makes me a little sad, I guess?

It's funny that "FOMO" has become a thing people say. But my feeling left out and left alone obviously has some deep roots. It's real and it hurts, if you're someone who has always felt left out. Which I have. It's a recurring theme in my life.

In my immediate family, I've always felt different. I've certainly always looked different. My mom and dad and sister all have dark hair and dark eyes, and here I showed up, this little blond-haired, blue-eyed weirdo. I remember hating when my mom would laugh and shrug and say, "I guess she must be the milkman's baby!" But also, like most of the weird things my mom would say, she would then immediately and kind of seriously say, "No . . . actually, Busy looks just like Joe's sister and my mother." (And I do look exactly like them, so *take that, milkman!*)

People (in the world, not People-mag-dot-com, which is my favorite online publication but also the source of so much agitation for me because they *insist* on posting horrible stories about children being murdered) have often made a point of how loyal I seem to be as a friend. And it's true. I'm one of those people who will friend you for life, if you'll have me. But that's in part due to my own fear of being left out.

I remember in fifth grade when all the girls turned against me in classic mean-girl puberty style. Girls who had been my best friends since I'd moved to Arizona were suddenly so mean to me that some days, on the playground at lunch, Noah Guttell and Seth Kasselman would take pity and let me hang with them on the bleachers while they talked about the Beatles. One morning, after my friends had been particularly cruel the day before, I was sobbing in my bed, not wanting to go to school, and my mom let me play hooky. She took me to the movies to see *The Little Mermaid* instead, which is one of the saddest/happiest memories of my life. I'll never forget sitting there in the dark, eating popcorn and watching my favorite Disney movie ever with my mom in the middle of the day when I should have been at school. In that moment, I felt like she fundamentally understood me, like she knew how best to take care of me.

Really, I think acting was the thing I clung to because I was a part of something. And also, it meant that I got the attention of the people I so desperately wanted to see me, for at least thirty to forty-five minutes every few months, when I would perform in whatever weird play or showcase I was currently doing. Plus, I was good at it. People always tell me I'm lucky to have known what I wanted to do since I was eight years old, but honestly, I think there's a piece of me that felt like it was all I could do because it's the only time I really ever feel like I'm a part of things. Because the girl who's the lead in the school play can't be left out, right? You would think.

But it's funny, because with acting—the thing I'm best at, the thing where I feel I belong the most—I still feel left out *all the time*. Somehow, I've managed to choose the absolute hardest profession for someone who tends to feel forgotten and worries about not being seen. I've had so many days in the past twenty years where I just want to stay in bed crying until my mom shows up to take me to see *The Little Mermaid* in the middle of the day.

But in all my therapy over the years and all my talking to friends and all my social media–ing, I've determined that just about *everyone* feels left out; it just comes down to how you handle it. I haven't handled it the best, historically speaking. But I'm trying to get better. And truthfully, isn't there something incredible about the fact that we *all* feel left out? Shouldn't that somehow make us all feel a little less alone??

Maybe I do need to change the way I see two-year-old me. Maybe I need to start looking at it more the way my mother does. But the facts remain. When I was two, I took a walk around the block. What's up for grabs is what it means to you. It's like a litmus test: Do you see a sad, left-alone baby wandering the streets, or a determined little kid who wanted to see the world and decided to ace out in her nudes and make it happen for herself?

I guess it really just depends who you ask.

SMELLS LIKE TEEN SPIRIT
(Nirvana)

There's no denying I was never one of the popular kids in school. I know that a lot of people who have gone on to become successful in whatever field they chose tend to have this same narrative. And I don't want to be one of those annoying good-looking people who's like, "I swear I was *such a nerd, guys!*" Also, I totally appreciate that sometimes people feel like outsiders even when they're the head cheerleader, or whatever. But, come on . . . be honest! You were still the head fucking cheerleader, you know?!

It's similar to when super-skinny actresses insist they just *eat whatever they want*! I mean . . . ! I used to fall for that, but now I know better. Yes. You can totally eat whatever you want. As long as it's literally like three bites of that thing and then you stop. I remember a friend of mine recounting a date he went on with an actress (*she's famous, guys*) and he was initially impressed when she ordered the fried chicken. But then she proceeded to pick the fried part off and eat like three bites of white meat before she declared how full she was. Those are fake eaters, my friends. And they are *everywhere* in my town.

Anyway, the point is, my friends and I were *not* exactly the head cheerleaders. Not that head cheerleaders even exist in elementary school. They don't. Unless maybe if you live in Texas. But you get it. We weren't necessarily nerds, but we *for sure* weren't considered popular. The popular girls did things like have coed parties and kiss their boyfriends in sixth grade and wear Esprit and big earrings and read Sweet Valley High. We played games like Store for the Stars, where we would take "business meetings" (which consisted of ordering iced teas and bread baskets at Buster's, a local bistro we could ride our bikes to), and we read the Baby-Sitters Club (way less cool) and the only boys we were friends with had no interest in kissing any of us.

My very best friend was Emily Bronkesh-Buchbinder. Our family moved into our rental house in Scottsdale in August 1985, and little Emily came around the corner with pigtails and a plate of brownies and that was it. We're the same age (she's actually like eight months older than me), but when we were in third grade, she skipped ahead a year. But we still spent most days playing Pound Puppies at each other's houses or riding our bikes around the neighborhood after school. That is, when she wasn't taking her "college classes" at Arizona State University. Emily was the smartest kid I knew (she's still one of the smartest people I know), and she was in some sort of after-school program a few days a week at ASU. But of course she made sure everyone thought she was taking actual college classes with college-age kids.

I had crushes, but nothing requited. None of my friends did, either. By middle school, the popular kids were all dating and "going out," but my friends and I were content to just hang out with each other, listening to Boyz II Men or watching *Pretty Woman* for the millionth time. Then seventh grade rolled around, which meant school dances. There were a few every year, held in the school gymnasium, with the eighth graders participating too. Mostly, my friends and I hung around the edges together. None of us really danced with any boys, and I would just goofily do the running man to make Rachel laugh.

Ever since second grade, Rachel Davidson had been my school best friend (Emily BB didn't count, since she was a grade above—she was my best friend in real life). Rachel was for sure the leader of our group, the queen bee of a hive no one really paid attention to. She was the one who was always egging the rest of us on to do mischievous things. But I loved to make her laugh. She was such a good audience. I can still see her, doubled over in laughter, her hands covering her mouth, tears in her eyes as I did something stupid, like tie my shoelaces to Brandy Payton's and run down the storm wash only to end up rolling and almost breaking our legs. I would do insane voices and characters on the playground at her request. As far as I was concerned, Rachel was the coolest.

Anyway, the Valentine's Day dance in seventh grade was coming up, and for some reason, it kind of felt like a big deal. It was all anyone could talk about, and there were student government posters up all over campus encouraging us to *get our tickets*. I can't remember what boy I had a crush on at that point. Maybe John Randall, who was Mormon and therefore seemed mysterious and exotic to me? In any case, my girlfriends and I were so excited, and we decided we would ask our moms if we could wear some makeup to the dance. I knew it wouldn't be a big deal for Rachel. Her mom was incredibly stylish, which meant *of course* she'd let her wear makeup. But it was a bigger deal for me.

My sister is four years older than me, so she was already a junior in high school when I was in seventh grade. Leigh Ann and I were (and are) very different. She was somewhat of a tomboy. She went to an all-girls Catholic high school and seemingly had zero interest in things like makeup or cool hairstyles or wearing heels. Meanwhile, I would spend my free time watching *Beverly Hills, 90210* or *Saved by the Bell* and then use my mom's makeup to try to replicate the actresses' looks. I would spend hours in front of the little mirror at her vanity, trying all her different products and using her perfumes. And then I'd use her Pond's cold cream and wipe it off my face, like I'd seen on *Designing Women*, one of my favorite TV shows. (I watched a lot of TV.) (Still do!)

My mom was fine with me playing with her makeup in the house, but she thought it was inappropriate for young girls to wear makeup out of the house. My parents were the type who had those weird age rules that in retrospect seem so arbitrary—like I couldn't get my ears pierced until I was twelve, I couldn't get contacts until eighth grade (why eighth grade? I had to wear glasses *forever*!), and I wasn't supposed to wear makeup until *high school*. HIGH SCHOOL! Like *two years* after *seventh grade*.

Anyway, I was nervous to ask my mom, and at first, as I had suspected, she said no.

"Elizabeth. No. You don't need any makeup," she said. "You're beautiful as you are!"

"But maybe just mascara? And lip gloss??"

"I don't know, Biz. Your dad won't like it."

"He doesn't even need to know! Come *on*! Mascara and lip gloss?!"

My mom sighed. "I'll ask your father."

I have a feeling she didn't ever ask him. I'm pretty sure my mom did whatever she wanted or thought was right and then later informed him what was happening. For his part, my dad generally thought that whatever she decided—especially in matters pertaining to girlhood—was probably the right call. So it was settled. I won. Mascara and lip gloss it was.

The day of the dance arrived. At school, everyone was discussing what they were wearing, who they wanted to ask to dance, who they wanted to hopefully try to kiss. I was personally excited about two things. One: the mascara and lip gloss. Two: Emily was going to let me borrow her amazing *brand-new* purple Guess jeans to wear with the super-intense patterned blue-and-purple shirt my mom had bought at Price Club but had somehow convinced me was cool.

Emily and I got ready together at her house. I cannot explain to you the layers of mascara I used on my poor little eyelashes. The fact that I could even open my eyes was a miracle. My mom had, for some reason, decided to be super rad before the dance and bought me *my own* blue mascara at the drugstore. That, combined with my Lip Smackers strawberry lip gloss and Emily's purple jeans . . . *well*! I don't think I need to tell you that I was really *feeling* myself.

Emily's mom dropped us off with our signed permission slips, and my mom was to pick us up at ten on the dot. Already there were kids streaming into the gym. As soon as we got inside, Emily headed to the right, closer to the speakers, which was where the eighth graders typically hung out. I very quickly found Rachel and our other seventh-grade friends on the left side of the gym, near the bathrooms and the snack table.

We must have gone to the bathroom at least seven times to look at ourselves with our "makeup" on and reapply our lip glosses and adjust our outfits and our hair—not that it mattered much, since the lights in the gym were turned off and there were only a few ambient pink-and-red lights and a disco ball.

We danced a little in our group and ate a few cookies. And then, just as I was starting to feel a little restless with my group of friends, the DJ switched it up from the usual pop R&B and put on Nirvana's hit single "Smells like Teen Spirit."

Now. I need to explain something about pop culture here. This was February 1992. Earlier that school year, in the fall of 1991, Nirvana's "Smells like Teen Spirit" debuted on the radio and MTV. Most kids were still listening to pop music like P.M. Dawn, Paula Abdul, EMF, R.E.M., and Michael Jackson but that video was *everything*. This was before the internet, so trends and music had a tendency to trickle in a bit slower. I mean, if you were a normal kid, you really had to rely mostly on MTV and regular radio. The cool high school kids, like Rachel's older brother, were already totally into Nirvana and Red Hot Chili Peppers. Not my sister, though. She was really into George

Michael and Color Me Badd. But in middle school, there was just a small faction of kids starting to get into grunge, mostly some cooler-than-average eighth-grade boys.

So the DJ put on "Smells like Teen Spirit." Most of the older kids went nuts, since they all could at least identify it was something considered cool, and truthfully, it's a fucking catchy song, even if you're just a suburban kid in Arizona. But when the song ended, something truly weird happened. The DJ put it on *again*. And then *again*. And *again*. It was as if he just hit repeat and went outside to smoke or something. Well, this made the cool eighth-grade boys get *really* hyped up . . . on Nirvana and hormones and fruit punch and cookies and as-yet-unidentified white male privilege. They started a mosh pit, something I'm sure none of them had ever really been in before but had only seen on TV. You know, *like in the "Smells like Teen Spirit" video.*

I wanted a better look. Did I want to be a part of it? I don't know, truthfully. I can't for certain tell you what provoked me to move from the safety of the seventh-grade side of the dance, where I'd been trying to make Rachel laugh and looking for John Randall. I know what I *said*. I said, "I'm gonna go see if I can find Emily."

But that was a lie. I knew it then and I'm telling you now. I wasn't going to find Emily. I wanted to see what the fuck those boys were doing. What that anger and aggression and music was all about. So I made my way in the dark over to the eighth-grade side of the gym.

Even now, I can see it like it's a movie. In slow motion. The music distorted. The lights flashing on my little baby-fat twelve-year-old face, full of mascara and too-shiny lip gloss. I want to tell seventh-grade me not to go. I want to tell seventh-grade me to stay in the comfort of my friends. There's nothing to see with those boys. There never will be.

But there's no time for that, because it wasn't in slow motion. One minute I was on the edge of the mosh pit, and the next I was in the middle of it. It happened so fast I didn't even know why I was on the ground. I just knew I couldn't get up. *I couldn't get up off the ground.* Just like that, my left leg didn't work. And *fuck* did it hurt! The searing hot pain combined with the blaring music made me panicky as oblivious kids stomped over and around me. I looked up for help. There was no one who could see me. It was just a swirl of sweaty bodies in the dark. I tried scooting backward a little on my butt, but the pain in my leg was too intense.

That's when I started to cry. Hard. The song ended, thank God . . . *and then it fucking started again.* And there I was, sobbing on the ground, these horrible boys all around me, unsure of what had happened or why I couldn't move, in *so much pain* I assumed my leg was shattered, but I honestly had no idea. I couldn't even see. I put my arms around my head, tried to curl up as much as I could, and just cried. I had no idea how or when this would ever end.

Then, all of a sudden, I heard a girl's voice.

"Hey! Are you okay????"

I looked up to see Lauren Ellis, an eighth grader, shouting over the music. She was short but superstrong, the kind of cheerleader who could do backflips up and down the football field. I literally couldn't even talk at this point. I just shook my head no. She crouched down next to me.

"WHAT'S GOING ON?" she yelled. "CAN YOU MOVE??"

I shook my head again, through sobs. She looked around.

"OKAY! I'M GONNA PICK YOU UP."

I shook my head again. I was in too much pain. I just wanted her to leave me there to die. That seemed way more reasonable.

"YES," she said firmly, and with that, little Lauren Ellis scooped me up and started screaming at people to get out of the way. She carried me, cradled like a baby, to the edge of the gym and set me down gently on the floor next to the bleachers.

"OKAY, LISTEN. I HAVE TO FIND A TEACHER OR SOMETHING. DON'T WORRY. I'LL BE RIGHT BACK!"

This time I cried out, "NO!"

I've been injured a few times in my life, like in a way that required ambulances and hospitals, and I know now that when I've been in one of those situations, when my body is going into shock, the person who comes to save me becomes very important. I just want that person to stay with me. It's helpful to have something consistent to focus on. (This is also true of giving birth with no pain drugs but *that is much later in this book*.)

"YOU'RE GONNA BE FINE! I'LL BE RIGHT BACK!"

And with that, Lauren Ellis disappeared into the darkness. A small circle of kids started to awkwardly form around me. The saddest group of kids at the dance. The ones who had been standing at the sides. And here I was now, in the middle of everything, mascara pouring down my face in sheets, pooling under my chin and dripping onto my patterned silk shirt that was now also stained with sweat.

A kid stepped forward and yelled, "WHAT'S YOUR NAME?" Oh, God. I shook my head. I needed someone I knew.

"DO YOU KNOW EMILY BRONKESH-BUCHBINDER?" I asked one of them. "CAN YOU FIND HER FOR ME PLEASE??"

She nodded and ran off just as a teacher finally showed up with a walkie-talkie. He was trying to assess the situation and figure out what was happening. All the while, "Smells like Teen Spirit" continued to play on repeat. Again. And again. And again.

Truthfully, this is where things get a little fuzzy. Emily showed up with her eighth-grade friends, concerned but also maybe a little wary of being identified with the injured seventh grader on the ground. Then the school nurse and one of the administrators arrived. Someone had the DJ turn the music down, then off all together, to the jeers of not only the moshing boys but also most of the student body population. Then the lights came on, garish bright fluorescent gymnasium light, illuminating me in the middle of a growing circle of kids. Rachel pushed her way to the front.

"OH MY GOD!" she cried. "What happened? We didn't know where you went, and then someone said you were on the ground—"

Just then, another teacher pushed through along with four or five paramedics, snapping their gloves on, rolling a gurney behind them. One paramedic took charge, a ridiculously good-looking dude who was probably only like ten years older than us. *Of course.*

"Okay. Everyone! Out of the way. BACK UP BACK UP. GIVE HER SOME SPACE!"

I didn't need space. I needed to disappear altogether. *Forever.* They kneeled down next to me and started taking my vitals, asking me my name and what happened. I told them I wasn't sure. I couldn't move my leg. I was in so much pain.

"Okay. I'm gonna need to get these jeans off of you so we can have a look, okay?"

I looked around in absolute horror. But before I could say anything, a female paramedic was using a pair of medical scissors to cut up the side of my jeans, past my knee, to my thigh, and was about to keep going when I screamed:

"WAIT! THESE ARE EMILY'S JEANS! YOU CAN'T RUIN THEM!"

The female paramedic looked at me sympathetically, nodded, and stopped cutting.

"Okay," she said. "You're going to need to get them off at the hospital, though, and I'm not sure how you'll do that without cutting them. Your knee is badly dislocated."

Then the hot paramedic said something dumb to try to get me to laugh. I did, but only to please him. I wanted to die. They secured my leg in a foam brace and loaded me onto the gurney. As they started to wheel me out, past literally every single kid I went to school with, my mom showed up with some teachers by her side. She was, as she likes to always say, *apoplectic.*

I wouldn't call what my mom was wearing her pajamas, necessarily; it was more like a leisure suit, a soft purple velour track-suit that she liked to watch TV in, which she had purchased at Price Club, obvi. Let's just say it wasn't the best thing for your mom to show up wearing to your school dance.

"Good Lord, *Elizabeth!*" she said, her eyes filled with worry. *"What happened?! Are you okay?"*

The hot paramedic knew how to handle this situation.

"She's going to be fine," he assured her. "It looks like she dis-located her knee. We don't think she hit her head, but they'll take a better look at her at the hospital."

When we got outside, I saw multiple fire trucks and three or four ambulances. I have no idea what the 911 call was like. Maybe they just said there had been an accident at a middle school dance and the fire department was prepared for mass ca-sualties? This was *years* before school shootings became a thing. (Ugh, that sentence is so upsetting. "Before school shootings be-came a thing." Horrifying.) It was a chaotic scene, and teachers were trying to herd kids back into the gym. As they wheeled me past, I put my face in my hands, overwhelmed by pain and the sheer humiliation of being carted out of my school dance on a stretcher, my mom in her tracksuit yelling at some administrator as she tried to keep up.

This is what I got for wanting to know what was going on, for wanting to be a part of things, for wanting more. I got my fuck-ing ass kicked. It's too bad I didn't realize the life lesson I was being handed. Because maybe, possibly, it would have saved me from even more pain in the years to come.

But at the time, it wasn't a lesson. It was just the worst thing that could have possibly happened to seventh-grade me. My mom met me at the hospital, along with my sister and my dad. My sister could be such a bitch sometimes, but with tears in her eyes, I could tell even her heart hurt for me in that moment.

Do you know how they reset a dislocated knee? Two doctors (or med students or nurses, I don't know) just yank your leg out straight as hard as they can while a third slams your kneecap back into place. It's disgusting and kind of violent and it hurts like hell, but as soon as it's over, you have immediate relief. It took a while to get to that point, though, because they had to x-ray my leg and make sure I hadn't broken anything and didn't need emergency surgery. When it was all over, the doctors put me in a temporary knee brace, handed me crutches, and gave my parents instructions to follow up with an orthopedist the next week.

I didn't go back to school that Monday. Or the Monday after that. Or the Monday after that one. It took me about three weeks before I was able to face it. My parents didn't press the issue. Emily picked up my assignments and brought them to me every day. I talked with Rachel and my other friends on the phone after school (I had my own line, guys, NBD). My mom turned Emily's purple jeans into jean shorts and Emily even generously said she liked them better that way.

When I did get back to school, it wasn't *as* terrible as I'd imagined. A few kids snickered when I hobbled by. There were stares and whispers, and one day some kids threw balled-up paper at me. I learned to handle my newfound infamy by keeping my head down and shutting it out almost completely. That is, until Scott Bell approached me one day in between classes.

Scott Bell was the worst. A Tracy Flick, if Tracy Flick had been a lanky boy who was obsessed with student government and randomly really good at calligraphy. I had no idea why he was walking up to me.

"Hey, Busy," he said. "Listen. I think you should know that if your parents decide to sue the school over your accident, we won't be able to have any more school dances. *Ever.* That's what Mr. Bataglia said in our student government meeting and I just thought you should know. Just because *you* fell down doesn't mean our whole school should be punished, you know?"

I stared at him. "I have no idea what you're talking about."

And I really didn't. I hadn't heard any discussion of my parents suing the school over my humiliation. They're not exactly litigious people, although my mother *does* like to bring up all the times she *should* have sued people.

"Yeah. Well, just make sure they don't. 'Cause, like, everyone would know it's because of you."

I realize this exchange sounds so fucking arch—like how could some seventh grader even *be* that horrible? But it's true. The *worst* part about that kid (who by the way, *never* got any better through high school) is that he actually lives in Southern California, and our paths have crossed a few times. About fifteen years ago, I ran into him at some cheesy sports bar in L.A. I was on *Dawson's Creek* at the time. He was drunk, and very flamboyantly came up to me saying, "*Look at you! You're just all that now, aren't you?!*"

Weirdly, my takeaway from that run-in was that he was gay and had come out of the closet, and I concocted this whole story in my head about how *that* was why he was so intolerable in school, because he was repressing who he truly was. I mean, he was *really* into *calligraphy*! *Of course he was gay!*

A few months after running into him, I was having a general meeting at a production company when one of the executive assistants poked her head in and said, "I just wanted to say hi and introduce myself. I'm friends with a bunch of your friends from high school!"

"Oh really? Who?" I already knew this wasn't true, since the girls I'd ended up friends with in high school all still lived in Arizona, with the exception of Emily BB, who was my roommate in L.A. by this point.

"Taylor Goldfarb and Nikki Eliot and Scott Bell!"

"Oh! Yeah! I mean, I *for sure* know those guys. We weren't really *friends*, though. I actually just ran into Scott. I'm so glad he's out of the closet and everything—that's so great!"

The air was sucked right out of the room. I knew I'd fucked up immediately. Her face fell and then she very tersely said, "Oh. Ummm. No. Scott's not gay. He's my fiancée."

I tried my best to laugh it off and back up what I'd said, but the damage was done. I've now heard from multiple people that he has it out for me. Oh well. Do your best, Scott Bell. You were always a fucking cunt.

Anyway, after my run-in with Scott, I confronted my mom that night in tears.

"No," she said. "I never talked to the school about getting a lawyer. But we did talk about there needing be *something* put in place for these dances. The fact that there were no teachers or administrators around to stop those horrible boys is unacceptable—"

"Mom! *Please!* If you do *anything* or say *ANYTHING* they're gonna *cancel* the school dances forever and it will be because of me!"

"Oh, honey, don't be ridiculous. It will be because the administration wasn't doing their job. That's not *your* fault."

"Mom! No!"

"Okay, okay. Calm down, sweetie. I promise."

I'm not sure if she ever talked to the school about it again, but it must've been dropped, because Scott Bell left me alone and the year-end dance went off without a hitch—not that I was there. My knee brace came off and I had to do some physical therapy, but it wasn't so bad in the end. It was actually kind of fun to go to a weird tiny office in a strip mall and do exercises and ice my knee with a bunch of septuagenarians who were recovering from hip surgery.

As seventh grade came to a close, bar and bat mitzvah season started to get going and I was relieved by all the invitations I got, and the fact that the boys who went to Hebrew schools knew nothing of my humiliation at the Valentine's dance. I went with my friends, and we stuck to the edges of the crowd, and talked about which boys we thought were cute, and took a million silly photos in the photo booths.

And in case you're wondering, I avoided the mosh pits.

MY SISTER
(The Juliana Hatfield Three)

One of my mom's famous stories about my birth has to do with her beloved poodle, Pierre.

"He took one look at you in your bassinet and KEELED OVER AND DIED! HE JUST SAID, 'NOPE! NOT GONNA DEAL WITH THAT! I'M OUTTA HERE!'"

Obviously, I know that isn't exactly true. I mean, a dog doesn't look at a baby and just decide to kick it. In truth, the poodle was like fifteen years old when I was born and I think my mom had basically kept him on life support for the months leading up to my birth. Plus, the fact is, Pierre was put down: he didn't just die naturally of disgust at the whole prospect of my birth. And I *believe* he was put to sleep a few months *after* I was born anyway. So, yet another one of my mom's favorite go-tos is a total fabrication for dramatic effect. Which I knew on some level as a kid. But the feeling I got whenever she told it to people was that I had killed her favorite thing on earth when I was born.

I mean . . . the *stories* about Pierre the wonder dog! Did you know that when my mom made beef stroganoff, she would give Pierre his helping and he would "SPIT THOSE PEAS RIGHT OUT AND LINE THEM UP ON THE PLATE WITH HIS NOSE! CAN YOU IMAGINE??!"?

And did you *know* that Pierre was "SUCH a GENTLEMAN, he JUST LOVED wearing his little tuxedo!" that my mom sewed for him? Many times I wondered if she ever loved me or my sister as much as she loved that dog.

The other story about my birth that my mom loved to tell was this: "*Busy* just popped right out! *She* couldn't *wait* to be born! 'HERE I AM WORLD!! READY OR NOT!!' "

The truth is that I was a planned C-section that *she* scheduled for the earliest date they would allow, June 25. My dad and my older sister were waiting for me patiently in the recovery room. There is the sweetest picture of my sister, wearing her pop beads and holding the baby blanket that she brought for her new little sister, which matched her own.

"*Leigh Ann*, on the other hand!" my mom always says. "Well, she tried to *kill* me! We *both* almost died! It was horrendous— just horrendous! We should have sued that doctor! The hospital! Everyone!! But you know, we were just so happy that Leigh Ann was alive!"

And here is where my mom—if she's in a particular mood— always gets teary at the memory. "That 'doctor' should have *never* induced me. Leigh Ann was upside down and backward! They tried to yank her out and they broke *both her hips*! And then I had the emergency C-section and it was just horrible. Your poor dad thought he had lost us both!"

If my dad happens to be around for this particular retelling, he usually just nods and adds, "It was very scary."

And so these are the stories of our respective births: My older sister Leigh Ann tried to kill my mother, and then I came along, popped right out, and killed her beloved dog.

My sister is four years older than I am and I think my mom was so traumatized by Leigh Ann's birth that it took a while for her to want to get pregnant again. I don't know the whole truth of it (how could I?). What I do know is that she was breech, which wasn't identified for some reason, and when they tried to yank her out, the doctor broke her hips and she had to be in some sort of cast/brace for many, many months as a baby. I can't imagine what that does to a person. To have that kind of trauma when you're born. Or to spend the first six or seven months of your life confined like that. My mom also had a hard time recovering from the birth. They were living in Connecticut at the time, but moved back to Oak Park, where both my parents' families still were, when Leigh Ann was about three.

My mom likes to say, "Everything was *fine* until we moved to Arizona. Moving from Oak Park was the thing that did it. Leigh Ann just was *so angry* at us. I don't think she ever really got over it, truthfully."

The amount of anger my sister had, and would display, was often scary to me. I know it didn't *feel* normal. I know my friends were always confused by my loud, fighting family. And I know I preferred to play at other kids' houses when I could.

Our mom had a thing about making everything "even" in our house. I think it was some prevailing parenting philosophy of the time. Or maybe it was something she had come up with to try to alleviate jealousy. She would make it known that she would allot the exact same amount of money for each of us for Christmas presents or back-to-school clothes. When she turned sixteen, Leigh Ann got my mom's old car, so when I turned sixteen, my parents bought me a used car that was pretty much equivalent. Or, for instance, if someone complimented me on a performance at a play in high school, my mom would pipe up and say, "*Both* my girls are *so* talented! *Leigh Ann* just starred in the Creighton University production of *Les Liaisons Dangereuses!*"

I would just stand there, rolling my eyes. *My friends' parents don't care about Leigh Ann, Mom. READ THE ROOM.*

When Leigh Ann got to redecorate her room as a teenager, it was determined that I would too, when I turned fourteen. I couldn't pierce my ears until I reached the age Leigh Ann had been when she got hers pierced. Same for contacts. It was in my mom's head that if she could make things feel equal, they somehow would be. But I don't need to tell you, that's not how kids work. You can't force them to be equal, and you certainly can't force them to be friends or even like each other.

I didn't understand my sister. I didn't know why she hated me so much. I know now that she didn't. But that's what it felt like for so much of our childhood. When she was mean, she was *so mean*. There were times when she was beyond scary, like when she got mad at me for some reason and flipped over everything in my bedroom. Or when she threw me into a giant potted cactus and I cut my leg so badly, I still have a scar running lengthwise down my shin. I remember my dad telling me to hide in their walk-in closet while they tried to calm her down. Our fights were almost always insanely physical, which was unfair given our age difference and hence our obvious size difference.

But it wasn't always like that. Leigh Ann was also incredibly creative and smart and funny and weird and occasionally sweet to me as a kid. And that was part of what was so confusing for me, especially since I was so much younger than her. She managed to fashion a pulley system between the shared air vents in our bedrooms so that we could pass notes back and forth to each other. She would always cast me in her video projects for her high school religion class and would laugh so hard at my Jim Bakker–like evangelical pastor impression. She was sweet to me when the girls in fifth grade were mean. She came to all of my plays.

I remember as a kid thinking she was an anomaly in our family, not yet recognizing my father's deep depression and occasional rage. Not yet understanding that not all mothers break down in tears telling stories. Not yet knowing that shaking my head to feel my hair hit the sides of my face over and over again until I got called to the teacher's desk, or ripping out my hair at the roots in a little patch on the top of my head wasn't exactly a "normal" thing for an eight-year-old to do.

I feel like my parents knew they should try to instill self-confidence in us, but at the same time, they still thought that spanking, or even a hard smack across the face, was acceptable. We were all on vacation recently (a Disney cruise, if you must know), and one day at lunch, all the kids were kind of cranky.

"You girls are lucky it's not like when Busy and Leigh Ann

grew up," my mom said. "You'd get smacked right across those mouths!"

And then she proceeded to tell everyone about the time she hit me while she was driving because I had talked back, and my gums got caught on my braces and my mouth started to bleed.

"And I just felt *terrible!*" she said, shaking her head. "Can you imagine!? *Your mouth full of blood?!*"

My husband's and daughters' mouths dropped open. *They* couldn't imagine. But of course I could.

For years, my own narrative of my childhood was that my sister was the one with the "problem" and we were all just swirling around her, trying to stay above water. Yet I've had anxiety for as long as I can remember. I would lie in bed at night as a kid and imagine the worst possible scenarios: my entire family being murdered, house fires, plane crashes, car crashes, my parents dying, my sister dying, my best friends dying, myself dying. I would become paralyzed with fear and unable to even go to my parents' room. Instead, I would just lie in bed, tears streaming down my cheeks until I finally exhausted myself enough to fall asleep, despite my worst fears. And what's so strange is that I don't think I ever really told my parents about this. Part of the reason may have been that Leigh Ann took up so much of the emotional space in our family. And another reason is, I think I just thought it was normal. Like probably no one likes bedtime and most likely everyone thinks horrible morbid thoughts before falling asleep.

I went through a period of time recently where I would become convinced right before sleep that my heart had actually stopped beating and I was seconds away from death. I would patiently wait *for hours* thinking that death was imminent, while my husband slept soundly next to me. I've always had issues falling asleep. But I'm also afraid of dying from sleeping pills, so I would *never* take anything to alleviate my fears or help me. I recently started using medical CBD and THC (*pot, y'all*) to help with my sleep anxiety, and it's legitimately the only thing that has ever helped and not made me feel like it would also kill me.

So, what I guess I'm getting at is that *maybe* my anxiety had to do with my volatile family. Or *maybe* I was just born with it. I used to think it was the former, before I had kids of my own. But now I'm not so sure. I see my daughter Birdie and her horrible sleep anxiety, which so closely mirrors my own, and I have *no idea* where it could have possibly come from for her. I think it must just be something she was born with. Or I somehow fucked her up when she was a baby. Either/or. *Or maybe both*.

My mom has one sister, who's quite a bit younger than she is, about six years. To say their relationship has always been strained is an understatement. My mom and her sister have never gotten along, as far as I can tell. The comparisons between my sister and me and my mom and her own sister started as soon as I was born. Leigh Ann looks exactly like my mom and was always a little on the chubbier side. And like my aunt, I was tiny and blond and blue-eyed. There was a feeling, especially from my mom's side of the family, that I was the cute one and Leigh Ann was the smart one. At my baby shower for Birdie, my mom *actually said out loud*, "Well, I know we're all hoping the baby gets Busy's looks and Marc's wit and intellect!"

She somehow managed to insult both me and Marc at the same time. No easy feat. But of course, when I expressed that maybe that was hurtful, she just laughed and said, "Oh, Biz! You know I'm just kidding! *Everyone* knows how smart you are!"

Okay. I guess? But maybe *I* don't? Because I've been jokingly told since I was a child that I wasn't the smart one.

My aunt is an artist, and part of the rift between them, at least as far as my mom was concerned, came down to that very thing. Now I am going to tell you something that should not shock you: My mother wanted to be an actress. IT'S TRUE, GUYS. She was the star of the theater department at Oak Park High and after school was accepted to the Circle in the Square Theatre School in New York. But her parents didn't think it was wise for her to go. So, instead, she went to college in the same town she grew up in, majored in English, married my dad, and eventually became a Realtor. Her sister, on the other hand, wanted to be a visual artist and ended up going to the School of the Art Institute of Chicago, which for some reason was fine with my grandparents. I don't think I can overstate the importance of this imbalance to my mother.

Now look, of course we can say, "Well, fuck it, Barb, why didn't you tell your parents where to put it and go to New York and follow your damn dream? *Or* do theater in Chicago? Or any number of things!"

But she didn't. It was a different time. My mom graduated high school in 1961, which was basically still the '50s. And I think that kids—especially "good" Catholic daughters—from that era kind of just did what their parents told them to do, no questions asked.

So when my sister and I came along, we were always encouraged to be and do whatever we wanted. But the irony isn't lost on me that even though Leigh Ann and I were both very involved in theater, I was the only one who pursued it.

I look at my own girls now and it seems so clear to me. Birdie is my older daughter. Full of her own anxieties, she is constantly pushing, pushing, pushing to be smarter, funnier, better. Our little one, Cricket, just exists. I don't know if maybe parents are in so over their heads with their first children that they project all this stuff onto them. I always thought a good book would be *How to Raise Your Second Child First*. Of course, I have no idea how one would actually do that.

I remember my mother saying to me once, "You know, Biz, I think you're here to help me heal my relationship with my own sister." Which *for years* I thought was really narcissistic. But weirdly, when Birdie was born, I kind of understood.

When I was in my early twenties, my sister wrote me a letter apologizing for our childhood and how she had treated me. I had very little interest in her at that point, to be honest. She wasn't there for my teen years, which were really painful, and she was an asshole to me when we were kids. I had no idea what kind of relationship we were supposed to have as adults. And here was this letter and my feeling was, *Okay. Whatever. It's fine.*

But then the strangest thing happened. I had Birdie. My sister was in L.A. at the time, living on the west side, working for a production company (which, truthfully, she should have stayed at, 'cause I think she'd be running it by now). She'd been living in L.A. for about a year at this point, and we would see each other every few weeks and honestly, I always looked at meeting up with her as a chore, like *I HAVE to invite my sister to that, right??*

She showed up at the hospital while I was in labor and sat in the waiting room for seven hours waiting for Birdie to be born. I didn't want her in the delivery room with me. I remember I was actually annoyed at the time that she had come.

"Why is she even here?" I asked Marc. "Why did she leave work?"

"Because, babe," he said, "I think she's excited and wants to be supportive of you."

She brought Birdie a baby blanket—she had found one identical to the one she'd brought for me when I was born. And she cried when she saw Birdie. Then, for those next few months, those long new-baby months where I was a mess, she would drive an hour three times a week—most days after working a full day at her assistant job—to come see Birdie and sing to her and hold her and love her. And it cracked me open. Leigh Ann's love for my daughter, who reminds me *so* much of my sister every day, allowed me to really love her too.

I cried for weeks when I found out I was pregnant with another girl.

"I can't do it, Marc. Birdie is Leigh Ann and now we're gonna have a *me* and I'm just gonna do the same shit my parents did and it's the same thing over and over and over and I can't do it."

"Yes, you can," he said patiently. "Birdie *isn't* Leigh Ann. This baby isn't you. You're not your mom. Or your aunt or your grandmother. You're you. And I'm me. I promise."

The truth is, Birdie *is* very similar to my sister. She is smart and funny and weird and creative and so sweet to her little sister. She also has the rage. And if we're being honest, Cricket is *so* much of me. But Marc is right. We're not my parents.

I called my mom the other night, sobbing because Birdie tore everything off her bed, including her mattress and box springs, and was screaming at me and I couldn't get her under control. She was hitting me and throwing things at me and I went into my bathroom and sat on the floor and cried and cried and cried. I told my mom that I didn't know how to help her.

"What am I going to do?" I sobbed.

"You're going to breathe, honey. And then go hug her. And you're going to do better than we did."

LIVE THROUGH THIS
(Hole)

The night before the last day of seventh grade, I slit my left wrist open with the Swiss Army knife my grandfather had given me as a gift the year before. Deep. Lengthwise. By accident.

My parents and I had gotten into some huge fight about who knows what. My sister wasn't involved, but there was screaming and name-calling and hitting. I had *had* it with my family. Leigh Ann and I shared a bathroom with a door that led to the backyard. I knew it would be unlocked, so for dramatic effect, I ran out our front door, slamming it behind me. I then stealthily crept around the side of the house, where I snuck into my bathroom, then quietly tiptoed into my bedroom. Through the closed door, I could hear my parents yelling for me, not knowing where I'd gone. After a while, I heard my mom go into the garage and start the car, and I sat back, so pleased with myself. She was gonna drive around our *whole* neighborhood looking for me! I imagined that just when they were about to call the police, I would emerge from my room triumphant and say, "DIDJA MISS ME??? I WAS HERE THE WHOLE TIME! SUCKERS!"

After a few minutes, though, I got bored and started to look around for something to do. I found a roll of clear packing tape that I had shoved a coin into—like in between the cardboard and the massive amount of tape—and for some reason thought, "Oh! It'd be a good idea to get that quarter out! *That's* a good activity to kill some time!" So I grabbed the Swiss Army knife out of my little metal bank that had BUSY painted on top in bubble letters, and I opened it up. I started to cut the packing tape, toward me, of course, when the knife immediately slipped and sliced through my wrist.

You know when you've hurt yourself so badly you don't even bleed for a few seconds? Or maybe you've seen that kind of thing in a movie? Like when Matt Damon smashes Jude Law's face in *The Talented Mr. Ripley*? That injury delay? That's what happened to my wrist. It didn't even hurt, to be honest. But I knew I'd really done it. I screamed "FUCK!!!" and grabbed my wrist as blood started to pour out of it; then I ran into the living room, where my dad and my sister were watching a car race together.

When she saw the blood, Leigh Ann jumped up screaming, "OH MY GOD, BUSY, WHAT DID YOU DO???!!!" My dad got on the phone and called my mom (who had a giant cell phone, since she was a Realtor and needed it for her business). Leigh Ann tried to make me run my wrist under water, which seemed weird, but was also a good instinct. She wrapped a ton of paper towels around it and made me press it really hard, then put me in the car with my dad.

"KEEP IT OVER YOUR HEAD, BUSY. AND KEEP

PRESSING REALLY HARD!!" she yelled as my dad peeled out for the hospital.

When we got to the ER, I was put in a room right away. My mom and sister showed up shortly thereafter. The ER doctor who had stitched me up was very kind, with a super soft, very soothing voice. I had to get two stitches internally and then around ten outside. There were a lot of questions from different doctors coming into my room, and I remember at one point a doctor shushing my mom and looking at me, like, *This is a safe space, say what you need to.* It literally didn't *occur* to me that they thought I had done it on purpose. The doctors, I mean. My parents and sister just thought I was an idiot.

It didn't help that I was so embarrassed by *how* I had injured myself that I initially lied and said the knife was open and fell off a shelf onto the inside of my wrist (COME ON, BUSY, I KNOW YOU'RE TWELVE BUT DO BETTER). After the truth came out, my parents were like, "Yeah. That's a dumb thing that Busy would do." Once the doctors were certain I was just stupid and not suicidal, they gave me some Tylenol and sent us on our way.

I ended the school year the next day, sitting in the final assembly with my hand all bandaged up and throbbing, too embarrassed to go to the school nurse to get more Tylenol. I was the girl who had dislocated her knee a few months earlier and now I had slit my own wrist open by accident.

So. Stupid.

I started eighth grade with a renewed sense of self. Over the summer, a couple weeks before school began, my parents finally let me get contact lenses. It was something I'd been begging for since I got glasses in the fourth grade (and had famously remarked, "*Mom!* The trees have *leaves!*"). I imagined that I would strut into eighth grade and that my classmates, most of whom I'd known since first grade, wouldn't believe my transformation.

That *can't* be Busy *Philipps!* She's so *beautiful and sophisticated without glasses*!!!

I remember sitting in my new homeroom, just waiting for someone to recognize the new me, when Tyler Bloom, the kid I'd had a crush on since fourth grade, leaned over and said, "Did you get new shoes? You should have beat them up more."

I *had* gotten new shoes over the summer. Brand-new kelly-green high-top Converse that my cool older cousin in Chicago had taken me to buy while we were visiting our family there. I loved them. I self-consciously rubbed one sole on top of the other shoe and said, "Oh yeah. I did. But also . . . I got rid of my glasses."

He studied my face.

"You wore glasses?"

And that was it. It was probably the best response I got from anyone.

Eighth grade was the year that my group of friends began to expand and change. I started to hang out all the time with a girl named Lacey, who hadn't gone to elementary school with us and whose parents had some unrealistic dream of their daughter being a cheerleader. Lacey introduced me to Kendra Cole, who was in Emily's grade and therefore already in high school.

The three of us became fast friends. On weekends, we would take the bus to Mill Avenue, where ASU is. We would wander around a bit before ending up in Trails, the local head shop. One of us would eventually get up the nerve to buy those bidi cigarettes, which weren't even really cigarettes, and then we'd sit on a stoop and try to smoke them. Both Lacey and Kendra had parents who were very lax about things like rules and curfews. My mom was way tougher to fool, but this was before cell phones and the proliferation of being in CONSTANT CONTACT, and I think she just assumed we were generally not up to anything too terrible.

I had a few crushes on boys, but nothing had ever happened, like, physically with any of them. By the end of eighth grade, Lacey and Kendra couldn't believe I'd never kissed a guy, and they became determined to make it happen for me. One Friday night, Lacey and I went to the bowling alley. There was a kid working there, probably sixteen or seventeen, tall and skinny with long hair. He kind of looked like an extra from the movie *Singles* and his name tag said ADAM. Lacey decided he should be my first kiss. He laughed at us as we kept coming over to the counter to flirt with him while he was spraying disinfectant into the bowling shoes.

"What time do you get off work?" Lacey asked him, and I rolled my eyes at her. I couldn't believe she was doing this to me, even though I did think he was cute.

"Uhhhh, like eleven."

Lacey's parents were supposed to pick us up at ten. We walked away, dejected.

"Wait. I have an idea," she said. "I'll just call my parents and tell them that *your* mom is picking us up and we're sleeping at your house. And then when we're done hanging out with him, we can call my parents and tell them there was a mix-up!"

I wasn't so sure about it, but I *did* want to make out with someone. Lacey handled the phone call and gave me a thumbs-up. And then we spent the next four hours doing nothing, waiting for this kid to get off work. Finally, he was ready to take off. The three of us wandered around the parking lot, which was empty-ing out by this point, and then decided to keep walking, over to a darkened office park. After what felt like forever, Lacey said, oh so casually, "I'm gonna be over here! You guys *have fun*!!!"

And she raced away. I sat down on a curb and Adam sat next to me. And then his mouth was on my mouth and there was so much spit and tongue that I was slightly horrified. I tried my best to figure my way into it, but it was just so *weird*.

As we leaned back, I saw Lacey running over to us.

"Busy!!!" she yelled, breathing hard. "YOUR MOM IS HERE! SHE'S ACROSS THE STREET AT THE BOWLING—!"

Before she could even finish her sentence, my mom's Audi screeched into the empty lot, her windows down.

"GODDAMMIT, ELIZABETH, WHERE IN GOD'S NAME HAVE YOU TWO BEEN?! I'VE BEEN LOOKING FOR YOU FOR AN HOUR! WE WERE ABOUT TO CALL THE POLICE!!!"

"JESUS! MOM!" I said, mortified. "WE WERE JUST HANGING OUT!!!!"

I glanced at my would-be suitor, my disgusting make-out partner, my first kiss, whose name wasn't even Adam, but it doesn't matter because I don't remember his name. He shrugged and half waved before walking away.

"GET IN THE CAR!" my mom yelled. "NOW! YOU, TOO, LACEY. YOU CAN CALL YOUR PARENTS FROM MY PHONE."

After dropping Lacey off, we rode home in silence.

"I'm sorry, Mom," I said eventually. And I truly was. That kiss wasn't worth it. (By the way, so few are.)

"I don't want to hear it, Elizabeth. What is *wrong* with you??"

I don't know if anything was "wrong" with me. But I knew that if I wanted things to happen, I needed to make them happen for myself. A few weeks later, in humanities, Julie Morgan—who everyone knew smoked pot and had probably already had sex—looked at me after I said something and wryly noted, "You're funny."

It felt unbelievably validating. But I didn't know how to repeat it. I was too self-conscious to actually be funny. She asked me if I wanted to come over that weekend and hang out.

My mom dropped me off and commented about the size of Julie's house in Paradise Valley.

"Well, *these* people sure have money."

We hung out in "her wing," as she called it. She had her own entrance to her room that went to an outside courtyard. There were a few kids hanging out, and Julie asked if we all wanted to walk to the Paradise Valley Mall and go to the Vans store. But first, she said—as it if were obvious—we should get high.

I had never smoked pot and was freaked out but also very excited and curious. I would occasionally steal the little airplane bottles of alcohol my parents kept above the refrigerator and take little sips with my friends at sleepovers, but I don't think we ever got anywhere near drunk. And Emily BB and I once tried to smoke oregano when I was in seventh grade.

But this was different. It clearly wasn't Julie's first rodeo, and her parents obviously didn't mind, because we did it right there in her room. I took a few hits off the joint as they talked me through it. I didn't want to overdo it. I thought I was stoned, but who knows now? We walked to the mall and hung out at the Vans store. I was trying *so hard* to *feel this pot*, you know? I grabbed a Baja pullover in the requisite red, green, and yellow and was feeling the fabric, really trying to focus in on my stonedness, when Julie came over and yanked the sleeve out of my hand, rolling her eyes. "Maybe, like, don't *try* so hard."

Doug Lisowski and Josh Ableman snickered. I was mortified. "I'm not! I'm—"

"It's fine, dude. It's just, you're not *that high*."

I tried my best not to try so hard for the rest of the afternoon, until my mom picked me up before dinner. But I never really hung out with Julie again.

Not too long after that, Lacey and Kendra met some skater boys at the mall who went to another high school. They were *so cute*, so obviously we decided we *had* to make them our boyfriends. The three of us started to spend every free moment we had at the mall. We'd share fries at Johnny Rockets and wait for the older skater boys to show up. There was a group of probably six or so, but Lacey and Kendra had already decided which three we should go out with.

Lacey had dibs on a boy named Trey, who was seventeen, short and stocky with a mop of curly hair. He was fairly dopey-looking and seemingly not terribly bright. Kendra loved Jacob, who was tall and skinny and I think the youngest of the boys, closest to our age. I picked a boy named Charlie, who had short black hair and was kind of a nice, quiet guy. For a while, we would just hang out in the parking garages and watch them skate and practice their kick flips or whatever. And then it got to the point where we would get in Charlie's car and drive around and hang out in deserted playgrounds or parking lots or strip malls. We got away with our parents not knowing where we were by telling them we were going to the movies. I must have supposedly seen *Free Willy* about four thousand times. To this day, I have not seen it once. I assume the whale lives, right?

I was nervous as summer rolled around, because I was going to a fancy performing-arts sleepaway camp in upstate New York. Emily had gone to it for the last two years and loved it, and we had convinced my mom and dad to pony up and send me too. I wasn't nervous about the sleeping-away part. I was nervous that while I was gone, Lacey and Kendra would achieve the goal of making boyfriends out of those high school skater boys and I would be left behind. A few nights before I was supposed to leave, I was with Kendra at the rec center, where kids tended to hang out at night. By this point, I had bought Etnies, a skate shoe, and had started wearing bigger jeans and baby T-shirts. My style was for sure evolving into skater girl. I had just never gotten on an actual skateboard.

As some of the guys from our high school, Josh and Doug and Jason—did their best attempts at tricks, Kendra and I sat by and made fun of them and laughed.

"You think you can do it better?" Doug asked. "You girls do it."

Kendra and I jumped up, defiant.

I watched as she stepped gingerly onto a board while Doug held her hand. Kendra was one of those girls who had a perfect flat tummy and a mouth that turned up on the sides so it seemed like she was always smiling. I was always jealous of the fact that she could wear Calvin Klein underwear out of her pants and look like Kate Moss. When I did it, it looked like a mistake.

"No fair!" I shouted, giggling. "I want to skate too!"

Josh Ableman shrugged and handed me his board. I got on and skated literally no more than two feet—*maybe*—when the board flew out from under me and I fell to the ground.

FUCK.

I knew immediately what had happened because of the year before. Except this time it was my other knee. I grabbed it with both hands as everyone raced over. Then I gritted my teeth and tried my best not to cry in front of the boys.

"Kendra, you have to call 911," I said, trying to sound calm. "I dislocated my knee. Fuck. And my mom. Call my mom."

You guys. I don't know what to say here. It's insane. Like literally what in the actual fuck?? Since we've already been through so many injuries and it's only chapter five, I'll give you the Cliffs-Notes on this one. Ambulance shows up, Mom arrives insanely pissed 'cause I'm leaving for camp in two days, I'm horrified and embarrassed, I cry, the boys are freaked out, Kendra feels terrible, Josh Ableman wants to make sure I'm not going to sue his parents (not a joke—WHY IS EVERYONE SO CON-CERNED ABOUT LITIGATION?!). A hot paramedic (HOW ARE THEY ALWAYS HOT?) tells my mom I've dislocated my knee (AGAIN), but this time, I may have cracked my kneecap in half when I fell, which means I'll need surgery.

AND SCENE.

Emily came over the next morning, so disappointed we wouldn't be going to camp together. My mom spent most of the day on the phone, talking to the doctor and scheduling my surgery. Then calling the camp to get them to defer my tuition until the following year. Meanwhile, I lay on the couch and watched *Saved by the Bell* reruns, my braced leg propped up on a pillow. I had knee surgery a few days later. It was supposed to be arthroscopic, but they ended up having to cut my knee open and put a pin in it, just below my kneecap. The next few weeks I spent on the couch or at physical therapy. Kendra and Lacey came over to visit me a bunch and regaled me with stories of the hot skater boys and the headway they were making with them. I was super jealous and ready to get back to that mall so I could hang out with those boys too. I hated being left out because of my stupid knee.

"Trey is having a party," Lacey told me one afternoon. "We have to go!"

"I can't even really walk. And I have this huge brace on, *how* are we going to go?"

"Kendra talked to Charlie," she said. (*My* Charlie. Ugh. Of course. Kendra was so hot. I'm sure that Charlie wanted nothing to do with me and my broken knee.) "And he said that if we get dropped off at the mall, he'll pick us up. We'll just tell your mom we're going to the movies."

My mom agreed that it seemed reasonable to go to the movies, and she dropped us off at the theater that night. But to be honest, I didn't feel great. I mean, I'd had major knee surgery two weeks earlier. I was embarrassed about the brace but still I just *didn't want to miss out*. (Are you sensing a theme here?) We waved goodbye and walked into the mall, waited ten minutes, and then went back to the parking garage to wait for Charlie. He picked us up and took us to the party. When we got there, Kendra and Lacey took off and I sat on the ground in a corner and tried to put pillows around my brace so that people wouldn't really notice it. Some high school girls asked me about it and I tried to be cool and say I fucked it up skateboarding. I mean, technically that was true.

"How *old* are you?" one of them asked, giving me an appraising look.

I was thirteen. My fourteenth birthday was in a week.

"Fourteen."

"Oh. You look like a baby."

She was right, in retrospect. I did look like a baby. I desperately didn't want to be one though. That's why I was there.

At a certain point, I realized we had to go back or my mom

would come get us and we wouldn't be there. There was a discussion as to who was the least fucked up and could drive us back and it was decided that Jacob would take Charlie's car to drop us off. He and Kendra ended up making out, which of course made me so jealous. That should have been me and Charlie! If only my stupid knee wasn't all messed up!

The rest of the summer, we had the same routine. Sleepovers at each other's houses. Watching so much MTV (it was the summer that both "Everybody Hurts" by R.E.M. and "Black Hole Sun" by Soundgarden came out and were on heavy rotation). Calling the skater boys and taking turns talking to them. Waiting at the mall for hours for them to show up. Feeling so dejected when they didn't. Planning how to make out with them. Charlie seemed less interested in me than the other two boys were interested in Lacey and Kendra, and it bummed me out. I wasn't sure why he didn't like me. Was I not hot enough? Maybe not. I was kind of awkward and weird, I guess. And maybe what Julie said was true. Maybe I tried too hard. I needed to relax.

In August, my sister was leaving for college in Nebraska and my parents were going to drive her out there. It was decided I could stay at home and their friend's daughter, Nicole, who was twenty-one could stay with me. I hugged my sister goodbye and waved as they drove away in my dad's Audi. As soon as they were gone, Nicole turned to me. "I assume you want to have people over. That's fine. I'll stay at my parents', but call me if you need anything."

What's so crazy is I don't think it had really occurred to me.

But *of course!* A *party!* I called Kendra and Lacey and we called the boys. That night, they came over and brought a ton of beer and vodka we got super drunk. I didn't have a bed in my room, because my parents had agreed to buy me a new one (from Z Gallerie!) and the frame hadn't come yet, so I just had a queen mattress on the floor.

At some point, Charlie and I were sitting on the mattress on the floor and Kendra came in and turned off the lights in my bedroom. Finally, the moment I had been waiting for! We started kissing and messing around. I reached into his pants, 'cause that's what I thought I was supposed to do, but I had no idea what to do with my hand once it was in there, so I took it out again. Then Charlie put his hand down my pants and shoved his fingers inside me. It didn't feel great. Just, like, fingers inside my vagina, not really doing much there. He pushed them around a little and then pulled his hand out and wiped it on his jeans. Then Kendra and Lacey burst into the room and jumped on the mattress with Jacob and Trey.

"ARE YOU GUYS HAVING FUNNNNNN??"

I don't remember much after that 'cause I was so drunk and everything started spinning, but at some point Charlie got up and left, and I felt so rejected. I had obviously done everything wrong. Jacob started kissing me and lifting up my shirt, and I let him, even though I thought it was gross and I was pretty sure Kendra would be pissed. She wasn't. She was laughing hysterically and thought it was all so funny. At some point Charlie came back in and told the other boys it was time to leave. They took off and Kendra, Lacey, and I passed out.

I woke up the next morning to the sound of bottles and cans and someone mumbling.

"*Jesus. Busy!* I said you could have some people over! I didn't think you would trash the house!"

Nicole had come back over to check on me and was furiously picking up empty bottles and cans and throwing them away. I wandered out into the living room, super hungover. It was trashed. I helped her clean up while trying to process my hangover and what was essentially my first real sexual experience, even though I was so drunk it was hard to remember what had happened the night before, who I had even hooked up with. Maybe I should like Jacob? He seemed more into me than Charlie did. For God's sake, I just wanted *someone* to want to kiss me.

It wasn't long before school would start, and Lacey—who was going to a different high school—told me and Kendra she was going to have to focus on making friends, which we thought was rude but whatever. We stopped going to the mall to see the boys. I tried calling Charlie a few times but he basically blew me off.

A few weeks into September, my phone rang. It was Trey, the skater boy that Lacey had called dibs on. Weird. I asked him if he had seen Lacey, since she was at the same school as him. He said he'd seen her around a little but he wasn't really into her.

"Yeah," I said. "We haven't really talked to her much since school started. She's got new friends there, I guess."

He told me she was hanging out with the cheerleader girls, which made sense. Then he said, "Well, we should hang out sometime."

What? This was so strange. Trey had never showed any interest in me whatsoever. I was thoroughly baffled but also obviously flattered. I hadn't ever really considered him before—he was basically like last on my list, but I guess he was pretty cute? I mean, he seemed a whole lot cuter now that he was showing some sort of interest in me.

I told Kendra about it at school the next day.

"Ewww. No," she said immediately. "You can't. Lacey would *never* talk to you again!"

The truth was, I wasn't sure if I cared. Lacey had totally abandoned us once she started at her new school. At least that's what I told myself when I dialed Trey's number a few days later. We talked for a bit and then he asked what I was doing the next night.

"There's a football game at my school," I said, "so I think I'm gonna go with Kendra and her new boyfriend. You wanna come meet us?"

"Yeah. I'll find you there."

I borrowed a dress from Emily, a red, thick cotton baby-doll dress that was super short. I wore my black-and-white striped over-the-knee socks that hid the hideous scar across my knee. I couldn't care less about sports and the game was of little interest to me. But finally, I spotted Trey in the crowd, wearing a white T-shirt and baggy jeans, looking out of place at a football game. I wandered over to him, trying to be cool. I mean . . . was this a date? I honestly didn't know.

"Hey," he said when he saw me. "You wanna go?"

"Oh. I mean, Kendra is over there. We were gonna go back to her apartment in a bit . . ."

"Yeah, I don't really want to do that," he said with a shrug. "So . . . do you wanna go or what?"

I shifted my weight to my good leg and sucked on the inside of my cheek. I wasn't really sure what was going to happen or where we were going to go. And Kendra was already being weird about me hanging out with Trey.

"Let me go talk to her."

He nodded, and I ran over to where Kendra was hanging with her arms around Dan, a new skater boy who had recently moved into her apartment complex.

"I'm gonna go with Trey. He doesn't want to watch the game—"

"Eww. Busy, *no*. Do *not* go anywhere with him! What's *wrong* with you!? He's *so* gross!!"

She laughed and Dan did too. My face flushed.

"Okay then," I said. "*You* don't have to hang out with him!"

Kendra rolled her eyes. "WELL, DON'T THINK YOU'RE JUST GONNA COME BACK AND HANG OUT WITH US AFTER!"

I glared at her, then turned and walked back to Trey, thinking, *You know what? Fuck you, Kendra! With your perfect stomach and all the boys that love you and hang on your every word.*

I looked at Trey. "Let's go."

And just like that, we got in his SUV and drove away from the school.

"So where are we going?" I asked, and he looked at me. Really looked at me, and I felt it.

"Is there like a park or a playground we could hang in around here?"

I tried to think of someplace not far from my school. "Yeah. Turn right up here."

He pulled into a playground, and we got out of the car. For a while, we just sort of awkwardly swung on the swings. Then he scrabbled up on one of those climbing structures and I followed. We didn't really talk. We were sort of just sitting there, not saying anything, not doing anything. *Oh, good.* Here was another boy who didn't want me. *Cool. Cool.*

"Oh. I guess I have to do everything?" I said, trying to be seductive. I reached over and clumsily started to unbuckle his belt. I have no idea why I didn't kiss him but instead just went for his belt. It was so weird. But then again, I was fourteen and painfully inexperienced. I had no idea what qualified as normal behavior. I took his dick in my hands. It was already hard. He lurched forward and put his mouth on mine. I tried my best to give him a hand job, something I had heard about from my friend Bailey. I thought I was doing all right. We made out for a bit and then he pulled away and said that he was really uncomfortable, that we should move to the car. I followed him and he opened the back door to his SUV and put the seats down. I climbed in, not sure of what to do or how to end it. I wanted to go back to Kendra's now, but I couldn't figure out how to say that without confirming all of my worst fears about myself. *I was unlovable. I was not attractive. I was a fucking baby.*

As soon as he got in and closed the door, he was straight up on top of me. He pulled my dress up over my head, exposing my purple bra that I loved so much. He weighed so much and was pushing me down so hard, into the carpet of his car. He pulled my underwear down and shoved two fingers inside of me, hard. I was still trying to figure out what I was doing. I had my hand back on his dick in his pants, and at a certain point he kind of pushed me out of the way and took his penis in his own hand, pulled it out of his pants, and started to push it inside me. I didn't know what to do. I put my hands under his shirt, digging my nails into his back. I hated it. I didn't want this. What the fuck was this? It was so, so painful.

"I don't think this is gonna work."

That was the most I got out in protest. That was all I said. That was it. Not no. Not stop. Not take me home. Not GET YOUR FUCKING DICK OUT OF ME GET OFF OF ME YOU'RE TEARING MY VAGINA OPEN YOU'RE PRESSING ME SO HARD INTO THE CARPET OF YOUR CAR YOU ARE RIPPING THE SKIN OFF MY BACK AND I CAN'T BREATHE AND THIS IS AWFUL AND FUCKING STOP IT RIGHT NOW.

He didn't say anything about it not working. He just kept doing it. I found a spot on the ceiling of his car and I sort of spun up to it and just focused on that until he shuddered and rolled off me. Then I pulled my underwear up and my dress down, already aware of the throbbing pain of my vagina and also my back, which felt wet and sticky against my dress.

I was sweaty and gross. I got into the passenger seat and he asked where he should take me.

My voice sounded very small. "To Kendra's, I guess?"

I was supposed to spend the night at her house. He pulled into her complex and nodded. "K. Talk soon." Then he drove off.

I walked up to Kendra's apartment. I could see that there were a bunch of boys inside with her, Dan's skater friends. I immediately started crying. I reached for the door, but it was locked. When I knocked, Kendra looked out of the shades.

"I TOLD YOU NOT TO COME BACK!" she shouted through the window. "DID YOU HAVE FUN BEING A WHORE WITH TREY??"

"Kendra—" I started to sob. "Please. Please. Let me in."

"NO! What do you think? I TOLD YOU NOT TO COME BACK. WHORE!"

She was laughing and telling the other boys not to open the door while I just stood there sobbing and bleeding, my underwear stuck to me already, my dress clinging to my back. At some point, Dan came out and said I could call my mom from his apartment. I told her that Kendra and I had a fight and I wanted to come home. Then I waited outside while Kendra and the boys made fun of me through the window. My mom showed up and I got in her car.

"Jesus. Busy," she said, looking concerned. "Are you okay?"

"I'm fine. Kendra's a bitch."

"Well, yeah. Kendra's an idiot. But are *you* okay? What happened??"

"Nothing. We're just in a fight."

She looked at me. She knew something was really wrong. She knew it. But she wasn't going to press it. Or she didn't know how to press it. We got home and I went directly into my bathroom. I peeled off my dress and looked at my back. The skin down my spine had been ripped off and was bleeding. I ran the shower. I peed, and so much blood and cum came out, I was momentarily fascinated. I actually didn't even know what the cum was. It took me a year to figure it out; I know that seems crazy, but it was just so disgusting and foreign to me. I rinsed my underwear in the sink and threw them in my hamper. I took a super-hot shower but was careful to avoid my vagina, which was swollen and throbbing still, so I got a washcloth and ran it under cold water and gently cleaned myself. Then I cried and got out of the shower and went to bed. When I woke up the next morning, I decided that what had happened was what I had wanted. I called Kendra and apologized for being such a bitch and leaving the football game. She was right to be so mad at me.

"What happened with you and Trey?" she asked, relenting.

"Oh," I said quickly, "we just hung out at a park and hooked up. It was fine."

I was very careful not to let my mom see my back, but a week or so later she came into my bathroom while I was changing and saw the scab running down my spine.

"Elizabeth! What happened to your back????"

I threw a shirt on.

"Nothing! It's fine. I was messing around at Kendra's apartment and she was dragging me around and I got a rug burn."

The lie was so immediate and came so easily it almost shocked me.

"What?! Honey, how is that possible??? Didn't you know that she was hurting you?? What's going on over there?"

"MOM. IT'S FINE! IT'S NOT A BIG DEAL."

I convinced myself not only that it wasn't a big deal, but also that it was normal and that's what sex was and Trey must be super into me. Like, he must want to be my boyfriend! How insane! Clearly he *loves* me! And I guess I love him, too? That must be what it means when you have sex with someone like that.

Obviously, I know now how ridiculous it was to think that, but I was fourteen, insecure, and painfully inexperienced. Also, I couldn't change what had happened. Or how it had happened. All I could control was how I decided I felt about it and him. My still-developing fourteen-year-old brain couldn't handle the trauma of what I had gone through, so I invented a new reality. And for the next few months, I became completely obsessed with him. I would call his number all the time and hang up—and by the way, this wasn't before caller ID, so he knew how much I was calling. A few times we had what I thought were meaningful conversations. I brought up the sex and said we should probably do it again because it was really uncomfortable and painful for me, and his response was, "Well, what do you think it was like for me? It was like trying to fuck a brick wall."

I fluctuated between my manic obsession and a deep empty hollowness, lying on the floor of my room and listening to the same songs over and over on repeat and sobbing. Or sometimes I would take a safety pin and scratch at my legs or arms.

"Cut that shit out, Elizabeth!"

That was what my mom said when she saw my arms. Then she

made me go to group therapy for teen girls. It was awful. Mostly, I lied in the group and tried to be supportive of the other girls, all while hating them because their problems sucked. I didn't talk about Trey or any of what had happened. I would just talk about my mom and dad. My sister. How hard school was for me.

Eventually, I told Kendra that I'd had sex with Trey and we were dating. She tried not to be judgmental, but told me that she thought he was a jerk. She was still friends with Jacob, and he said Trey had showed off the scratches on his back to illustrate how hard he'd fucked me and how into it I was, and that I was such a little slut. I laughed it off, then swallowed hard, pushing my rage and sadness down to my stomach. It didn't *exist*! I was *fine*!

One Saturday, Trey came over and picked me up in his SUV; then he drove around to the back of a strip mall where the dumpsters were and I gave him a blow job. My dad, who had recently started a consulting job in Salt Lake City and was only home on the weekends, happened to pull into the lot as we were pulling out, and the look on his face was so horrified I still to this day remember it. It wasn't that he'd seen anything—at least I'm almost positive he didn't—but he knew this loser kid was up to nothing good with his fourteen-year-old daughter. And he wasn't wrong. But neither of my parents talked to me about it.

One night, my sister was home from college on break and had gotten tickets for us to see Nirvana. I was so excited. After school, my phone rang. It was Trey. He told me that he had night school that evening but could maybe come by and see me afterward. I immediately marched into my sister's bedroom and told her I wasn't going with her to see Nirvana.

She stared at me. "What? Busy! Come *on*! You're so excited!"

"No. It's fine. Take someone else. I have a lot of homework and school tomorrow and I don't want to go—"

"WHAT?! WHY?! Come—"

"NO! JESUS, LEIGH ANN, LEAVE ME ALONE!"

I slammed her bedroom door. I don't think I need to tell you that Trey didn't show up that night, and I guess adding insult to injury is the fact that I never did get to see Nirvana, since Kurt Cobain killed himself like four months later.

For Christmas that year, my dad gave me Tori Amos's *Little Earthquakes*. He'd heard the songs on NPR and said, "It just seemed like something you would like, Elizabeth."

It's weird. I wasn't close with my father at all, but that Tori Amos CD basically saved my life. I remember listening to it over and over and just finding everything I needed in there. Like she had written it *for me*. I understand how dramatic that sounds, but it was. It was. It all was. It was truly a gift to fourteen-year-old ripped-apart me.

Around New Year's, I decided that I was done calling or seeing Trey. I was done trying to be his girlfriend or thinking that I was. I actually wrote in my diary something to the effect of "I'm sick of this little game that Trey and I are playing and I'm done with it!" Oh, sweet baby Busy. There was no game, honey. But here is where I found my true talent. Because what I was able to do was cut it off, all of it, everything that had happened. I shoved it down so far inside myself, it barely even existed anymore. It brought me no pain. I didn't feel it. It was like it never happened. Any of it.

After winter break, I stopped hanging around with Kendra as much. Emily invited me to come sit under the olive tree in the quad and eat lunch with the kids she was friends with. Kids who were the opposite of the skater boys. The AP weirdo kids. Not nerds, just kids who were super smart and interesting and all ended up going to Wesleyan and Brown and NYU and Reed. Right before Valentine's Day, one of them—a junior named Chris—asked me out. He was so nice and smart and had plans to go to Cornell University. I said yes.

I remember not being sure what was expected of me sexually, but he was so sweet, and I didn't feel like I had to do anything. Mostly we just made out at his mom's house. Like how it should be, I guess. But after a month or so, I got bored and broke up with him over the phone. I wanted something more . . . what? Exciting? Challenging? Dangerous?

Eventually, I started hanging out with Kendra again, mostly to avoid the awkwardness of seeing Chris under the olive tree, since I felt like he always gave me weird puppy-dog eyes. Even though I had been trying to reinvent myself as the girl who hung with the smart kids and dated nice guys who aced their SATs and weren't trying to pummel me in the back of a car, I missed Kendra and the freedom of roaming around Scottsdale at night, smoking cigarettes in the washes and hanging out doing nothing with skater boys.

One day, I went with my friend Nelson—who I knew from

theater—to the mall so he could buy a new bathing suit. Nelson's claim to fame was that he was the original Hobie on *Baywatch* but had been replaced by Jeremy Jackson. Which was a pretty great claim to fame since no one could prove him wrong. We were riding the escalator up when I instinctually turned around and looked below. I knew it was Trey before I saw his face—I knew it from the back of his brain-damaged head. I started to panic. I got shaky and sweaty and short of breath. I didn't know what to do.

I grabbed Nelson's wrist. "That's Trey."

"Where?"

"Down there. What do I do??"

"Nothing, why? He's just your ex-boyfriend, right?"

Yeah. That was the story I had going. That he was just a regular ex-boyfriend.

But then, before I knew what I was doing, I screamed out, "HEY, TREY, FUCK YOU!"

I grabbed Nelson's hand and ran to the mall exit. I looked for Trey's car in the garage, thinking I'd key it, but I don't remember if I did. Still, it was pretty satisfying. It felt good to scream at him, at least once.

I saw him only one more time after that, when I was a senior in high school and my dirtbag on-again/off-again boyfriend and I went to some random house in Phoenix to buy drugs for a rave we were going to. There was Trey, sitting fucked up on some dirty beanbag chair on the ground. Again, the immediate shaking and panic and shortness of breath.

"We have to leave now," I said. My boyfriend was annoyed,

but he'd already scored the drugs and could tell I was freaking out anyway, so we left.

For a few years, I pushed it down and my narrative mostly was, "Oh yeah, when I was fourteen I lost my virginity to some random seventeen-year-old I was dating in his car." But then, at my senior prom, I was in a deep red wine–fueled conversation about losing virginities with a friend's date when he abruptly stopped me and said, "Dude. That guy *raped* you."

It was hard for me to wrap my head around that word. I mean. No. Not really. Rape is what happens to girls in alleys screaming *no*. I unbuckled his belt. And I followed him to his car. And I got in. And I didn't say no. And I didn't say stop. And I blew him after the fact. And I called him all the time. And I was obsessed with him. And I said we were dating. And I told him we should do it again. And I was a slut. And I was a slut. And I was a slut.

And I unbuckled his belt.

I wish I had some definitive thing to say about what happened. What it was. What I call it. Or what it meant then and what it has meant to me the last twenty-four years of my life. How it has fucked me in the head again and again, almost always in new ways. Showing up when I least expect it. In college! Night terrors in the months before my wedding! As I'm pushing my baby out of my vagina with no pain drugs! And how it has fucked with all of my relationships, both sexually and emotionally. But it has never been one thing to me. And it certainly has never stayed one thing for long. Even to this day. Even as I'm writing these words. How I feel about it changes yearly and monthly and weekly, sometimes hourly. My only hope is that my girls grow up in a culture that truly understands consent and that they're never left to question if violence means someone cares for them.

Last year, my therapist asked me if I knew where Trey was or if I ever looked him up. My answer was immediate. No. I've never trolled Facebook or Twitter or Instagram for him. Which, if you know me, is a little weird, since I initially only got on social media in order to look up people from my past. So that night, while Marc put Birdie to bed, I did. And there I found him, smiling with his wife and their two little boys. I clicked to her page. He's the love of her life. "Dreams do come true!" she wrote under their wedding photo. "I finally got my happy ending!"

TEAR IN YOUR HAND
(Tori Amos)

I was raised Catholic and I *loved* church when I was a kid. I loved taking the body and blood of Christ. I loved listening to the priest give his sermon, trying to always make it relatable and modern. I loved putting dollars in the little wicker donation basket and passing it down the aisle. I loved lighting a tea-light candle at the little altar and saying a silent prayer for someone who needed it. My mom was a lector at our church, and my sister and I would sit together as kids, pressing our legs into each other's to keep from laughing as my mom over-enunciated the scripture in front of the parishioners: "THE GOSPEL ACCORDING TO *LUKE*!"

When I was little, I wanted to be an altar boy, and I remember my mom arguing with Father Brian about why they should let me, even though the church hadn't technically allowed girls to do that yet. But I had pretty much stopped going to church by the time I was in high school. It was hard to find the value in sitting there. I thought God had abandoned me in the back seat of an SUV.

Ben Miller was also raised Catholic but had ditched it in his teen years, for reasons different than mine, obviously. He wore pants that were bigger than his head, and they hung super low, suspended like magic under his flat ass. His head was shaved and he was prone to acne, especially around his nose. But he had a smile and eyes that melted my soul when we would talk in the halls or when I would "happen" to walk past the breezeway between third and fourth periods because I knew he would be there smoking with his friend Grant.

He had a girlfriend—a really scary girl named Samantha, who seemed like she would kick your ass for looking at her the wrong way. (In fact, I later based Kim Kelly on her.) But I knew they would eventually break up and he would be mine. I was sure of it.

I had to do one session of summer school that year. Considering the emotional toll of the year, I'm surprised I didn't have to do more. Ben started showing up at noon to skate in the parking lot of our school until Dennis, the security guard, would run him off. Sometimes I would walk with him over to Chop and Wok and we'd eat egg rolls in the 105-degree heat. He started calling me at night when he'd get off work, and I'd stay on the phone with him for hours. He told me he wanted to kiss me every time he saw me.

"But you can't," I said. "You have a girlfriend." (And I really didn't want to get my ass kicked.)

"I know," he said with that irresistible smile of his. "I gotta take care of it."

A few days later, Kendra called me with the news. She knew

before me, because Ben told his friend Grant—who she was now dating—that he'd broken up with Samantha. That night, we all walked from Kendra's apartment to Denny's, and on the way back, Ben grabbed me and kissed me.

I was in heaven.

Afterward, I went home and called him, and we talked until we were both falling asleep on the phone.

"So, listen," he said. "I want you to be my girlfriend. You know, like officially."

My heart was beating out of my chest.

"Yeah. I mean. Yes. I would like that so much."

It was June 9. We spent every moment we could together. I would stay on the phone with him until two in the morning and then wake up at six for summer school. I was running myself ragged but I didn't care. I was so in love with this boy. I have no idea the things we even talked about. Jim Croce? The Grateful Dead? His asshole dad? What his relationship with Samantha was like? How my ex-boyfriend was a real jerk who wasn't very nice to me?

My mom liked Ben all right. His parents were also Catholic, even though they went to a church where my mom "didn't like the music." But Ben certainly knew how to be polite around them, calling them Mr. and Mrs. Philipps and looking them right in the eyes.

"He seems like a very nice boy, Biz. I just *do not* understand those pants! But you know, your grandmother *never* understood the way my girlfriends and I liked wearing our glasses down on our noses in high school. We thought we looked so great!"

"Cool, Mom," I said, rolling my eyes.

As the month wore on, I was getting ready to leave again for the fancy performing arts camp in upstate New York. This time Emily wasn't coming, but I'd gotten my friend Ami to go with me, since we both did theater. We were super excited, but the idea of leaving Ben for three weeks was really painful to me. I promised I would call him as much as I could and write him every single day, and he promised to do the same. He even gave me a letter to open on the plane.

The Saturday before I was leaving for camp, my favorite band of all time, the Stone Temple Pilots, were playing at Desert Sky Pavilion, and Kendra scored us third-row seats for my birthday. I was feeling super run-down, but I thought it was just summer school and the heat and staying up late every night on the phone with my new boyfriend. Kendra's dad dropped us off and we made our way down to the front. I had scribbled a message on a shirt that I wanted to throw onstage. The hope being, obviously, that Scott Weiland would *get* the shirt, read the message on it and then what? Call me and Kendra maybe? I think we put our phone numbers on it. Anyway, I don't remember much of the concert. I *do* remember passing out against a huge sweaty dude, really the first and only time I've ever passed out. He yelled at Kendra, "Get your drunk friend off of me!!!"

The thing is, we weren't drunk.

"Kendra. I think I have to go. I feel really weird. . . ."

"No! You just need some water! It's like a million degrees out! Plus, they haven't played 'Creep' yet! We can't leave before that!"

She had a point. We went and bought some water and I started to feel a little better. We heard them play "Creep" and hugged each other and cried and I lamely threw the T-shirt onto the stage and then watched as it just sat there sadly for the rest of the show.

When I got home I went into my mom's room and started crying hysterically. This is actually a trait that I still have. If I have a fever, sometimes the only way I'll know is because I'll start hysterically crying out of nowhere.

"Oh, honey!" she said, putting a hand to my forehead. "You're burning up!"

She took my temperature: 103. She gave me Tylenol and put me to bed, and then, since I was supposed to leave for camp in two days, she took me to the doctor the very next day.

"It looks like it could be strep or it could be mono or maybe just a viral infection," he said. "We won't know until the tests come back in a few days."

"Well, Busy's leaving for camp tomorrow," my mom told him. "She's *going* to camp. We already had to defer last year because of the *knee incident*!"

I slept the rest of the day, waking only to talk to Ben on the phone when he got home from his job at the grocery store where he worked. The next morning, bleary eyed and with my throat almost swollen shut, I said goodbye to my parents and boarded a flight to New Jersey. I found the camp bus easily when I got off the plane and made it there with no issue. I was excited to see Ami, but I felt terrible. It didn't seem like I was getting better. In fact, I felt much, much worse.

I took a top bunk but had no energy to put away any of my things. I skipped the welcome bonfire and instead fell asleep immediately. When I woke up the next morning, the whole cabin was discussing my insane snoring. On the way to breakfast, I threw up twice. I tried my best to make it through the rest of the day, until finally my counselor found me and led me to the infirmary. My parents were called; options were discussed. My mom felt terrible. I spent exactly one week at French Woods Festival of the Performing Arts, the whole time in the infirmary. I remember hearing a few years ago that Adam Levine attended French Woods, and since we're the same age, I like to think he was there while I was, out living his best future-rock-star camp life, while I was asleep in the only building with air conditioning, trying not to die. And maybe, if I hadn't been so run-down and so *me*, I would've been out there too. And maybe Adam Levine would've become my camp boyfriend and I would've forgotten all about Ben Miller and everything that was about to happen wouldn't have happened. But I wouldn't meet Adam until many, many years later, and, as it turns out, I'm not really his type.

My mono test came back positive, and since it was then clear that I wouldn't be getting better anytime soon, it was decided I should leave camp. My dad used his miles to upgrade me to first class for my trip home, since my parents both felt so terrible about how sick I was. The drive to the airport was super weird—they had a groundskeeper take me in his van. He immediately asked if he could smoke on the drive, which I thought was strange, but since I had a hard time seeing a way to say no, I said of course it was totally cool! I wish I could smoke! I'm just too sick! Otherwise, PASS THOSE SMOKES! He smoked the whole way and talked nonstop. I was trying to keep my eyes open but I was just so sick.

Later, as I was waiting to board my flight, I saw a business-man chatting with the flight attendant. He had gray hair and an easy smile, and I remember feeling oddly comforted by his presence. Adding to my terrible case of mono was the fact that I was an incredibly nervous flyer. The summer between third and fourth grade, one of my best friends and her whole fam-ily were killed in a commercial plane crash. I remember I knew there was a crash from the news, and I knew that my friend and her parents and brother were coming back from visiting family in Detroit, because she and I were supposed to play My Little Ponies that week. But my parents didn't know that they were on the flight until the newspaper printed the names of all those on board a few days later. My mom was trying to figure out how to tell me when I snuck into the kitchen and read the article myself, scanning until I found my friend's name: Megan Briggs, 7. It was obviously devastating and almost impossible to understand as a child. But what I did understand was that plane crashes hap-pen, and since they're so random, they can happen anytime. For years, every time I would be on a plane taking off, I would think of Megan and her family. So needless to say, I always looked for things to comfort me on planes, and still do. A baby or a group of teenagers or a priest or someone really famous, and I would decide that my plane, this plane, couldn't possibly go down. I know it doesn't fully make sense but that's how these things work. They don't really make sense.

• • •

On board, I settled into my seat, and just before they closed the doors, the older businessman slipped into the seat next to me. We exchanged hellos as the flight attendant offered us orange juice. As she left he looked at me and said, "Tell me about her."

"The flight attendant?" Great. My day was not getting any less weird.

"Yeah. I feel like you're the kind of kid that knows things about people. What's her story?"

Look, I don't know how to explain this without it sounding totally crazy. But I *was* a kid who knew things about people. I am a *person* who knows things about people. My imagination has always been such that I can invent and create whole narratives and worlds for strangers to live in, and a lot of times, my imagination lines up with the reality. People fascinate me. They always have, and I'm really good at paying attention and listening. The same stories are happening all over, just to different people. If you figure out the type of person you're dealing with, you can guess at some approximation of a narrative that fits. I don't know *all* people's stories, obviously, but I think it's a talent. You just have to pay attention.

So this man asked me to tell him about our flight attendant and I did. I actually went back and read my diary from this time, because I needed to remember exactly what I thought right after it happened. Basically, I ended up talking to him for most of the flight from Newark to Dallas (where I had to change planes), and this guy told me, among other things, that my heart was in

New Orleans (okay, I mean, I really *do* love New Orleans. Maybe I should move there now?), that few people have the ability to make their dreams come true in life but I was one of them (a classic thing to say), and that I was about to enter a dark period in my life but there was a light at the end of it (I *was* fifteen, so that seems like a given, but still . . .).

Finally, he asked me if I was afraid of flying and when I said I was, he replied, "Well, I don't want you to concern yourself about that anymore. Nothing will ever happen to you or anyone you love on a plane again."

I hadn't told him about Megan Briggs but maybe he just guessed that's why I was afraid of flying? All of these things have logical explanations, for sure. But it was such a wild experience, made even crazier by the fact that I was so sick. All these years later, I'm still slightly baffled and awed by the whole thing.

As we got off the plane, he turned to me and said, "It was so nice talking with you, Busy! You're going to have a wonderful life and I'll be thinking of you often."

I know that could easily sound creepy coming from an older businessman, but it really wasn't. I called my mom from a pay phone and told her about it, and my mother, in her typical dramatic fashion said, "Oh *Busy*! You were sent a guardian angel to take care of you since I couldn't be there with you!!"

The rest of the summer I spent mostly in bed, getting better and taking visits from friends. Rachel and Emily would come play board games with me when they weren't at their own sleepaway camps. Kendra would come over, and we'd call whatever boy she was currently interested in and cut out pictures from *Spin* magazine to hang on my wall. And *of course* Ben came to see me as much as he could. He wouldn't kiss me for a few weeks since I had mono, but eventually he did. I was so in love with him. I wrote in my diary that I sometimes felt inadequate because I was sure that he and Samantha had "fucked all the time and everywhere" and I wasn't like that and he knew it. I asked him in August if he loved me while we were on the phone, and his response was, "Yeah . . ." Which was good enough for me.

The love I felt for Ben was that all-encompassing first love. He was all I could think about, the only person I wanted to talk to or see. But I was also very aware that I didn't want to be a slut with him. He was my boyfriend and I wanted him to love me and respect me. I wanted the opposite feelings that Trey had left me with.

I waited until September to have sex with Ben. It seemed like an eternity. My friend Ella's parents were going out of town and leaving her alone in the house (seriously, parents of the '90s, get your shit together!!). Ben and I talked about it and I told him I was ready. He brought over a bunch of pot and we got super stoned and hung out. He told his parents he was sleeping over at Grant's house and so he was able to spend the whole night with me.

The sex was fine, I guess. We were in Ella's brother's bedroom and I remember looking at his Red Hot Chili Peppers poster hanging on the wall and noticing how his sheets were soft, like they had been washed a million times. I derived no pleasure from it, really—I certainly didn't have an orgasm, but I made a lot of noise and we did it a few times, and truthfully, I was just so happy to be that close to him and to be able to give him what I knew he wanted.

For the next few weeks, Ben and I would have sex whenever we could. I mean, he was sixteen and it never lasted long, so we did it a lot. I started to have a creeping feeling like maybe we should use something so I didn't get pregnant, but it never occurred to me to say something to him. That would be *embarrassing*. Plus, I was so lucky he loved me. Little unlovable me. I didn't want to bum him out by telling him he should use a *condom*. Ugh. I wasn't totally lame!

I guess I thought that sex was something that just *happened* to you if you were a girl. That it was something that the boys controlled and your job was to do your best to please them. I was never taught any different. Not by sex ed in school, not by the movies I watched, and certainly not by my parents.

"What if I get pregnant?" I asked him one night while we were lying on the side of the storm wash by his house, smoking pot and cigarettes and looking at the stars.

"You won't. I promise."

I already was. I've now been pregnant three times. And all three times, I knew immediately. Again. I'm one of those people. I knew the whole time I was pregnant. I knew the morning I woke up at Ella's house. I was just hoping against hope it wasn't true. I waited a few weeks, and then one night at my acting class, I told my teacher, Mary, that I thought I could be pregnant. I'm not even sure if I had missed a period. Mary had known me since

I was seven years old, over half my life at that point. She looked at me, not heartbroken exactly, just resigned like, *Oh, fuck*. Then she said, "Well, I guess we're not gonna get much work done until we figure this out. I'll go buy a test at Walgreens."

I took the test in the bathroom of the theater and those two fucking lines showed up long before the three minutes were up. I started crying and then went outside with my friend Bailey and we smoked a million Marlboro Reds. Mary told us a story of an abortion she'd had in her twenties. She told me to talk to my mom.

"Are you *crazy*?" I said. "I can't do that!"

I mean, I literally had *never* talked to my parents about anything having to do with *down there*. When I got my period, I hid it for *months*; I just stole my older sister's pads and figured it out. I don't know why exactly. My mom was so cool about so much, but she was also raised very Catholic and it wasn't ever discussed in a real way. We had the where-do-babies-come-from discussion when I was little, but sex was just something that I knew was shameful. Bodies were shameful. There was no fucking way I was going to tell my parents I was pregnant.

"Well, then," she said. "I think you need to go to a Planned Parenthood."

I need to interject two separate entries in my diary here. Written in gray marker in my messy swirly teenage-girl handwriting, the first is dated October 8, 1994: "I think I may be pregnant. I'm really scared. Oh well."

The second, dated October 11, 1994; "Mary got me a pregnancy test at Actor's Lab tonight. I'm pregnant & I'm getting an abortion on Fri. Ben's paying for it and he's been great. I'm glad I know he's there for me. That's all now. —Busy"

When I read those entries again recently, I was truly shocked. I'm not sure why I wrote about it so casually when I know that I was freaking out. But I think there was a part of me that was trying to do emotionally the same thing I'd done with Trey: to keep it under control so that it wouldn't affect me.

Bailey had agreed to drive me to Planned Parenthood on Friday after school. As it turned out, another friend of ours, Tasha, ALSO thought she was pregnant and needed to go in for an appointment. So the three of us hopped into Bailey's open-air Jeep and drove to the Planned Parenthood in Scottsdale, smoking cigarettes on the way. We went in and the two of us filled out paperwork and waited our turns to pee in a cup and talk to a counselor. My name was called and I went in. She asked me how many sexual partners I'd had (two), if I'd ever used protection (no), if I knew my options (yes, ONE ABORTION, PLEASE).

It turned out it wasn't as *easy* to get an abortion as I thought in my diary entry. She gave me a phone number for a clinic I could call and make an appointment. Then she also encouraged me to talk to my parents about what was happening. I explained that they would *not* understand this *at all* and that I didn't want to bother them. An abortion at the time was around three or four hundred dollars, I think. I called the clinic from the pay phone in the mini mall where the Planned Parenthood was and made an appointment based on the information they had given me. Bailey said she would drive me. I would have to skip school, but that was okay. I would probably get in trouble, but that was the least of my worries. The worst part, as far as I could tell, was that I had to wait almost three weeks before I could get the abortion, so I had to be pregnant for two more weeks. When we left, Bailey said she'd drive me to Smitty's so I could tell Ben what was happening. Tasha hopped in the car with tears in her eyes. I offered her a cigarette and she shook her head no.

"So. I . . . ummm. I think I'm gonna have the baby, guys."

We agreed that it was the right decision for her and that we would be there and help in any way we could. We dropped Tasha off at her house. She was going to tell her mom that night. Then Bailey drove me to Smitty's, where Ben was pulling carts in from the parking lot. He came over to give me a hug, and then I told him I had to wait and go to a clinic in a few weeks. Neither one of us knew how it worked, clearly.

"I'm so, so sorry, baby. I can get the money. Did they tell you how much?"

I told him, and he assured me he would get it as soon as possible. Then he kissed me and promised to call when he got home from work.

The next week was fucking awful. I had to go to school, obviously. I had to pretend I was fine to my parents, obviously. I started getting morning sickness and my boobs felt like they were going to explode. I threw up in the trash can in the main building of my school in between first and second period as Kendra and our other friend Kate were walking over.

"Holy shit! Are you okay??"

"Yeah. I'm fine now," I said wiping my mouth. Kate gave me some water from her backpack and I went on my way.

Ben had started hanging out with an older girl named Melanie from his econ class, a horrible-looking girl with terrible pocked skin and hair that was thinning from how many times she'd bleached it. She had a car, though, and so she could drive us off campus for lunch. That day, Ben and Melanie insisted we go to Arby's, and I remember picking at my fries and trying not to vomit as Melanie ate her roast beef sandwich with extra Horsey sauce, all of it getting stuck in her clear braces as she chewed with her mouth open and laughed at Ben's dumb jokes.

"I don't want to go to lunch with Melanie anymore," I said to Ben that night on the phone. "She's weird and I don't know. . . . I don't have anything to say to her. Can we just hang with Kendra on campus tomorrow??"

"Yeah. Sure, whatever, babe. But she's cool, you know."

The next day at lunch, I waited for Ben in the quad with Kendra and Kate and our other girlfriends, but he never showed. I didn't even eat; I was just waiting for him, like an idiot. When the bell rang, I couldn't help the tears and just let them flow freely as I made my way to the theater building. I ran into Tim Lochran, one of the nice older kids who I used to sit under the tree with.

"Hey! Hey. Are you okay? What's wrong??" I still remember sweet Tim, looking at me through his round, tortoiseshell glasses, like Harry Potter.

I started to sob for real. "I can't. . . . I just . . . I didn't eat and I really—"

"Oh jeez! Do you want me to get you food?"

"I don't know. . . ." I said in between sobs. "I just really want an egg roll . . . I guess?"

"Well, I can do that. Come on, I'll drive you to Chop and Wok."

It was such a small thing, really. But it didn't feel small. I ate my egg roll on the way back to school and thanked Tim as we walked back from the parking lot, careful not to let any administrators or security guards see us. When I thanked him, he gave me a big smile.

"No problem," he said. "Feel better! It's all gonna be okay, especially now that you've eaten!!"

Ben called me after school with some story that it was a misunderstanding and he had looked for us but had eventually gone with Melanie to Burger King. I told him it was okay, I understood and wasn't mad at all.

On Friday at school, Ben found me before the first bell. "Ummmm. We have a problem. My mom and dad found out and they won't give me the money and they're insisting that you come over after school and talk to them."

I stared at him. "What? What the fuck, Ben? No!"

"Look. If you don't, my mom is going to call your mom and tell her. This was the deal I made with them—it was *hard enough* to get them to agree to *this*, Busy. You have to."

I couldn't fucking believe it. I tried to understand *how* they found out, but it didn't even really matter. I was so scared the rest of the day. Kendra and Kate prepared me for what to say to Mrs. Miller. Ben's friend Alex assured me it would be fine, that the Millers were reasonable people. I called my mom from my drama teacher, Mrs. Carrick's, office and told her that I was going to Ben's house after school and that she could pick me up there when she was done with work.

We walked along the wash and smoked cigarettes as we made our way toward Ben's huge fucking house. When we got there, Ben's mom called from her bedroom, "I'm in here, Ben. You and Busy come in here now. And close the door behind you, please."

Ben gave me a look and we headed back. She motioned for us to sit on the bed and she settled into a chair across from us, looking right at me.

"Well," she said, "you've gotten yourself into quite a situation, haven't you?"

I was actually dumbfounded. I had done this by myself?

Ben shifted uncomfortably. "Mom—"

"*Enough, Benjamin.* You have nothing to do with this. I'm sorry, Busy. But you cannot kill this child. I won't let you murder a baby. When I think about Billy and what would have happened if *his* mother had been like you . . ."

And here she got choked up and started to cry. Of course. They had adopted their older son, Billy. *Right. Well, fuck. FUCK.*

"Ummm. I know. I just . . . I'm not going to have this baby. I can't—"

"YOU CAN. You're being *selfish* is what you're doing. You're going to MURDER A BABY because *you* didn't prevent this. We are a good Catholic family and there is *no way* that I can let this happen in good conscience. Ben's father agrees with me."

Then I started to cry. "Please. Mrs. Miller. I don't have the money and—"

"And you're not going to get it from us. Or Ben. You need to tell your parents. I was going to call your mother today, but I wanted to talk to you first. You clearly have no idea what you're doing. The ramifications of this *act*. You will go to hell. I will not stand by while you kill a baby! I'm sure your mother will agree."

"She can't—I—please. Let me tell them!" All I could think was my mom hearing I was pregnant from this horrible woman. I had to tell her. I just had no idea how I was going to do that.

"Fine. When? I need to speak with her and make sure we're on the same page."

"I don't know—I'll tell them this weekend. My dad is home this weekend."

"You have until Monday. I'm calling her first thing Monday morning. I know you'll make the right decision. I know you don't want to go to hell. I know you don't want Ben to go to hell, either. You can give the baby up for adoption. And give this child a *wonderful* life."

I collected my things and headed for the door, Ben following me like a puppy with his tail between his legs. We sat outside and waited for my mom to show up. I asked if maybe he could get the money from Melanie or Alex, who both had jobs and then maybe he could convince his parents over the weekend not to tell my parents. He thought maybe he could do that. When the car pulled up, I hugged Ben goodbye and got in, barely looking at my mom.

That night, I went out to the movies with Bailey and Tasha

and I told the girls what had happened. Both of my friends were horrified. I mean, it was actually insane, when you think about it. But also, in my gut, I knew there was some truth to it. I knew it was a baby. Or rather, that she would become a baby, if I didn't put an end to her. Somehow I also knew it was a girl. I could feel it.

By the end of the night, when Bailey dropped me off, I'd decided I wasn't going to tell my parents. I would take my chances that Ben could somehow talk some sense into his mom and I'd be able to handle this on my own. When I went into the house, my parents were already in their room with the door closed and the light off, so I just got into bed and called Ben. He didn't answer his line. I fell asleep crying.

Sometime in the night, I heard someone whispering my name. "Busy. Busy. Wake up, sweetie. I need you to wake up now."

I half opened my eyes. "What?! Mom! What time is it??"

"Honey. It's three. I need you to promise you won't be mad. Okay?"

"What?!"

"Promise me you won't be mad."

I sat up, looking at my mom silhouetted by my hall light. "Mad about what?"

"Honey, your dad read your diary. Tonight while you were out. We need to know if it's true."

My heart sank. I wrote everything in there. The drugs. Sex. And of course, that I was pregnant. I lay back down and turned away from her and curled into a ball.

"Yes," I said, meekly.

"Oh, honey."

I started crying. My mom pulled me up and held me to her and let me cry, like how you hold a little kid when she's skinned her knee.

"I'm sorry, Mom."

"I know, honey. I know. Okay. You have to go tell your dad."

"*What?* Can't you???"

"No. Come on. Neither one of us has slept tonight. Let's go."

My mom and I walked across our house to my parents' bedroom. My dad was curled up in bed. As soon as I hugged him, he started sobbing. My parents sandwiched me between them like they used to do when I was really little and I would sneak into their bed. I told them about Ben's mom and what had happened. I told them that I had scheduled an abortion at a clinic.

"Busy. No. That is *not* happening. I'll call Dr. Fisher in the morning and we'll find someone good and private."

I gave her a hug, weak with relief.

We stayed in bed talking until the sun came up and decided that we should go eat breakfast at the Good Egg. I slid into the booth and made my mom sit next to me, cuddling into her, and for the first time in a year felt like I could breathe. At one point, my dad said something about "other options" and my mother literally almost jumped across the booth to strangle him.

"There are *no* other options for Busy. Not another word about this."

I looked at my dad, who shook his head and lowered his eyes. I knew he thought I was murdering a baby, too. And that I was probably going to hell. But he was willing to go along with it for my mom. And for me.

That night, my mom went into her home office to call Ben's mother. I listened through the door as she started off in hushed tones. Then as her voice got louder and louder until she was yelling at the top of her lungs:

"*MY DAUGHTER* DID THIS? WHAT ABOUT *YOUR SON*?! DO YOU KNOW HE GAVE HER *DRUGS*?!"

and

"YOU HAVE NO PART IN THIS DECISION. THIS IS ABOUT *MY* FAMILY. AND WE WILL DO WHAT IS BEST FOR *OUR* FAMILY AND *MY* DAUGHTER."

and

"QUITE FRANKLY, I DON'T THINK INTIMIDATING A SCARED FIFTEEN-YEAR-OLD BY TELLING HER SHE'S GOING TO HELL IS A VERY CHRISTIAN THING TO DO!"

and

"DON'T YOU *EVER* SPEAK TO HER THAT WAY AGAIN OR YOU WILL HAVE SOME SERIOUS PROB-LEMS ON YOUR HANDS. HOW *DARE* YOU!"

She hung up the phone, muttering to herself, and came out of the office.

"It's fine," she said. "That woman is crazy. I'm sorry she was so awful to you."

The truth is, my mother is who you want in your corner when shit goes down. The way she put aside any of her own feelings about what was happening and just supported and loved me was staggering. I wish I had trusted that she would have taken care of me the year before, but there was no point in bringing up Trey now. One trauma at a time.

My mom was referred to an ob-gyn who performed private abortions. We went to his office and I had an internal ultrasound. I saw the little bean I would be getting rid of, her little heart fluttering. Mine fluttered too.

"I take it this was a rape situation?" the doctor said as my mom and I sat across from him afterward. I looked at my mother, aghast. *What had she told them?*

But she just reached over and grabbed my hand and said, "No. No. What we have here is a case of two *very* young people letting their emotions get the better of them and making a bad choice."

If this abortion didn't kill me, my mother's description of me becoming sexually active certainly might.

The doctor explained the procedure so I would know exactly what was happening. He said I could be put under, in a twilight sleep, if I wanted. I did. A series of rods would then be used to open the cervix enough to get the tools needed into the uterus to remove the fetus. Before you leave, they make sure they've gotten it all. All of the baby fetus. That's also why you have to wait a bit for a traditional abortion; they need it to be big enough that they can make sure it's all out. It's still super tiny, by the way, like only an inch and a half, maybe. Then there might be some cramping and bleeding for a week or so after. Maybe not. You can't use tampons or have sex for four weeks.

Mine was scheduled for the following Thursday morning.

On Wednesday, Ben brought me a flower to school, which was nice but also, like... what the fuck am I supposed to do with this? Plus, then people at school kept asking me if it was my birthday. Nope! Just getting an abortion tomorrow!

My mom took me in early the next morning. I was already crying. The nurse petted my head softly while I got the IV. I went to sleep and woke up to some juice and the nurse telling me that my mom was waiting outside and that it was over.

"It's okay, baby," my mom said in the waiting room. "Let me help you put on your shoes."

I nodded gratefully to her.

We went home and I slept the rest of the day. Ben didn't call me that day or the next. I lay in bed all day Friday crying. My mom had to fly to Omaha, where Leigh Ann was in college, because she was in a play that weekend. I begged her not to go. I didn't want her to leave me with my dad. I needed her to take care of me.

"I'm sorry, Busy. I have to go."

My parents told me that Leigh Ann didn't need to know about my abortion, because it would just upset her. We should just move forward like it never happened, and since I was now on the pill, it wouldn't happen again. My dad tried to check in on me, but I didn't want to see him. He couldn't comfort me; he didn't know how. He sort of just lingered by my door, asking if I wanted anything.

"No. Thanks, Dad."

He nodded and headed off. Ben finally called Saturday morning before he went to work. He wanted me to come out that night with him to his sister's high school theater production.

"It's just like people reciting poetry and monologues they've written, I think."

I asked my dad if I could go out and he looked at me sternly and said, "You know, I'd rather you not, Elizabeth."

"Well, it's like a school thing," I told him. "So I'll be *fine*."

The truth was, I wasn't fine. But I wanted to see my boyfriend and make sure he still loved me and what was I going to do at home all weekend with my dad? Sit in my room and cry? I was still bleeding and cramping, but it was just a school thing.

Ben and Melanie picked me up in her car, which smelled like menthol cigarettes. Ben pulled his seat forward so I could squeeze in the back. I hadn't realized she was coming, or, I guess I should say, that we were going with her.

"What time is the thing?" I asked as I got in.

"Oh . . ." Ben said as he lit up a cigarette, ". . . we're not going. That seems so lame. We're gonna go to Melanie's friend's party."

"Oh." I tried my best not to cry. We pulled up to a dingy house in Phoenix that was decorated cheaply for Halloween. As soon as we walked in, Ben took off to see if he could find Grant, and I lingered by the door.

"How do you feel?" Ben's friend Alex was suddenly next to me. "You want a rum and coke or something?"

"Oh. No. I'm okay. Thanks for asking, though."

"Yeah. It's rough. My friend Kelly had an abortion last year— do you know Kelly? She said it was fine and everything, but it still sucked. So . . ."

In retrospect, this conversation was fairly evolved for a

sixteen-year-old boy to even strike up. I mean, he could've just ignored it all together, but I really think he was doing his best to try to make me feel better. I waited a while and then went to find Ben, who was in the back of the house with Grant and Melanie, getting high.

"Can we go? I don't feel great and you're not even hanging out with me so—"

He jumped up and put his arm around my neck and kissed me on the forehead. "Yeah. Of course. Maybe in like a half an hour?"

"I guess. Sure. I'm gonna go to the bathroom."

I found the gross dirty bathroom with its ugly chipped Spanish tile and sat on the toilet and bled into it and cried. For myself. For my unborn baby. For the fact that I was pretty sure that my boyfriend might be a drug addict. What the fuck? Why was I here in this house with these people? I got up and went out front and found Alex again.

"Hey. Can you drive me home? I feel like shit."

"Yeah, dude. This party sucks anyway."

I bummed a cigarette off him and got in his car as Ben was coming out the front. He looked annoyed. "What the fuck, Busy?"

"Alex is gonna take me home. I couldn't find you and I don't feel well." My eyes welled with tears.

"Well, okay. Why didn't you just say that?" He hugged me. "Is it cool if I stay?"

I nodded yes. What else could I say?

Here's the thing. I should have broken up with Ben that night. Or the next week or the week after. But much like the Trey thing, I had made the decision that the only way all of this would be okay was if Ben and I stayed together and I don't know what . . . got married? Had babies? And then we could tell the story of how we met when I was fifteen and we just *knew* we were meant to be together??

I hung on wishing, willing it to be different or better. Ben was disappearing more and more with his friends, and I was left waiting for phone calls that inevitably never came. Finally, one cold January night, I called and broke up with him. I'm sure it wasn't a surprise, but he was still so mean on the phone. Afterward, I hung up and walked into the hallway and called out for my mom. I didn't know what else to do. She came running from her room in her robe.

"Busy! Honey! What is it? Are you okay??"

I folded into her, sobbing. When I told her, she started to cry too.

"Oh, honey. If I could take it away, you know I would. You know I would take it *all* away if I could." Then she put me in bed and got a cold washcloth for my head and scratched my back until I fell asleep.

As the school year wore on, I had a reminder every day in geometry class of my abortion. I watched—our whole school did, really—as Tasha got bigger and bigger. She was keeping her baby, not giving it up for adoption. Her family was being supportive, and her boyfriend, for his part, was sticking around. She would bring in sonograms and show them to me before class, and the day she told me she was having a girl, I congratulated her and told her how excited I was for her, and then I went to the bathroom and sobbed in the stall. Bailey and I threw her a baby shower. I made a little peach cake with baby booties on top of it; my mom helped me to get the icing right.

Ben's friends would yell stupid shit to me as I walked through the quad. (They liked to say, "Watch out! There goes *Jizzy Philipps!*" Cool, dudes.) And occasionally they would toss gum wrappers or balled-up notebook paper in my direction. Even Alex, who I had thought was pretty cool. But I guess I was wrong. It became clear that Ben was dating another girl. A friend of Melanie, I think. But I didn't see them much around campus. Our school wasn't small, and it was fairly easy to avoid people you didn't want to see.

One day, though, I walked into my science class and saw Mrs. Miller standing there. She was our substitute teacher. I felt like the wind had been knocked out of me. I took my seat and started to panic, but I wouldn't allow myself to cry in front of her. *Do I really have to sit here for the next forty-five minutes with this woman who told me I'm going to hell??* I grabbed my bag and started to run out. When I heard her call after me, I spun around and looked at her. "I'm going to the counselor's office and I'm going to call my mom." And then I did just that.

When I was done telling my mom, she said, "Put your guidance counselor on the phone."

Then I watched as she nodded, listening to my mom. "Uh-huh, uh-huh, uh-huh. Okay, Barbara. Yes, thank you."

She hung up the phone and looked at me. "So listen. You can

stay in here or go to the theater building. Whatever you want. You're excused from that class, and any time Mrs. Miller is sub-bing, you just come right in here, okay??"

I still have no idea what my mom said. But I was so glad she said it.

Soon after that, Kate and her boyfriend James decided they wanted to set me up with a senior named Shawn Harris. I knew him a little because he was in a play I'd done that spring and we had hung out a bit backstage. I thought he was super cute. He was dating one of Kate's friends Becca for a while, but they were broken up.

Shawn and I started hanging out, and before long, we were going out. Becca was pissed at me, especially since she thought maybe she and Shawn would get back together at some point. In order to keep the peace of our friend group, Kendra suggested a dinner at the Village Inn to smooth things over. All of us girls went. Becca showed up with Kelly Yi, Samantha's best friend, whom she had become good friends with in art class. As the conversation began to get heated about who was allowed to date who, I started to tear up.

"Becca, I'm sorry," I said. "I know you loved him, but you guys are broken up and . . . Look, I've had a really shitty year. After my abortion I felt like I would never recov—"

Kelly Yi cut me off. "Wait. *You* had an abortion, too?? *When?*"

We all looked at her, confused.

"What do you mean, *too*??"

"No—I mean. Wait. With Ben Miller?"

"Yeah. Who else?"

She looked at us, with wide eyes. "Samantha had an abortion in June. When you and Ben started dating. He knew. He gave her some money."

My face fell. We all just sat there in stunned silence. Then I jumped up and ran to the pay phone and dialed his number. He picked up on the second ring. "Did Samantha have an abortion? Like when we started dating?? Like four months before I had one???"

"What the fuck, Busy? YEAH. I *guess*. So what?"

"*So* what?! So you got me pregnant like three months later???" I tried to compose my thoughts, but I was just so disgusted by him it was hard to get anything out.

"Well, what can I say? My family were Vikings."

"What the fuck does that mean?"

"I have strong sperm. Whatever, Busy. *Prove that it was mine*."

I slammed the receiver down and ran out of the restaurant and up the street. I just wanted to get the fuck away from everything and everyone. Kendra ran after me and grabbed me and we tumbled to the ground and both cried on the side of Shea Boulevard, as cars whizzed past us. After that, Becca was okay with me dating Shawn Harris. Not happy about it, but okay with it. I avoided Ben at school, which wasn't that hard.

Toward the end of the school year, my French teacher announced that she would be taking a small group of students on a two-week tour around Europe in June. Kate and I both decided we should go. Our parents agreed. I think my parents were rightfully not looking forward to the summer with me. I was dreading my due date and would be glad to be out of the country for it. I still cried regularly in bed at night, sure not only that I had murdered a baby but that I was also going to hell. *How would God ever forgive me? How would my own father? How would I?*

Our tour of Europe was only about ten kids from my high school. In every town and every city we visited, we would be taken to the cathedral in the center of town. And in every single one, I would light a candle and pray for forgiveness. Pray for my baby. Pray that God would allow me to have beautiful children in the future. Sometimes I would cry, and Kate would wait patiently for me in the pews until I was finished, and then we would go explore with the rest of the group and buy chocolate and postcards to send home before getting back on the bus and continuing on.

Our teacher was very cool about letting us drink so we could truly experience "European living"; after all, we were almost sixteen. I felt such freedom walking around these beautiful old cities with my friends, having coffees and gelato in cafés and wine in the afternoon, visiting places we had only read about and seen in movies (basically just *The Sound of Music*!). In Florence, we met up with my aunt—my mom's sister—who was living there at the time. She came to meet us at our hotel, ate breakfast with us, and smoked about a million cigarettes. I could tell my French teacher was impressed with her worldliness, and I felt cool that I was related to her, even if we didn't really have much of a relationship because of my mom's complicated feelings about her.

By the time we got to Rome, we were tired, but I was feeling pretty good. Our first morning there, we visited the Colosseum and Kate and I took pictures standing and smiling where all the tourists do. Then it was off to the Vatican. When we arrived, our tour guide turned to us and said in his cheerful Italian accent, "Oh. It seems there is extra security today! Bags open, everyone!"

Everyone went through one by one, but I was stopped by a security guard. There was conferring back and forth in Italian with another guard, and my teacher called our tour guide back to intervene.

"He says you mustn't go in! We have a bit of a problem here. Let's see . . ."

He then explained that I was wearing overalls, really nice cream overalls that I had borrowed from Emily (of course) for the trip. *Overalls* are not allowed in the Vatican. It's a rule that has something to do with farmers not going to church in dirty overalls or something. Honestly, I have no idea. But we didn't know what to do. We weren't close to our hotel. I couldn't change into anything. And I *had* to see the Vatican!! After a bit of discussion, the tour guide came back to the little group that was waiting with me while everyone else had gone in ahead.

"Okay. We *maybe* have a solution! Does anyone have a sweater???"

Kate pulled one out of her backpack and waved it around. "I do! I have a sweater!!"

"Okay! So, Miss Busy, you just put the sweater on and it must remain on the whole time inside, okay? Are we good??"

I pulled Kate's sweater on over my head, the guards gave us a nod of approval, and in we went. As soon as we entered the Vatican, I was awed by not only the sheer size and beauty but also the number of *people* crushing in there. We could barely see anything. Someone in front of us turned around.

"The *Pope* is here!!!!!"

The Pope? THE Pope? Pope John Paul II? THAT Pope???

I grabbed Kate's hand. "*Come on.* We're getting a picture for my grandma."

And around we scooted, weaving through the hundreds of people all clamoring to do the exact same thing. We made our way to the right side of the church and pushed forward. At some point I lost Kate, but I kept moving ahead, determined. This was it. I was about three people deep behind the rope. There was lots of jostling and shoving, but I kept pressing forward.

Then something insane happened. Well, a few things actually. A woman turned around, looked me straight in the face, and said, "Go! You need this more than I do."

And with that she grabbed me and shoved me in front of her. You already know I clearly don't have the best balance. I fell forward as the man who was in front of the woman stepped to the side. I would have fallen to the ground, but someone from the other side of the rope grabbed my right arm, the arm where I wore the little ball chains I'd bought at the hardware store with my dad and wrapped around like a bracelet because I thought it made me look punk rock and cool. It was a large security guard. He pulled me up, and just like that, I was face-to-face with Pope John Paul II. Inches from him in fact. I was staring into his eyes.

"Es Deutches?"

I shook my head.

"No. I'm—"

"Oh! Americano! Americano!"

He smiled and laughed and then took my cheeks in his hands and said something softly in Italian, I guess? A prayer for me. He made the sign of the cross on me and put his palm to my forehead and then nodded at me and turned and walked away, back through the door where the Pope goes to do Pope stuff. I remember his eyes. They were soft. I remember that he really had love for me. Truly. I remember I knew it was okay.

I've never told this story publicly; I haven't even told people I'm very close with. It almost feels sacrilegious for me to be typing these words now, giving this to the world. Imagining having to talk about this in an interview for a gossip magazine to sell my book, or seeing the headline, reducing what was the most incredible thing that has ever happened to me to clickbait. But I don't exist without this story. And the story doesn't exist without this ending. It doesn't work for me without getting the absolution I needed. And from the only person in the world who could give it to me: the Pope in Rome. When we got back to the hotel I called my parents and woke them up. It was June 14, 1995, in Rome; June 13 in Arizona. It was my due date.

INTERSTATE LOVE SONG
(Stone Temple Pilots)

I had been begging my mother to let me get an agent ever since I was in third grade. How did a third grader in Arizona know what an agent was, you might ask? Well, my friend Ami had an agent in Los Angeles and would fly out for auditions and put herself on tape. She even *screen-tested* for Wednesday Addams in the Addams Family movies, the part that eventually went to Christina Ricci. Ami *also* sang the jingle for her dad's window-tinting company on the radio. To the tune of "Stupid Cupid," her little voice would ring out from 104.7 FM, "Polyglycoat you're the one for meeeeeeeee!"

Third grade was when I landed the role of Wilbur the Pig in our grade's production of *Charlotte's Web*. Actually, I wasn't the only Wilbur. The whole play was double cast, in order to give more kids parts. Jeremy Babendure was the other Wilbur. Jeremy also had some professional experience. The year before, he'd been cast as "Scamp with Squirt Gun" and had gotten to deliver *three whole lines* in the classic Coen brothers film *Raising Arizona*. I felt a little bit of pressure, sharing the part with such a seasoned professional, and I became determined to shine brighter as the *other* Wilbur.

The week before the play, the teachers explained to the two casts that one would be performing at the morning assembly in front of the kindergarten through second-grade kids, while the other would perform for the fourth through sixth graders, and that it was up to me and Jeremy to decide who would perform for which group of kids. Well, I'm not an idiot. Obviously, the power move is to perform for the older kids. Who gives a fuck what a bunch of babies think about my portrayal of Wilbur?? I wanted the fourth, fifth, and sixth graders to know how talented I was. I remember this moment of manipulation so clearly, it still makes me laugh. I immediately turned to Jeremy and very earnestly said, "I think you should do the morning show; you really have a way with younger kids that I just don't have. Honestly? I just think they're going to like your Wilbur better. They'll understand 'cause Wilbur is a boy and you're a boy. I think they might get confused by me playing it since I'm a girl, right?? Don't you think???"

I mean. Jeremy didn't stand a chance. It *was* way more satisfying to have older kids come up to me in the weeks after the play than it would've been to have impressed a bunch of kindergarteners. I also made sure I took off my pig snout for curtain call so that kids who maybe didn't know me before would be able to recognize me in the halls. I was one hundred percent hooked on the love of performing, but I think the recognition was more important. Sometimes it still is. SEE ME! LOVE ME! TELL ME I AM THE BEST! TELL ME YOU LOVE ME!

I knew that in order to procure work as an actress, one must have an *agent*. After Wilbur, my mom *did* take me into the local Ford agency, where I was rejected by the agents working there. I clearly wasn't meant to be a child model: too short but not tiny, not conventionally or uniquely pretty enough. So I kept doing my theater programs, auditioning occasionally for an open call that my mom would find in the paper. But she wasn't about to figure out how to take me to L.A. to get me an agent. My parents didn't really have the expendable income to have a child actor. Especially back then, if your kid really wanted to act, one of the parents would essentially have to give up their lives and move to L.A. to live in one of those horrible apartment complexes that the out-of-town kid actors all live in and devote all of their time and income to making the impossible happen. No. My parents weren't interested in that.

"When you graduate from high school and make it through at least *two years* of college, Busy, *then* you can really try. But your dad and I will *not* be paying for *that!*"

I was convinced the only thing that could somehow redeem *any* of the previous few years of my life was if I were to become famous doing the thing I'd declared I was going to do in third grade, and as soon as possible. Honestly, the only time I'd ever expressed interest in being something else when I grew up was when I'd decided at age three that I was going to be a *red bucket*. The final straw in my high school years—which had, more often than not, fucking sucked—was having Shawn Harris cheat on me repeatedly after he went away to college, and then give me

HPV (because OF COURSE HE DID). I was due for something good.

One morning, I was listening to the radio on my drive to school when the entertainment reporter had a bit about how they were making a TV show from the movie *Clueless*. I was beside myself all day. I should be the new CHER! OF COURSE! I'M MORE LIKE ALICIA SILVERSTONE THAN ANYONE I KNOW! This was my plan. I was sure of it.

"You have to get me an agent," I said when I got home that day. "And headshots. I need headshots."

My mother looked up from the giant piles of house listings she was sorting through. "Actually, you know what? Dixie's friend told me about this woman you should meet! She's got her own little agency in Paradise Valley. I think she's more of a manager, but her daughter is an actress."

A week later, my mom took me after school to a normal-looking house in Paradise Valley, where I met Ellen Anderson. That day at school, I'd dressed up more than I normally did, saying to some girls in the theater hallway, "Oh, yeah, it's not a big deal but I'm going to meet a new *agent* today and see about an audition. They're making a TV show from the movie *Clueless* and I'm probably going to put myself on tape for it." I had *no basis* whatsoever for this other than what I'd heard on the radio, but I had convinced myself this was a very real possibility for me.

Inside of a dimly lit, fairly messy home office littered with headshots with résumés stapled to the back, Ellen gave me the once-over and decided that I could probably find some local work. In my head now, she's basically Joey's agent from *Friends*, but I know she was just a nice lady in Arizona whose daughter wanted to be an actress and she figured out how to do it all herself, probably so she didn't have to deal with small-time agents, who are terrible anyway. She asked me what kind of work I was interested in. I took a deep breath.

"Well . . . I heard they're making a *Clueless* TV show. Like from the movie? I think I should be on it. Can I audition for that??"

She looked at me. "Okay . . . ummm. Let me look into it. It may already be cast. But you know, if there are things that are casting in L.A. that you're right for, we can see about putting you on tape for them and sending them over."

She told me I needed headshots that showed different characters I could play. (A cheerleader! A nerdy girl! A fun girl!) Also, I needed to make up a résumé using the plays I'd been in and to really beef up my special-skills section in order to make up for my complete lack of actual experience. Oh, I had *special skills*! Singing? Obviously. Dancing? All the damn time! Good with kids? Yup. Some French? *Oui!* Ice-skating? Roller-skating? YOU BET! BIKE RIDING?! OH, I CAN FUCKING RIDE A BIKE.

My mom and dad agreed to pay for headshots since they'd paid for my sister to get some pictures taken recently. (And you know, EVERYTHING HAD TO BE EQUAL!) Leigh Ann had recently been signed by the local Ford agency as a plus-size model. She was getting a ton of catalogue shoots and had even been on the cover of a local magazine. So my parents got me headshots. They were ridiculous. I'm wearing so much makeup I look *way* older than seventeen, with dark lipstick and heavily contoured cheeks, an attempt to give my baby-fat face some angles. At least I didn't actually wear costumes, like people did in some of the other composite cards I saw in Ellen's office. I figured that you could tell I would make a good cheerleader without me having to actually put on a uniform.

Ellen liked my pictures and assured me auditions would be coming. They weren't, exactly. I had a few, for commercials that were shooting in Arizona and therefore nonunion. Ellen encouraged me to be an extra on a made-for-TV movie about an alien invasion that Luke Perry was starring in. I strutted onto that set and immediately figured out that the AD (assistant director) is the one who you want to be friends with if you're looking for some screen time or to be "featured." I worked so hard to try to be noticed. And even when I wasn't, I decided I could put "featured extra" on my résumé because A) who the fuck even knows what that means, and B) who the hell will ever even see this insane movie?

A month later, Ellen called with what she described as a great opportunity for me. The Mattel toy company was coming to Scottsdale to have their annual "pre-toy fair" and they were looking for local actors to present the new toys to buyers. Specifically, they were hiring women to be live versions of the dolls they were trying to sell. Live Barbie dolls.

"Look, mostly, they bring actors and actresses in from Los Angeles for this, but it's a good job, and you make *great* money for two weeks of work. I think it could be a good fit and they were excited about you. The only thing is that I told them you were eighteen, so just say that."

The auditions were held in a ballroom at the Phoenician, one of the nicest resorts in Scottsdale. I went to my appointment with my headshot in hand and signed in. The casting director came out and handed some material to me and another woman who was waiting. It was basically a monologue filled with sales projections for a particular Barbie, explaining to the buyers why this doll would sell so well. It was completely generic in tone. What I didn't know is that apparently, the toy business is *very* serious, and toy espionage is actually a thing of concern. So my audition piece was the generic Barbie audition piece that all the girls received. I did it in what I thought was my best Barbie voice. When I was finished, the woman who was clearly in charge pulled a script out of a manila envelope.

"Busy!" she said, beaming at me. "That was really great! You know, part of the job is that you're portraying the *live* version of a new doll to our buyers." Here she looked over to her cohort, who nodded. "And one of the dolls that's coming to market *isn't* actually a Barbie. It's a doll from an upcoming TV show that we think will be incredibly popular. I assume you've seen the movie *Clueless?*"

Was this woman fucking with me?

"Well, we're launching a line of dolls to coincide with the show's premiere, and we've been looking for a girl who could play the live version of Cher. Will you take a look at this material and see what you think?"

Do I even need to tell you what happened next? As you can well imagine, I fucking killed it. My Cher impression had been AT THE READY for MONTHS. And here we all were. It wasn't *exactly* how I'd imagined I would be putting this particular talent to use, but it would do. The job paid like two grand a week! I'd been working as a hostess at California Pizza Kitchen for over a year and still hadn't made that much.

I had several fittings before the pre-toy fair in order for them to build a life-size version of the outfit the doll came in. Also, four full days of rehearsal. Yes. Rehearsal. My script was one of the longest, about nine pages total. And *in* those nine pages—which I was to deliver in my VERY BEST CHER impression—were tons of statistics and projections and also just a basic explanation of *who* these characters were and *why* toy shops all over the world would want to sell them.

The two giant ballrooms at the Phoenician were transformed into a toy wonderland, a maze of perfectly art-directed lands for the dolls and their human counterparts to live in, to do their *very* best to be sold to buyers from around the globe. I learned fairly quickly what the deal was from the Barbie girls who were flown in from L.A. and had done the circuit before. Basically, different groups of buyers were to be shuttled through the various rooms with a guide from Mattel. The Mattel marketers responsible for your doll would almost always be in the room with you, in case there were questions that weren't in your script. But if the question *was* something covered in your script, they preferred if *you* answered the buyer directly and in character.

My marketers were two fun young women in their late twenties who thought everything I was doing was amazing. I mean, not to toot my own *Clueless*-doll horn here, but they did basically win the fucking lottery with me. My impression was spot-on and really funny. Plus, I have an *insane* ability to memorize *anything*. Great big hunks of dialogue have never been an issue for me. (I sometimes thought the writers on *Cougar Town* were trying to fuck with me just to see if I would be stumped, but *nope*. I always got it. Even when I was handed new half-page monologues while I was sitting in the makeup chair.)

By the time the pre-toy fair opened, I was beyond ready. I loved the different groups of businesspeople coming in to listen to my spiel, and I felt so proud when one of the more experienced Barbie girls said to me, "Wait. You do your whole thing every time? Normally the buyers just cut you off and start talking with each other about the doll. You must be really good."

The day the CEO of Mattel, Jill Barad, came through was especially exciting because she brought SHARON STONE with her. *The* Sharon Stone. This was 1996. This was PEAK SHARON STONE. The two impeccably dressed women watched me with bemused expressions as I gave my little performance, and then Jill raised her hand to stop me and they both clapped. Sharon swept her scarf over her shoulder and as she was walking out turned back to me and said, in her very best Sharon Stone, "You're very talented and I think you're going to be a big star someday."

When the doors closed behind them, my marketing reps and I almost died. If Sharon Stone said it, it *must* be true. I could barely contain my excitement.

I felt so grown up, getting to work at six-thirty in the morning, grabbing coffee and a cheese Danish from the catering they had for everyone working the fair, chatting with the other actresses as we got dressed in our Barbie outfits and then making it to the showroom floor by 7 a.m. sharp to go over the schedule for the day. I was finished at 6 p.m. and would drive home, windows rolled down, air-conditioning blasting (it was summer in Arizona, after all), smoking cigarettes and listening to music with the volume turned up all the way.

The two weeks flew by, and before I knew it, the toy fair had packed up and left town. How was I supposed to just go back to my job at CPK and then to my senior year of *high school*? I was a real working *actress* now!

As senior year started, I began working at another restaurant, an upscale Mexican place that was in the same strip mall as CPK. Kate and I both moved over there together. I can't exactly remember why. Maybe we were offered more money. Maybe we were tired of BBQ chicken pizza. Maybe we were sick of the low-grade sexual harassment we were subjected to at CPK by one of the managers. WHO KNOWS? What I do know is this: I was seriously *done* with being in school and I couldn't wait to graduate and get the fuck out of Arizona.

I had to figure out what colleges to apply to that I had a shot of getting into and that—even more important—were in Los Angeles. There wasn't a chance for UCLA or USC, which I didn't have the grades for and which were also prohibitively expensive if you were applying from out of state. So that left only a few places. CalArts, which had a conservatory program that I had to audition for, and Loyola Marymount University. I had a few older guy friends who were all attending LMU, so I decided to apply there. Also, since it was Jesuit, I knew my parents would be into it.

"The Jesuits love to drink, but they are *the best* at education!" my mom would always say.

I started spending a lot of time with my friends Brett and Craig, who were friends from theater. Brett was also in my French class and we would sit together and make fun of our crazy French teacher and pass nonsensical notes back and forth. Craig was tall and skinny with floppy curly hair. The two of them were fairly nerdy; they mostly just hung out with each other, making weird movies on Brett's parents' video camera or recording slightly offensive comedy songs on Craig's boombox. Still, I liked both of them a lot and occasionally would drive us all off campus for lunch. Sometimes I thought I must seem like an alien to sweet Craig, with his art-house movie theater job and his love of Charlie Chaplin. He was the lead in the school play that fall, and I had volunteered to be the assistant director. I actually ended up having to replace one of the girls in the cast when she basically refused to memorize her lines and kept ditching rehearsal. Also, she was pretty terrible, and I think our theater teacher was happy to have a reason to get rid of her and have me step in a week and half before the show went up.

After rehearsal one day, I was talking with Craig in the school parking lot and sort of apologizing for being a crazy mess the year before, when he revealed that his mom had been diagnosed with cancer again and this time they thought it was terminal. Maybe six months to a year. I was so devastated for him, standing there as the sun was setting behind the mountains and turning the sky pink and purple and orange. I remember his face so clearly, and I remember just having an overwhelming feeling like I needed to be in his life. That I needed to take care of him. I committed to myself in that moment that I would.

There was something so sweet and innocent about Craig's crush on me. We were the same age, but you know how it is with boys and girls when you're a teenager. I was seventeen, but I seemed like I was twenty-five. My girlfriends and I would get served alcohol in restaurants. Shawn's sister Britney taught me that if you just ask for a pinot noir, they assume you're old enough because you know what you're talking about, and she was almost always right. On the rare occasion that we got carded, it was embarrassing but not the end of the world. We weren't trying to get into bars. We were ordering *wine* in Italian restaurants. They were always happy to make a wine sale.

I was still dating random guys who were older, and occasionally going down to Tempe and fucking Shawn Harris in his dorm room. Lord knows why. I guess it was just something to do. So while I knew Craig liked me, I wasn't sure what I wanted to do about it. I loved hanging out with him, and as we worked on the play I found him more and more attractive. He was really cute and really talented and so funny and smart, which was probably more attractive to me than anything else. And he thought I was so funny. I loved making him laugh, and I loved watching him watch me tell stories. And I loved the fact that I could tell he was so into me but wouldn't do anything about it. And I loved him. I just loved him.

I was really into raves that year, and Brett started coming with me more and doing drugs, which drove Craig crazy. He thought we were so dumb for wasting our time like that. I mean, he wasn't wrong. But it was fun as fuck, and what else were we supposed to do in Arizona but waste time? But as the school year went on, I started to like staying in and making popcorn on the stove with Craig and watching movies that his older brother Jeff, who was already studying screenwriting at NYU, would recommend. To my surprise, I liked it just as much as I liked getting high on E and staying out until the sun came up.

One night, after watching Noah Baumbach's *Kicking and Screaming* for the millionth time, Craig walked me out to my car. It was freezing, and while I was wearing my fuzzy black coat from Delia's, he was just wearing a sweatshirt. We were leaning against the car as we talked, and I said something that made him double over laughing, which I always loved. (You might be sensing a theme here: I love a good audience, especially one-on-one.) And then I felt that thing. All of a sudden, I wanted him to kiss me more than anything. But I knew he wouldn't. So I looked at him and narrowed my eyes.

"Do you want to kiss me?"

He glanced at me and then up at the sky. He shivered, and I couldn't tell whether it was because of what I'd just said or because it was freezing. I didn't need to ask. I knew the answer. But I wanted him to say it. He didn't. He just looked back at me. And then I moved in front of him and put my hands on his face and kissed him against my car.

He would tell me later that after I left he went inside and wrote a note for himself that said "THAT REALLY HAP-PENED" and placed it on his nightstand, in case he woke up in the morning and thought he had dreamed it.

I wish I could tell you that he became my boyfriend and everything worked out, but that wasn't exactly what happened. We kept hooking up, off and on, with everything being a first for him. And then I would get annoyed that he didn't seemingly want to be my boyfriend, even though he said he did. I mean, he wouldn't hold my hand in public, at school he didn't want people to know we were dating, and we didn't really go "out" places. We mostly just hung out at one of our houses. It was really confusing, and it also felt like I was always trying to convince him it was okay for me to like, give him a hand job or whatever. I know. When has a seventeen-year-old boy ever needed to be convinced of that? But he did. He was very inexperienced and nervous about it all. So I kept dating older guys, including stupid Shawn Harris.

In the winter, my agent called and said that Mattel wanted to hire me for the huge toy fair in New York! They would fly me and my mom out and put us up at a nice hotel, and I would work for two weeks. It was the start of the second semester of my senior year. The only catch was that I had to convince all of my teachers to excuse me for that long, and I also had to convince Mrs. Carrick, my drama teacher, to still allow me to star in the spring musical even though I would miss two weeks of rehearsal. *Guys and Dolls* was only one of my FAVORITE MUSICALS of all time, and I'd been waiting my WHOLE LIFE to play Adelaide (or at least since eighth grade, when I had seen the touring production).

Most of my teachers said it was okay, that they would just send my work with me and I could turn it in when I got back. Except my asshole Republican sexist Government teacher. He flat-out refused, which put me in a real tough spot since I wouldn't be able to graduate without completing Government. I asked my mom to help me, and she called the vice principal, who agreed to meet with me to discuss my options. She was a humorless older woman who had been in administration for so long that I'm sure she'd forgotten what it was like to deal with kids who actually had dreams that extended beyond just going to ASU and becoming a CPA or something.

She looked at me flatly. "I don't understand why you have to do this."

"Well, I don't *have* to do anything. But, you know, I want to be an actor and this is experience working *as an actor*, so—"

"You *do* understand that you're *not* going to be an actress, right? That's not a viable career. You'd better start thinking about what you actually *could* do, because college will go by quickly and you'll need to declare a major."

I looked at her and wished my mom was there. Barbara Philipps would have put this lady right in her place.

"Okay. Well, I just need you to sign this paper saying I can leave school for two weeks and get paid to DO THIS ACTING JOB."

"Fine. When you get back you'll have to sign up for the online computer course, where you can finish Government on the computer. It won't be easy for you."

"That's okay. I can do that. Thank you, Mrs. Weber."

Of course I could fucking do that. This woman had greatly underestimated me. My conversation with Mrs. Carrick, however, did *not* go the way I thought it would.

"I'm sorry, dear," she said. "Of course I know you would make a fantastic Adelaide. That's not the issue. You just can't miss two weeks of rehearsal when we only have four, which is barely enough time to put this show up anyway."

I was devastated. But I didn't want to miss my chance to go to New York City. I'd never been there! Plus, I was told that the BIG NEW YORK toy fair was even cooler, and the other actors who worked it were all REAL BROADWAY ACTORS, people who were living the dream. *My* dream! So I decided it was worth it to miss out on the last musical production of my high school career and go to New York.

My mom and I flew into the freezing cold New York winter on a Saturday night. After we checked into the hotel and I got the package with my updated script and call time for the morning, I went downstairs to try to sneak a cigarette outside without my mom knowing. I stood against the stone wall and looked up. All the buildings seemed to be caving in on me and the ground felt like it was swirling beneath my feet. I took a deep breath and put my hand against the wall behind me to steady myself. It was vertigo, just for a moment. I was totally overwhelmed by the enormousness of it all. I put the cigarette out, bummed to be wasting it, and went back upstairs.

I started work super early the next morning, not really prepared for the jet lag. The Barbie girls from Arizona were right: this toy fair was *way* bigger and more impressive. It was so much fun to be in the dressing room with the actresses from New York, talking about what Broadway workshops they were doing next and who had gotten offered what part. There were a few of the girls who would always sing in the dressing room in the morning as we were getting ready. One of the Barbie girls I knew from the Arizona toy fair, who had been flown in from L.A., turned to me and gestured toward one of the singers. "You see that girl? I heard she turned down the part of Maureen in *Rent* because of her *religious* beliefs. Can you believe it???"

I shook my head. No. I certainly could not imagine turning down the role of Maureen in *Rent* because of religious beliefs!! I've tried to figure it out for years and I haven't been able to confirm this, but I feel like there's a *really* good chance the petite singing religious girl was Kristin Chenoweth, two years before the revival of *You're a Good Man Charlie Brown*, for which she won her first Tony Award. Though it also could've been someone who never worked again after TURNING DOWN A ROLE IN *RENT*!

My mom would wander around the city during the day while I worked, occasionally getting tickets for matinees in the cheap-ticket line. I was off work every night at six and would meet her back at the hotel for dinner. A few times, I went across the street with the other toy fair actors to have a drink after work. I didn't really know what to order, since I mostly just drank red wine in Arizona with my friends. My Barbie friend, Lisa, smiled at me and said, "Let me get you a cosmo; you'll love it!" This was at least a year before *Sex and the City* made cosmos something I would've known about, and I remember my mind was JUST ABOUT BLOWN at how amazing that drink was. In fact, I'm not kidding, can we bring them back? They were so delicious! I was careful not to overdo it, though. Even though I was fairly reckless in Arizona, when I was working, I had my shit under control. It was hard work and I had to wake up early, so it was better to just have one and say good night.

I didn't know many people in New York, obviously. But one night Emily took the train in from Connecticut, where she was in college at Wesleyan, and we went to the Harley-Davidson Cafe for dinner and took pictures in front of the billboards for Crunch gym because we thought they were funny, I guess. She took the late train back, because she had class in the morning and I had to work. But it was fun to see a friendly face.

Craig's older brother Jeff was in school at NYU, so my mom and I took him out to dinner one night. Then he met just me for dinner another night after work. The toy fair was closed on Sundays, so I asked Jeff if he could take me out to some clubs or something Saturday night. I was dying to go dancing. My mom had no problem with me going out with Craig's older brother; why would she? I was going out in Arizona on the weekends until 6 a.m. Even though this was New York, I know she felt comfortable with Jeff and told us to have fun. We went to a bar near NYU that he knew wouldn't card me and had some drinks

(I ordered my new favorite: a COSMO), and then we went to a club that was eighteen-and-older to dance. I got in easily, even without a fake ID (this was the late '90s, things were easier).

When we came out of the club, it was super late and starting to rain. Freezing rain. We hopped into a cab, and before I could really think about it, I was making out with him. I know, I know. You hate it. I get it. It was a shitty thing to do to Craig. Not just on my part. Jeff knew how his little brother felt about me. But you know, I was in NEW YORK. Starting to LIVE THE DREAM. And Jeff was super cute. And it was raining and we were in a cab and we were mostly drunk and for sure young and maybe Craig wouldn't have to ever know? It wasn't like he was my *boyfriend*. He wouldn't commit to that, remember? It made him uncomfortable. He was basically just like my best friend. You know, a best friend who I was in love with and who was in love with me, except we didn't say that probably because we didn't really know it yet. And who wouldn't fuck me, even though I wanted to. So I would fuck other people (not that I particularly enjoyed it). And now here I was making out with his brother in the back of a cab in New York City. Ugh. Busy. Get your shit together, girl.

We went back to Jeff's dorm and made out some more but didn't take it much further, mainly because as we both started to sober up, I think it dawned on us how truly fucked up this was, what we were doing to Craig. We promised we would never tell him—this was a what-happens-in-New-York-stays-in-New-York situation.

I finished the toy fair and went sadly back to Arizona with my mom. My Mattel toy reps told me that I would be joining them at the E3 expo in a few months to help them with the *Clueless* CD-ROM that was going with the doll. And the pre-toy fair would happen again in the summer, before I went to college.

When I got back to Arizona, I was really excited to see Craig and Brett and get back to school. I had to do that weird government class online, but it was so insanely easy that I finished it in ten days, which apparently had never happened before, since the only ones who had to take the online class were usually burnouts and kids who had been kicked out of regular class for behavioral issues. I was called back to Mrs. Weber's office.

"Well, clearly you cheated on this," she said, giving me a disapproving look over her glasses. "You couldn't have done it in this short of a time. It's a whole semester of work."

I looked at her blankly. I mean. What the fuck was I supposed to do here? I obviously finished it in ten days because it's for stupid kids and I wasn't stupid.

"I didn't cheat," I insisted. "I wouldn't even know how to do that. But what do you want me to do? There's no way to prove it to you."

I was so fucking done with high school and all this bullshit I knew didn't mean anything. I just wanted this to be over.

"You'll have to do it all again," she said. "And we'll make sure the teacher is watching your work."

I rolled my eyes. "Great. Thank you *so much*."

I flounced out of her office as only a privileged kid who knew she was destined for better shit could do. *You want me to do the online government class for stupid kids, again? Fine. And acting isn't a viable career? Well, I guess we'll see about that.*

The Saturday night after I got home, Craig, Brett, and I had tickets to see the Cardigans. An hour before Craig was supposed to pick me up, my phone rang.

"Hey. What's up??"

"I just got off the phone with my brother . . ."

His voice was shaky. Oh, fuck. THANKS, A LOT, JEFF! Of course his brother broke down and told him everything. "Riddled with guilt" is how Craig described him. Look, it wasn't like I felt *great* about it. But I'd been willing to keep up my end of the bargain. I guess Jeff couldn't.

Craig was (rightfully) super pissed at me and didn't want to go to the concert, but he was also kind of cheap and the tickets to the Cardigans were like twenty-five dollars, so he begrudgingly agreed to still go. I spent the show trying my best to get him to look at me or let me put my arm through his but his gaze was *withering*. I even cried a bit when they played "Lovefool." Not to be manipulative, but truly because I just wanted him to love me and I knew I had done something reckless and stupid and I should have known better, but couldn't he understand it didn't *mean* anything??? I guess not. Not that night, anyway. I got him to agree that he didn't want to throw away our friendship over this and I worked *very* hard that next week to make sure he understood how sorry I was. One week later, he was in my bedroom, sitting on my bed, when I cuddled up next to him and he kissed me again. I was so relieved. He was annoyed at himself that he caved so soon after declaring it was over for us, but I was just so happy that he was back that I vowed not to do anything to hurt him again. At least, nothing that he could find out about.

I had to fly to L.A. for my CalArts audition, and Brett's older brother, Eric, agreed to pick me up from the airport and drive me out to Valencia for it. He also was going to show me around LMU afterward, and then take me back to the airport that night. I didn't really have the grades to get into LMU. I mean, my grades were fine and my SATs were okay, but they still left a lot to be desired. I worked really hard on my essays, though, and even put together a picture collage to submit with my application. Instead of mailing it in, I just figured I'd drop it off in person while I was there.

My CalArts audition went great. I did a Shakespeare monologue—I think from *Romeo and Juliet*, although it's possible it was from *Hamlet*—and I also did a dramatic monologue from some play in which I was a girl talking about being raped, but using birds being killed as a metaphor or something? Who knows? I really thought I was going to be a VERY SERIOUS DRAMATIC ACTOR. The CalArts people were seemingly impressed, and I felt very confident that I would get in. (Why wouldn't I? WHO WOULDN'T WANT ME IN THIER SCHOOL?)

After my audition, Eric and I went to the Venice boardwalk and sat in the sun and had lunch and I remember breathing in the salty air and looking at all the weirdos wandering around the boardwalk and just thinking, "*This* is about to be my life." We went to the LMU campus, which isn't far from Venice, and

Eric took me on a tour, introducing me to his friends. Then we walked over to the admissions office for me to turn in my application. There wasn't anyone behind the desk but after a moment, a man poked his head out of a back office.

"May I help you?"

"Oh, hi!" I said brightly. "I just wanted to drop off my application for next year. I'm in town 'cause I was auditioning for CalArts and I thought I'd bring it by."

"Great!" he said with a smile. "Save some postage!"

He grabbed my application and started to open it as I introduced myself to him.

Have I talked about being a sparkly human yet? Well, I have a theory. There are certain people who are what I call sparkly humans. These are people who have things just happen for them or to them because other people see them and seemingly inexplicably *want* to help them. Because they sparkle. From the inside out. I was always a sparkly human (still am, for the most part, on most days). Adults just liked me and wanted to help me. Not kids at my school. Sometimes sparkliness isn't recognized by peers until much later. Sometimes sparkly people are even bullied as kids. Because other kids want to put that light out. They don't understand it and they want to kill it. The secret is, if you're truly sparkly, you survive all that bullshit and you don't let them put it out. And at some point, you start to get rewarded for it. Sparkly humans aren't always entertainers, and they don't always become famous. There are sparkly humans everywhere. And there are also plenty of people who are wonderful and amazing, but aren't sparkly. It's a very specific thing.

So anyway, I'm sparkly. And in this case, the man who took my application turned out to be the head of admissions at LMU, and even if my grades and SATs weren't *exactly* what they were looking for, he thought I was funny and engaging and loved my essays and my collage of pictures from my life. I got accepted to LMU for one reason: because I was sparkly.

Soon after that, Mrs. Carrick announced that there was an open casting call for an anti-smoking commercial and that they were looking for *real* teens to star in the spot. All of the kids from the theater department went after school to audition. I brought my headshot and trumped-up résumé and waited my turn with all my friends as they brought us in one at a time. They asked me to dance around while miming smoking and burning some-one with my cigarette. They asked me if I smoked and I lied, "Only sometimes, if my friends are." They seemed satisfied with that. They called my mom the next day and she told me that I'd booked the lead part in the commercial.

"BUSY! Congratulations, honey! That's SO GREAT!"

I was beyond excited. We shot all day, in a warehouse in downtown Phoenix called the Icehouse that I had spent many Saturday nights dancing in, high off my face. In the commercial, I was dancing in a mosh pit (thankfully, it was a *faux* mosh pit, and since I was the star of the commercial, I wasn't in any danger of dislocating my knee) and accidentally burning people with my cigarette until two dudes got fed up and crowd-surfed me and dumped me into a trash can. For the dancing, they played the White Zombie song "More Human Than Human" on repeat, and to this day, when I hear that song, I immediately think of being in that anti-smoking commercial.

I was positively high at the end of the day. *This* was what I wanted. I wanted to be on sets and work so hard I could barely see straight and hang out with people who I would probably never see again and eat craft services and get my hair and makeup done and get paid to *act*.

I found out I got into both CalArts and LMU and decided that LMU was the better call since I wanted to start acting professionally as soon as possible, and in the conservatory program at CalArts, working was frowned upon until you graduated.

I was chosen to give a speech at graduation, which in and of itself was fairly hysterical, since it was questionable whether I would be able to graduate at all, with the whole Government debacle. But I finished the course online to the satisfaction of the vice principal and was cleared to graduate. Afterward, my parents took me out to dinner to celebrate with Brett and Craig and also Shawn Harris, who wanted to come to my graduation. There's a super-hilarious picture of all of us, standing in front of the Chart House in Scottsdale where I'm in between Shawn and Craig, my arms around both and smiling this shit-eating grin, like, *Oh fuck!* I don't think I was even still sleeping with Shawn, although I guess that's possible. Craig was more or less my boyfriend by that point.

I had one moment of panic over the summer that maybe I should stay in Arizona and just go to ASU with all my friends.

Plus, Craig was a year younger than me, and I didn't want to leave him. I actually looked into it, but my mom was having none of my cold feet.

"Elizabeth. Absolutely *not*. You've been waiting your whole life for this! Don't be an idiot."

She was right, obviously. I had been waiting my whole life to move to L.A. and try to make my dreams come true. And as we've already established, I'm a lot of things, but I am *not* an idiot. So in August, right after my eighteenth birthday, we packed my car, I kissed my parents and my friends and Craig goodbye, and I drove myself to my new home, a dorm room at Loyola Marymount University in Westchester, California, which was about as close to Hollywood as I could get.

BAD REPUTATION
(Joan Jett)

"Busy Philipps, everyone!"

Almost every audition for producers or directors starts the same way, with some variation of "Say hi to Busy Philipps!" or "Here's Busy Philipps!"

And freshman year, this was all I wanted. To hear them call my name. To get *started*. A few years ago, Colin Hanks told me he remembers me crying hysterically in my dorm-room bed and sobbing, "YOU DON'T UNDERSTAND! I JUST CAN'T WAIT ANY LONGER TO BE AN ACTRESS!!"

I'm rolling my eyes right now, but that's who I was. It's who I am. I have a hard time just existing. I always think that *if only* I could be somewhere else, with someone else, doing something else, *then* I would be happy, finally. The hole would be filled. I know that's not how life works. But it's always been the thing that drives me.

Colin and I met when my new college friends and I went to see the LMU theater department production of *One Flew Over the*

Cuckoo's Nest. There was a kid in it playing Billy Bibbit, and as soon as he took the stage, I was in. Listen, I know. But there's just something about talent—real talent—that gets me. Also, he was tall and skinny and adorable. At intermission, I looked in the program and found his name.

"Do you know him?" I whispered to my friend Joe. "What year is he?"

"That's Colin *Hanks*. Tom Hanks's son."

After the show, Joe introduced us. I told him he was great in the play (which he was). He told me he liked my skate shoes. And, just like that, I had a crush on him.

I had a boyfriend back home, and he had a girlfriend back home. But it soon became clear that we liked each other, and we started finding ourselves in the same places at the same time. One night, we hung out at a party and then stayed up all night, walking to the bluffs that looked out over the lights of L.A. and talking until the sun came up. By seven in the morning, we had kissed and decided we would both break up with our significant others back home.

And that was that.

Around that time, one of the Barbie girls I'd met at the toy fair very sweetly offered to give me some advice about getting started in the business. I ended up meeting with her manager, Lorraine Berglund, at her home in the Valley. She was petite and stylish, and she and her husband were from London. I immediately loved her. She told me all about the kind of clients she represented and how I would need to get real headshots, since apparently the ones I'd been using in Arizona wouldn't work for

L.A. She even offered to split the cost with me, with the deal that I would pay her back when I started making money.

Eventually, she got me a meeting with Marilyn Szatmary, who was the head of a small talent agency, and who did not disappoint in terms of being intimidating. She looked at me skeptically over her desk and narrowed her eyes. "Well, you're very attractive. But can you *act*? Because I don't take on pretty people who can hit their marks, I represent *actors*."

I shit you not. Twenty years later and I can *hear* her saying those exact words to nineteen-year-old me. In fact, I believe that I committed them to memory while I was sitting there, because I knew what a fucking iconic thing that is to say to a young actress trying to break in to this business. Marilyn Szatmary did *not* suffer fools.

I assured Marilyn that I was, indeed, an *actor*. She then asked me to prove it by coming back and auditioning for her and the rest of the agents. I was elated. And I nailed it. Just like that, I had a manager and an agent, and I was ready for everything else. But it wasn't until the second semester of my sophomore year that the auditions started to roll in.

Dawson's Creek had been *such* a huge hit that all the networks were attempting their own versions of a "teen" show, hoping they would discover the next Katie Holmes. (I wouldn't be cast on *Dawson's Creek* for three more years.) In the span of those first few months of 1998, I was sent on over *ninety* auditions and callbacks. It seems impossible, I know, but sometimes I would only be reading for an assistant and then I would have to come back for the actual casting director, and *then* they would bring me back for producers or the director. Sometimes I'd audition for the same TV show four or five times. It became essentially a full-time job. Forget about making it to Intro to World Religions or Psych 102. I was in Glendale in a random office park, reading the same angsty teen drivel for the forty-seventh time. I got very used to hearing feedback like "They want to put a pin in you" (which means they like you but aren't ready to pull the trigger yet) and "You're not right for the lead but they want you to come back in for the *other* girl."

I had an audition one day for a pilot called *The Acting Class*. Lorraine told me the show was for NBC with Imagine Entertainment and Steve Martin producing, which was already exciting enough. But when I got the script, I couldn't believe it.

Writers: Carlos Jacott and Noah Baumbach
Director: Noah Baumbach

ARE YOU FUCKING KIDDING ME? NOAH BAUM-BACH? FROM *KICKING AND SCREAMING*?! I was dying. Plus, I was *perfect* for it. I skipped my classes and worked on it all morning and then went in for my pre-read, which was just for an assistant. She loved it and had me come back a few hours later for the casting director, who also loved what I did and asked if I would be able to come back the next day for the director and producers. I was literally losing my shit. *This* was what I was supposed to be doing. I was sure of it. *This* was my TV show. It was poetic, really.

I knew I had to call Craig and tell him. He was in Chicago

by then, studying acting at DePaul. Even though we weren't really talking much at that point, he was the only one who would understand. We loved Noah Baumbach and had watched that movie together a million times.

"What do you think I should do?" I asked. "Do I say something to him?"

He laughed. "Yeah. I think if it feels right, just say how much you love that movie. Jesus. This is so cool. Break a leg!"

At the audition, the casting assistant brought me back to the office where they were reading people. She walked in ahead of me and announced to the room, "This is Busy Philipps, everyone!"

I was ready. Noah and Carlos laughed heartily at all the right places as I did my reading, and afterward, as they clapped, I gave an awkward little curtsy/bow.

"That was really great, Busy," Noah said. "Thanks for coming in."

As the casting director showed me out, I thanked them and waved goodbye again. The door was almost closed when I put my arm out and stopped it.

"Wait," I said, half stepping back in. "I don't know if you're allowed to do this kind of thing, but this might be my only chance, so can I just say that *Kicking and Screaming* is my favorite movie of all time? Seriously. I've seen it a million times. And *Mr. Jealousy*, too. And I'm just such a huge fan of yours and this has been the most exciting thing that's ever happened to me so I just wanted to say that . . . OKAY, 'BYE!"

"Ummmm. Thank you?" Noah said with a smile. "That's really nice. Great work, Busy."

I flew back to campus, high on the whole thing. Later that day, Lorraine called and told me that not only did they love me but there was something a little strange that they were hoping I would be up for doing. Apparently, NBC hadn't officially green-lit the pilot, so Imagine wanted to put together a table read with all of their first choices in order to prove they should shoot it. I was so excited I could barely breathe.

Two days later, I drove to NBC, where I met the other actors cast in the read-through: Adam Scott, Nia Vardalos, Carlos, John Lehr, and a few others. Noah worked with us for a couple hours and then, in the afternoon, the executives at NBC filed in and we did a table read of the script. Afterward, I walked with Adam (who I'd just met that day) to the parking lot. I asked him what he thought was going to happen and he looked at me, "Oh. They're not picking this up. No way."

He was right, and I was really crushed for about ten seconds, until Lorraine told me that the head of casting for NBC, Grace Wu, had been very impressed with me and wanted me to come in and have a general meeting with her. General meetings *generally* feel like bullshit to me: I've been on a million of them. I've always thought that mostly they don't lead to anything, but that agents and managers like to set them up to prove they're actually doing something on your behalf.

But as it turns out, my meeting with Grace Wu was fairly productive. Especially the moment when she looked at me and said,

"We have this pilot called *Freaks and Geeks*. I'm going to give you the script. You should read it. I think it could be a great fit."

A week later, I drove to the Pacific Palisades armed with my audition scenes (commonly called sides) for the lead character, Lindsay Weir. I was brought in directly for the producers and director.

"Busy Philipps, everyone!"

I did my best Lindsay Weir, even though I was mad at myself for not managing to get the tears to roll down my cheeks in the scene where Lindsay tells Sam about their grandmother dying. When I was done reading, Paul Feig, the creator of the show, said, "Hey! That was really great, Busy! We actually have this other character. She's probably not in the pilot you read, but we're adding her to the show. Will you take a look at this and come back in and give it a shot?"

I took the new sides and stepped outside into the waiting area. I looked over the scenes. In one, Kim Kelly, the character they wanted me to play, was trying to mess with Sam Weir by asking him if he wanted to kiss her, and in another she was being a bitch to Lindsay. I spent about five or ten minutes looking it over, but honestly, it was getting late and all I could think about was how long it was going to take me to drive back to LMU on the 405. I kind of shrugged to myself, and when the casting director, Allison Jones, came back out, I told her I was ready.

I read the scenes once for the guys. The director, Jake Kasdan, laughed silently (I have come to know over the years that's the way he laughs), and producer Judd Apatow gave an approving "HA!" and then I thanked them and left.

The next day, Lorraine heard that I was the first choice for Kim. THEY WERE PUTTING A PIN IN ME! But they needed to secure the rest of the cast before they pulled the trigger. Since Kim Kelly was a new character and technically a guest star for the pilot, they weren't going to test the part in front of the studio and network, which is what series regular characters have to do.

Two weeks later, my agents and Lorraine called me together to tell me I'd been officially offered the part of Kim Kelly on *Freaks and Geeks*. Lorraine had actually talked to Judd, who wanted to make sure we knew that they imagined the part would be a series regular, but that for the pilot, it would just be a guest star.

My agents were feeling like maybe we should hold out a few more weeks and see if I got any test offers for bigger parts, since I was already doing one guest star on a WB pilot called *Saving Graces*. But Lorraine really loved the show and thought it would be the right move for me. Personally, I had no idea. I couldn't really tell tonally what the show was; it wasn't like anything I'd ever seen on TV, and I didn't know if that was a good thing or a bad thing. I'd been going on all of these auditions for teen shows and this was just *so different*. Lorraine said to take the weekend to think about it.

Coincidentally, that weekend, Colin flew up to Sacramento to visit some friends, and I was picking him up from the airport on Sunday night. At the baggage claim, we ran into a girl who had gone to LMU, but was taking a year off to work: Linda Cardellini. We knew Linda because she was on campus a lot and was roommates with some upperclassmen in the theater department. She was also pretty much a legend, since she had left school to work professionally. Also, she was just the coolest and best. Linda beelined for me: "Oh my God! Hiii! I heard you got offered Kim Kelly?! Is that true??? You have to do it! I'm playing Lindsay!"

This was all new information to me.

"What?! Oh my God. That's amazing! Yeah. I mean, my agents maybe want me to wait and see if I get a series regular, but I don't know. . . ."

"No! Dude! You HAVE to do *Freaks and Geeks*! It'll be so much FUN! We'll do it TOGETHER!"

The next morning I called Lorraine and told her I wanted to do the part. It's crazy, because at the time, it didn't seem like a decision that would change my life. But of course, being on that particular show would eventually change everything. For all of us. And even beyond how successful everyone has become in the years since, it's just incredible to have been part of something that's turned into such a cultural touchstone and such an iconic high school show.

My first day on the set was kind of a blur. Ben Foster (who was playing Eli) and I hung out outside of our trailers and smoked a cigarette together. I was insanely nervous, but tried my best to chill out. We were shooting the school-dance scene, which was essentially the end of the show. I was comforted by the fact that Linda was there, even though she was busy working and we didn't really have anything to do together in that scene. Mostly, I hung out outside on the steps of my trailer, looking over the script for the rest of the pilot.

Finally, at nearly the end of the day, I was called in for my shot. Jake Kasdan was behind the monitors with Judd and Paul, yelling out direction to me and Shaun Weiss while they were rolling. They gave us an eyeline of a piece of tape on a metal stand, which all seemed very weird to me, but I pretended like I knew exactly what was going on. A few years ago, I told Jake that it was my essentially my first day ever on a real set and he stared at me for a second; then his shoulders shook as he began to laugh. "I had no idea! You should have said something!"

But that was just it: I didn't want anyone to know! I wanted them to think I belonged. I was terrified someone would change their mind about me, so I was just doing my best to fit in and play it cool. Especially since I wasn't technically a series regular yet. They'd assured me that if and when the show got picked up, that would change, but on the day they shot the initial cast photos and opening credits, I wasn't included. My feelings were hurt, but I tried not to let it get to me.

Linda had been right: shooting the pilot was a lot of fun, and I was so happy to be doing this with her. The boys were okay. James Franco was weird and intense and his whole vibe both annoyed and intimidated me. Seth Rogen was sweet and laughed a lot, and Jason Segel acted like the old pro, since you know, he had been in like two movies before. At the end of the shoot, they played us a little bit of the pilot edited together so we could see what we'd been doing. It was the last scene—the school dance—

and they had already cut it together. The crew and cast gathered in the cafeteria of the middle school we were shooting in and Paul gave a little speech and then they showed it. I remember watching that ending and just knowing it was something great. I mean, obviously, since it was my first TV show pilot, I suppose I could have felt that way about anything. But it felt like there was something different about this.

Beside me, Linda was crying. She gave me a hug and said, "I really hope we get to do this for real."

A few weeks later, I shot my part in a WB pilot called *Saving Graces*, where I met Chyler Leigh and Lauren Ambrose. I loved Lauren immediately; she was such a cool girl. She taught me that it's okay to politely ask the makeup artists to do things a little differently if you don't like the way it looks. And also that Tabasco sauce on craft service tuna salad is a really good snack. We got along really well and remained close after the shoot. In fact, she introduced me to two of her close friends from boarding school at Choate, Abdi Nazemian and Sarah Shetter, who became two of my best friends and remain so to this day.

Meanwhile, Colin was shooting the pilot for *Roswell* for Fox. We were both just so excited to be doing this, and couldn't believe that everything seemed to be coming together for us at the same time. I was still supposed to be going to classes at LMU, but since auditioning and shooting were basically taking up all my time, I was flunking out of most of mine. The only exceptions were my literature class, because the teacher liked me and allowed me to turn in everything late, and my pottery class, because the studio was open to students twenty-four hours a day.

In the end, the only class I got credit for that semester was pottery. I got an A, and to this day, my mother refers to it as my twelve-thousand-dollar pottery class.

In May, I found out that *Freaks and Geeks* was picked up, and although I wasn't going to get to travel to New York for the announcements with the rest of the cast, Judd told Lorraine that they would be giving me the title of series regular, which was super exciting. Around the same time, Colin found out that *Roswell* was going to be picked up by the WB. We were both so insanely excited that we were going to be on TV the next year and also that, obviously, we wouldn't be going back to school in the fall. We would be REAL WORKING ACTORS!

Years ago, there was a show on HBO called *Unscripted* that followed a group of actors around Hollywood as they tried to break into the industry with varying degrees of success. Frank Langella plays an acting teacher, and in one of the episodes, he gives a speech that I think about all the time. I'm going to have to paraphrase here because I haven't watched the show since 2005, but basically he says, *Remember to savor the call. Because the call is when you're validated. The call is full of possibilities. The call means they want YOU. And you can't control anything that happens AFTER the call. You don't know what the picture will turn out like, you don't have any control over how many people see it or how it affects your career but the call is a unique moment and a triumph and you should enjoy it and savor it. And then get to work.*

There is TRULY no feeling greater than answering the phone and hearing an assistant on the other end say, "Hi Busy, please hold for Greg and Marilyn and Lorraine." Because that's how you know you've gotten a job. And then your heart pounds and you get to just wait to hear them say it out loud: "YOU GOT IT! CONGRATULATIONS! ARE YOU READY TO GO TO WISCONSIN????" (Or Vancouver, Atlanta, New York, Calgary, Michigan, London, Morocco, Mexico, L.A. . . . !)

I didn't know it then, but getting the call about *Freaks and Geeks* was the first of many you-got-it calls I would get over the course of my career.

I'd been guaranteed I would be in ten out of thirteen episodes, which isn't exactly a series regular (series regular typically means all episodes produced). One of the questions I get asked the most about *Freaks and Geeks* is why I'm not in the opening title sequence. Since they didn't initially shoot me getting my school picture taken, and they couldn't do a reshoot of it, they instead added a special title card for me that said "AND ALSO STARRING Busy Philipps as Kim Kelly."

It wasn't quite the same, but my roommates all cheered when my name came on the screen, and I tried to convince myself that maybe it was even *more* special to be singled out in that way.

I was invited to a limited press day with the rest of the cast, where I was asked by the NBC publicist to do an interview on *Entertainment Tonight* with James Franco. I overheard Franco ask Gabe Sachs, a producer and writer on *Freaks*, "Hey, does De Niro do *Entertainment Tonight*?" Franco had come back from our few months off and was clearly set on being a VERY SERIOUS ACTOR. Not that he wasn't before, but it felt like over the summer he had read *Easy Riders, Raging Bulls* or something and had decided that the only way to be taken seriously was to be a fucking prick. Once we started shooting the series, he was *not* cool to me, at all. Everything was about him, always. *His* character's motivation, his choices, his props, his hair, his wardrobe. Basically, he was a fucking bully. Which is what happens a lot on sets. Most of the time, the men who do this get away with it, and most of the time they're rewarded. Because ultimately, they get to give the performance *they* want to give.

I've watched time and time again as the squeaky wheel gets not only the grease but also EVERYTHING ELSE. It was hard for me, because I don't really know how to handle that kind of thing except to push back at it. People love the contentious nature of Kim and Daniel's relationship from that show, but it was coming from a very real place. It became clear that James was going to do his own thing and that it was up to me to figure out how to fit into that. In the episode "Kim Kelly Is My Friend," which was the third episode we shot, James was insistent that I really hit him as hard as I could when our characters fight in the end. I slapped him repeatedly, so hard that his skin was turning bright red. I felt really weird about doing it, but at the same time, he asked me to, so I went for it. I just wanted to be a good actor. Honestly, I thought he was weird and annoying, but maybe he knew better than I did? It didn't feel right, but what did I know, really? Linda and I would talk a lot about it, since I didn't really know how to handle it. James respected her, for the most part, because she was the lead of the show. And he was cool with the other dudes on the show because, you know, guy code or whatever. But he treated me as if I were inconsequential, barely there. I was insecure because I thought he didn't think I was a good actor, and it drove me crazy.

James was being particularly contentious with me when we shot the school-spirit episode. We were working together all morning, and in the scene, he kept taking one of my lines. I was so frustrated because I felt like no one would *ever* do anything to stop him. The script supervisor tried to tell him a few times, but he kept doing it and it was the first day a new director had been on set, so he didn't really know what he was walking into. I don't know why James kept taking my line. Maybe to fuck with me. Or maybe he really thought it was his. Or maybe because he's a guy and figured he can take whatever he wants. Finally, I spoke up to him: "Dude. Will you *stop* taking that line?? IT'S MINE."

It's not like I had *that* many on the show. I wanted my fucking line. He was annoyed and gave me a dirty look, but then didn't say it the next take, although I could tell he was pissed at me. We moved on to the scene where James and Seth and I get pelted with water balloons by kids from a rival school and then we run after the car. For one take, the director asked me to sort of hit James in the chest as we ran after the car and say my line: "Dammit, Daniel, *do* SOMETHING!"

We got hit with the balloons, we ran after the car, and I did what the director asked. I hit James in the chest as I said, "DAMMIT, DANIEL, *DO* SOMETHING!"

James did not say his line in response. Instead, he grabbed both my arms and screamed in my face, "DON'T EVER TOUCH ME AGAIN!"

And he threw me to the ground. Flat on my back. Wind knocked out of me. Immediately, I could feel the wet hot stinging of tears, but I tried like hell to suck them back in. He stormed off to the bathroom to change as the ADs and cameramen and my makeup artist rushed over to help me up and see if I was okay.

"I'm fine. I'm fine."

I smiled to prove it.

The cameraman looked at me carefully. "Are you sure? That was *so crazy*."

My makeup artist started wiping under my eyes to get rid of my tears as the director came over.

"Hey," he said, looking concerned. "Are you okay?"

I nodded.

"Listen, I hate to do this, I wish we could just call it, but we really need one more. Can you do that? Can you change and do one more?"

I went to the bathroom and changed into dry clothes and went back and did one more take, barely looking at James, who said nothing to me. They yelled *"Cut!"* and I ran to Linda's trailer, where I burst in and dramatically sobbed as I told her everything. She was appalled and told me to call my manager and tell her what had happened. Judd and Paul weren't on set. Gabe Sachs showed up and asked if I was okay and told me Paul was on his way. The director had called everyone. I was finished for the day and just wanted to go home. James was full of bad behavior, so why would this be treated any differently? Judd called me that night. Everyone had watched the tape. They had talked to James's manager. They were going to talk to James. He would need to apologize to me. It was barely a slap on the wrist. But that's how a boys' club works. I already knew there was no sense in trying to express to Judd and Paul how humiliating it had been on set. How James continually made me uncomfortable and got away with it because of his "talent." I knew there was only one thing for me to say.

"Okay."

We were shooting in the school gym the following day, and James found me and said he was sorry. He said he didn't like that Daniel was always getting hit by his girlfriend or something and he reacted badly. He told me Judd had him watch the tape and "it was pretty mean."

And then he smiled at me and hugged me, and I don't need to tell you this, but James is a fucking movie star. He was horrible to me, yes, but he's also gorgeous and charming as hell. That's where the manipulation lives. These dudes so often get away with their shitty behavior because they smile at you and stare into your eyes and for a second you're totally transfixed and you just say, "Yeah. It's okay. I get it. You were in the moment. I'm sorry I don't understand. I'm sorry I'm not a better actor. I'm sorry I'm not a prettier girl. I'm sorry." And you accept their apology and somehow end up apologizing to them.

But the Franco weirdness aside, working on the show was beyond fun. We all felt like we were a part of something really cool. We knew that what we were doing was totally different from the unrealistic teen shows every other network was putting out. I read a review of *Freaks and Geeks* that said something to the effect of, "You won't find any polished pretty people here. These are *real* kids." I was vaguely insulted. Like, I know I didn't look like Katie Heigl on the cover of *Maxim*, but I felt like I was fairly attractive. Honestly, it didn't occur to me that I might want to lose weight now that I was on a network TV show, but Linda was on Jenny Craig and I figured maybe I needed to do it too. I liked it for about three days and then I was annoyed and wanted to just eat whatever I wanted to eat. Paul Feig found out that Linda and I were *on a diet* and came to talk to us about it one morning. In a very awkward conversation, he tried to tell us that we'd been hired because of what we looked like, that we were perfect the *way we were*, and that he wanted to make sure we didn't feel any pressure to be thin from anyone, because that wasn't what they wanted. We assured him that we wouldn't get too thin. I think I quit the diet shortly after that conversation. My first diet failure.

I used to go into Linda's trailer and hang out in the mornings. She always had the heat turned up really high, and after hair and makeup, we would lie on the floor cuddled up next to the heater and talk and wait for camera to be ready. It was on one of those mornings that Linda said something to me about Hollywood that I probably should have gotten tattooed on my arm. We were talking about how the show wasn't a huge success even though it was critically acclaimed and how hard it is to get jobs and how much rejection there is and Linda said, "Yeah. But we all hang on because it only takes one job to change your life. It only takes one."

I hadn't thought of it in that way before, but hearing her say it made so much sense. It only takes one. So you keep going. Because if it's not this one, maybe it's the next one. Or the next one. Or the next one. And she's right to a certain extent. But I certainly haven't been in the ONE THAT CHANGES EVERYTHING. I haven't even really been *up for* the one that changes everything. I've built a career slowly over time, and I've been lucky enough to keep working and working and working. So it's not always the *one*, but fuck if we don't all wish it would be.

We knew the show wasn't doing well in the ratings. While we were shooting, no one in the industry seemingly cared about any of us, or even knew WHAT *Freaks and Geeks* was. (By the way, I am publicly calling bullshit on all the people who claim they loved it when it first aired on TV, because guess what? If everyone who claims they watched it in 1999 actually *did*, we'd be on season 17 by now!)

It was pretty clear we were going to be canceled, so as a special treat for all of us kids on the show, Judd took us to the *Man on the Moon* premiere, starring his good buddy Jim Carrey, which in and of itself was insanely impressive. *But* it also starred COURTNEY FUCKING LOVE. Now, you have to understand, I had been beyond obsessed with her in high school. I had every picture of her from every magazine plastered on my bedroom walls. I wore red lipstick, Wet N Wild, obviously. I painted my nails black and cut bangs and wore baby-doll dresses with fishnets and my Doc Martens. Courtney Love was literally the coolest, most badass woman in entertainment, and I not only wanted to be her, I wanted her to want to be my best friend.

In my head, I thought that a giant movie premiere would be the perfect place for me to introduce myself to Courtney Love and that *obviously*, she would recognize me for the true star I was on the inside and she would want to be my friend and that would fucking be it. So, I got a few vodka cranberries in me at the after-party and I spotted her table and made my way over to introduce myself. I walked up and smiled nervously.

"Ummm. Excuse me, Ms. Love? Hi! I just wanted to introduce myself. I'm Busy Philipps. I'm an actress and I just thought you were so great in the film and actually, I've, like, been such a fan for such a long time and I just think you're so—"

Her look literally cut me off. She narrowed her eyes at me and said, "This is my friend Paul. Isn't he hot???? Don't you want to FUCK HIM?"

I was so mortified that I barely looked at her friend. I muttered something like, "Oh, ha ha, yeah? You seem really nice . . ."

I slunk back to the corner with the rest of the *Freaks and Geeks* crew, and Samm Levine pointed out that the guy she was with, the one she asked me if I wanted to fuck, was Paul Rudd. Ugh. Of course. Obviously, in retrospect, I couldn't have asked for a more Courtney Love encounter. She didn't give a fuck that some blond teen actress from a TV show no one had ever heard of idolized her. I felt so dumb. But I shook it off and promised myself I would be cooler in the future.

All of us, minus Franco, would hang out after work or on the weekends, going to a diner called Swingers and getting breakfast burritos at 10 p.m., or to Jason Segel's condo in Westwood to hang out and smoke pot. Colin and I still hung out all the time, though we'd broken up the year before, and Gabe Sachs told me not to be an idiot and just be Colin's girlfriend officially. Everyone loved Colin. I mean, he *is* a super-lovable guy but I always weirdly felt jealous of that. I felt like people preferred him to me and that if they had to choose (why would they, btw??), they would pick him. After a picture of us from a movie premiere was printed in the *Hollywood Reporter* with the caption "Colin Hanks and GF Busy Philipps," I remember being so annoyed that I was reduced to being *his* girlfriend. Like why didn't it say "Busy Philipps and BF Colin Hanks"? I was wildly insecure about it.

But eventually, we became official boyfriend/girlfriend again. We would hang out with the other actors from *Roswell* and some of the actors from *That '70s Show*, Wilmer and Danny and Topher. Those kids seemed like they had it made. They were on a hit show, their jobs were secure, and they always knew what clubs to go to. I became friends with Rashida Jones and Jason Schwartzman after their respective guest starring roles on *Freaks*. Jason and I went to a party together at Rashida's place in Hancock Park and I thought it was the most beautiful apartment I'd ever been in. It was the bottom floor of a Spanish-style duplex, with hardwood floors and a real fireplace. I couldn't imagine ever having enough money to afford something that seemed so lavish. My gross apartment—which was in the flight landing path of LAX—hardly cut it. My roommates and I threw a party at our place one Saturday night, and I invited all of my new friends to come. With the exception of Linda, who had gone to LMU and knew other people living in the complex, I could tell that my TV friends were slightly horrified by where I lived.

As the season was wrapping up, it became clear that we probably weren't going to get to do a second one, even though Paul and Judd weren't told that officially. They wrote an ending for the season that could work either way, just in case. It didn't seem like a great sign when NBC put Martin Starr, who played Bill Haverchuck in *Freaks*, on a TV pilot they were producing that starred Newman from *Seinfeld*. I asked my agents and Lorraine about pilots, but they said there was nothing we could really do until we knew if *Freaks and Geeks* was getting picked up or canceled.

Judd and Paul threw a prom-themed wrap party for all of the cast and crew. I wore the Betsey Johnson dress I'd worn to my real prom with a hot-pink wig. Linda wore her mom's prom dress and an amazing beehive wig. The boys all wore cheesy tuxedos. Seth and Martin got their diplomas from high school in the middle of the party—they had finished high school with the on-set tutor while we were shooting.

Afterward, Colin drove me back to my shitty apartment, and I sobbed and sobbed and sobbed the whole way, drunk and sad and scared that I was never going to work again. Somewhere, in my cardboard boxes of photos, I have a picture that I took in his car from that night. It's me, looking directly into the camera, pink wig slightly askew, tears and makeup streaming down my face. A selfie years before I would know what it was or where to put it.

I have a confession. I've never seen all the episodes of *Freaks and Geeks*. People are often truly shook when I reveal this. Especially those hard-core fans who own the commemorative "Yearbook" DVD collection and have all the lines memorized. But the reason is simply that I wasn't home most Saturday nights! I was out partying with my friends. And DVRs obviously didn't exist then. In fairness, I was given VHS tapes of the episodes while they were airing, and I later got the DVD collection too, but it always seemed weird to just sit down and watch a show that I was on. I mean, I was there while we were filming it, right?

It's not often that a show finds its audience after it goes off the air, but it's been wild to see the impact that *Freaks and Geeks* has had on people over the last ten years. So I've decided that when Birdie turns thirteen, I'm going to watch the entire series with her.

I can't imagine anything better than both of us watching it all for the first time, together.

I DON'T WANT TO WAIT
(Paula Cole)

After *Freaks and Geeks* was officially canceled in May, I started auditioning for anything I could. I did a small guest spot on *Malcolm in the Middle*, but other than that, work was far and few between. I hadn't made that much money for *Freaks and Geeks*, and in spite of the fact that the show had been critically acclaimed, it didn't seem to be translating into anything career-wise. James was off to play James Dean and seemingly become a movie star. Linda was doing a new show for AMC. Jason was shooting a movie I had auditioned for like four times and not gotten. I felt like a loser. And I was running out of money.

Emily BB graduated from Wesleyan and got a job working at an ad agency in L.A., and we moved together to an apartment near Brentwood—a sort of neither-here-nor-there part of town generically called West L.A. She was feeling conflicted about moving to L.A. because her college boyfriend, Chuck, had wanted her to go to Boston and live with him. She almost backed out the month before we were supposed to move in, and we got into a huge fight on the phone about it. I had put down money for this apartment and had told my current roommates I was moving out. I knew she loved Chuck but *come on!* She had a job offer! I had an apartment for us!

She agreed with my logic and moved across the country. She and Chuck knew long distance was probably impossible, so they broke up, although they still talked almost every day. And we ended up having a lot of fun, making dinner every night when she got home from work on our George Foreman grill and doing weird arts-and-crafts projects. We didn't want to pay for cable but we had a DVD player so we would walk to the video store and rent *Sex and the City* DVDs. We probably watched the first several seasons of that show at least three times.

Eventually, we became friends with the girls who lived next door, law students at USC, who *did* pay for cable, and when *Sex and the City* started back up, they would have us over on Sunday nights to eat dinner and watch the show with them. One of the girls was named Stephanie, but Emily and I decided that she seemed more like a Penelope, so we started calling her that.

In June, Colin flew me to Toronto, where he was shooting a movie with Kirsten Dunst. I remember hanging with Kirsten while Colin was doing a scene, when Harvey Weinstein came in to her trailer and sat down to talk to her.

"You know," he said, "you have a really unique talent and ability, NKAY, and you're clearly a beautiful girl, but it's not always just about that, NKAY. You should really look at how we've shaped Gwyneth's career, NKAY. I mean, first *Shakespeare* and now we're having her do this movie where she's a flight attendant, NKAY, and it's amazing to see her in this new way, NKAY. That's what's possible for you, and you just need to remember that we're here for you, NKAY. Like I always say, you know, do one for them and one for you, NKAY??"

If you've spent any time with Harvey Weinstein—and I unfortunately have—he would always say "nkay" in the middle of his sentences, almost like a tic or how some people say "like" a lot. I remember that it didn't feel creepy to me, him coming into her trailer, just SCARY AS FUCK. Like this is the MAN WHO RUNS HOLLYWOOD. I was sitting there while he was talking, not sure what I should be doing, if I should leave or stay, so I just stayed there, eating Doritos on the leather sofa. I was secretly hoping he would notice me, and say, "You know, YOU should be a star like Gwyneth too, NKAY?"

Obviously, I didn't know what I was spared in that moment, that he *didn't* see me, or see an opportunity to, you know, cum on my leg, NKAY. I wouldn't know for years. Even after I'd gotten to know him fairly well and had worked with him, I wasn't aware of the depth of his depravity. But in that moment, I will tell you for certain I would have gone to his hotel room to talk about my career without thinking it meant something gross. I was twenty. I wanted a job. I wanted to work. I would have met anyone anywhere. Thank God I didn't.

In August, I was about to apply for a job at the department

store Fred Segal when I got an audition for an MTV movie called *Anatomy of a Hate Crime*, which was the story of the murder of Matthew Shepard, a gay college student in Wyoming. I was cast to play Chastity Pasley, who was the girlfriend of one of the murderers and an accessory after the fact. Ian Somerhalder played my character's boyfriend, one of the killers.

MTV was making a lot of these made-for-TV movies back in the late '90s and early 2000s, but only a few of them were dramatic. Most were comedies, and there were a few musicals (Beyoncé even did a version of the opera *Carmen*). I took the job very seriously, feeling the weight of the true story of Matthew Shepard's death. We all did, really. We filmed in Calgary, Canada, which was freezing, but when I wasn't working, I liked wandering around alone and shopping (I was pretty good at burning through my per diem). Colin came to visit me, and so did my manager, Lorraine. It was fairly low-budget, so the shoot wasn't too long and we were finished before winter really hit.

Back in L.A., Colin and I were still dating, and still hung out with all of our college friends, so it was weirdly like we hadn't stopped going to school. Colin and I had both moved farther from campus, but we would still go to all the parties on the weekends, and were essentially living the lives of students who just happened to have real jobs. Meanwhile, I signed up for some classes at Santa Monica College, credits that could transfer to LMU if I ever wanted to finish my degree—I took Women's Studies, and another pottery class. (Luckily, this one was less than twelve thousand dollars.)

My auditions were going pretty well, even though I kept getting really close on things and then not getting the part. Weirdly, auditions have always been one of my favorite things. Many actors hate them, or say they hate them. But I love it. When you're an actor for hire, you don't get a lot of chances in your daily life to *act*. And I LOVE ACTING. So, to me, there's nothing better than going into a room with someone's material and getting the chance to perform it. It's fun, or at least it should be. And look, *most* of the time, you're not going to get the part. That's just statistics. But if you can let go of that *expectation*, then you can just enjoy the actual *doing* of the *thing you love*.

I auditioned many times for an independent movie called *Home Room* about two girls becoming friends after surviving a school shooting. Mass school shootings were a relatively new concept. Columbine had only happened a year and a half earlier. Erika Christensen was cast as well. She was coming off her part in the movie *Traffic* and was very highly sought after. To be honest, I think the writer/director was hoping to get a bigger name for my part, but after all the actresses he offered it to turned it down, he offered it to me.

It was emotionally really difficult. Independent films often have a shorter shooting schedule than bigger-budget movies, and many times you only get one day off a week. That was the case with *Home Room*. The subject matter wasn't easy either, not to mention that my character's backstory was that she had a baby when she was fifteen that died. I *mean*. I was in a terrible mood most of the month we were shooting, exhausted and sad and panicky, and Emily was just about over it.

Colin was in England working on the *Band of Brothers* TV show and as soon as I wrapped, I went over to see him for Thanksgiving. I was only there a few days, but it was so much fun. We ate yakisoba noodles (I'd never had them before, and I don't know, they made an impression on me), he introduced me to a new band that hadn't hit the U.S. yet called COLDPLAY (I'm not kidding), and we hung out with all the guys and their wives and girlfriends from the show and had a big Thanksgiving feast together. (I packed Stovetop stuffing in my suitcase and felt like a real *hero*.)

Right after the holidays, I was offered another movie for MTV, a terrible "comedy" called *Spring Break Lawyer*. But it was a job and I needed the money and it was being offered, so I couldn't turn it down.

Finally, pilot season started again, and I went out for *everything*. This time, I was getting asked to test for a ton of them. I tested for *nine* pilots that year, and every single one of them I went to studio *and* network. That's an absurd amount, just so you know. That's eighteen of the most high-pressure auditions you can go through as an actor. And every *single* time, I thought, "THIS IS THE ONE."

Of all the shows I tested for that year, I can remember two of them very clearly. One of the pilots was called *Close to Home*, and I was testing to be the best friend of the main girl. In the script, the writers had written in what songs would be playing over the scenes, and it was all the same indie rock that my roommate from college Diana and I listened to nonstop. So in my audition, I commented on the music. It was a writing team, a guy and a girl who seemed like they were adults but were probably just a few years older than me. The guy writer smiled when I brought up the music. "Yeah," he said. "That's me. I like to put the music in so you can get a feel for the tone of the show."

I didn't get the part, but at least they knew I had good taste.

Another pilot that season was called *The Education of Max Bickford*. It was starring Richard Dreyfuss and I was testing to play his daughter. It was between me and an actress named Katee Sackhoff, but I was positive this was my part, not hers. Turns out I was wrong. I still remember the phone call I had with my agent Greg, "Honestly, Biz, they said you were *wonderful*. They said you *both* were. They said it was basically an arbitrary decision. It could have been either one of you."

It was ARBITRARY? WHAT THE FUCK? It didn't FEEL ARBITRARY TO ME, FUCKERS. I was heartbroken. I sobbed and sobbed. I called Colin, who was working on *another* movie. He couldn't believe it and said he was so sorry.

The premiere for the Kirsten Dunst movie was actually *that night*, but it turned out he'd be stuck at work, so he said I could just skip it if I didn't feel like going without him. But I thought, "No. This is what we do. We don't get parts sometimes and life goes on." So I got dressed up and went.

At the after-party, Emily and I were getting some vodka sodas when Katee Sackhoff walked up to say hi. I couldn't believe she was there, but I hugged her and congratulated her on the part. She was so excited: this was her very first show. And I was happy for her, really. It's just that I was sad for myself. I knew I had been good. I'm a good actor. And I knew I was supposed to be doing this. So why was it so fucking hard to get a job? What was it about me that wasn't enough? Or maybe, more accurately, what was it about me that was TOO MUCH? I didn't know how to be anything other than what I was. What if no one wanted that again? What then?

I am not a quitter. I don't quit anything. All I could do was continue to audition and have meetings. Colin was working nonstop and I was seeing him less frequently. Not because he didn't want to see me, but truly, his schedule was crazy and he was so tired. Jake Kasdan, my director from *Freaks and Geeks*, gave him the lead in his movie *Orange County*. I auditioned for Jake too, but didn't get a part in it. WHAT ELSE IS NEW?!

A few days later, I was driving over the 405, on my way home from YET ANOTHER AUDITION, when my phone rang, I knew it was Emily's office from the number, so I picked up, expecting to hear her voice. But instead it was her boss, who sounded shaky.

"Ummm. Busy? Hi. This is Susanne. I—I'm um Emily's boss? Can you come to our office right now?"

"Hi. Yeah. What's going on? Is everything okay?" I knew it wasn't. I could tell. My stomach started sinking.

"You know Chuck? Emily's Chuck? I— He's dead. He, uh, died and . . . she . . . ummm . . ."

My heart fell. "I'll be right there. Susanne. Fifteen minutes, okay? Can she talk?"

There was a pause. "No."

"Okay. I'll be there as soon as I can."

I hung up. Chuck was dead. Chuck was dead? *What? WHAT??*

When someone dies young, out of nowhere, it doesn't make any sense. Ever. I didn't ask questions immediately, because it didn't matter. How? Why? Who fucking cares? Chuck was dead. Emily's Chuck. Her first love. Her only love. I loved Chuck too. He was the greatest. So funny. So cool. So weird. So punk rock. So smart. I called my mom and started hysterically crying, repeating, "Chuck died, Mom. I don't know what to do, I don't know what to do, I don't know what to do—"

"Busy. *Busy! Stop!* Listen to me. This isn't about you right now. Okay, honey? I'm so sorry. You need to go get Emily. I'll call her mom and have her call you. *You* have to stop crying, okay, honey? You need to just go get her and take her home and put her in bed. And get her water and cold washcloths for her face. And just be with her. But you have to get it together right now."

I did what my mom told me to do. Emily couldn't talk. She couldn't stop shaking. Her face was already puffy and red and there was no end to the tears. I talked to her parents and helped make a plan for her to go back to New Jersey for the funeral. Chuck had died of a seizure in his sleep. A freak thing. I sat with her while she talked to people on the phone and cried. It was a lot to handle by myself. But that's what you do, right?

I remember feeling relieved when she left for New Jersey, because I knew she was going to be with people who had loved Chuck as much as she did, and they could grieve and cry together. My heart was truly broken for her. I knew how much she loved him. I knew she thought that if she had just moved to Boston with him and not to L.A., he wouldn't have died, which of course wasn't true, but I felt like I was the one who forced her to move to

L.A. It was so, so beyond horrible. When she came back from the funeral a few days later, she went straight back to work. She had to. Life goes on, even when you don't want it to. But Emily was different somehow; there was a weight that she couldn't shake. She still carries it with her, I think. Even all these years later.

Right around then, Craig had decided to leave school in Chicago and move to L.A. to see if he could break into the business. We started hanging out a little, even though I was dating Colin and he was still dating a girl in Chicago, long distance. Brett lived in L.A. now too, so he and Craig and I would go out dancing to '80s nights or go to Manhattan Beach and get coffee and walk along the beach. It felt like we had never been apart. Like the three of us were still in high school, best friends in the theater department.

One Saturday night, my old roommates were having a huge party. Craig and I were sitting outside, drinking and getting high. I can't remember if Colin didn't want to come, or was too tired, but he wasn't there. Craig and I walked back across the courtyard to his apartment together so he could get cigarettes and as soon as we got into the stairwell, we started kissing.

Well. Okay. I know. This is a thing with me, maybe? A, WHAT DO YOU CALL IT . . . PATTERN?! Yes. It is. But you know, I'm not a quitter. So I think in terms of relationships, I often have a hard time *ending* them when I think I should, and instead I just sort of *move on* to another thing, and then *that* ends up being the decision that's made for me.

We both felt like shit the next day. Not just from the hangover, obviously. We both had significant others. Colin and I were planning a huge trip to Europe in a few weeks. We hadn't been seeing much of each other, but I knew he was really looking forward to going away with me. I was such a fucking coward. But hooking up with Craig was the thing that made me realize that Colin and I weren't working *at all*.

So I broke up with him. When I told him I wasn't going on the trip, he was fairly (understandably) upset. I didn't even tell him about the Craig stuff. I didn't have the guts. (Even though, you know, he didn't have much room to talk, since I had cheated on Craig with him only a few years earlier.)

It would be years before Colin and I would be able to be friends, but eventually, he forgave me and we moved on. Now, Colin and his wife are two of Marc's and my closest friends and our kids all go to school together. I sometimes think how amazing it would be to go back in time and show the two of us a flash of the future: all of our kids playing together, his wife, Sam, and I having wine and laughing, Marc and Colin talking about bands and artisanal coffee places. Recently, I found a birthday card Colin wrote me after we broke up the first time. In it, he wrote, "I love you and know we're going to be in each other's lives for a long time." He was right in a way neither of us could have predicted at nineteen, but I am so much better for having him in my life today and feel so lucky that my kids get to know him too. He's really just one of the best people I've ever known, and I'm sorry I was such an asshole to him but grateful he understood and forgave me.

After Colin and I broke up, Craig and I started dating right away and were pretty much inseparable. I liked that he would spend every night at my house and was up for whatever I wanted to do. I didn't even mind that I almost always had to pay.

In June, I got a call from Jake Kasdan's little brother Jon, who had written on *Freaks and Geeks*. He and I had become good friends in the year after the show. He'd been hired by Tom Kapinos, who was the showrunner of *Dawson's Creek*, which was now going into its fifth season.

"*Hypothetically speaking*," he said, "If we added a *roommate* for Joey at college, would you move to Wilmington, North Carolina????"

"Jon," I told him, "I tested for *nine* fucking shows this year and didn't get one. I would move wherever the fuck you asked me to."

He laughed. "Okay, okay, okay. That's what I thought. Tom's a huge fan from *Freaks*. We're writing this part and it's perfect for you."

Not that I didn't have to audition and test for it. I did. But Audrey was my fucking part. I remember going into my test at Warner Brothers, and seeing the girl they were testing against me, who was obviously super talented. But all I could think was, "Good luck, girl, but you may as well just go home now because this is my part. I'm due for it. IT'S MINE."

IS THIS IT
(The Strokes)

A few nights before I left for Wilmington, North Carolina, Craig and his brother Jeff and Emily and I went out to dinner at Islands, a burger chain with a Hawaiian theme. I was feeling nervous about leaving Emily but also about leaving Craig, who I was newly in love with (again). Not to mention, I wasn't sure how much I was going to be able to fly home. In my deal I was only guaranteed a plane ticket back to L.A. if I wasn't in an episode.

We were talking about the show at dinner. None of us had ever seen it. I knew kids in college who really liked *Dawson's* and *Felicity*, but my friends and I weren't really into it. I mean, *obviously* I knew what a big deal it had been when it premiered, how hugely popular it was. The *Rolling Stone* cover with Katie Holmes swinging on a tire swing was *iconic*, but I think I thought of the show as something for teenagers, not me. Craig looked around at the table and kind of laughed, "We don't have to, like, start *watching* it now, do we?"

The way he said it was so mean, and so seemingly out of nowhere. I didn't yet understand that Craig had a hard time being happy about any of my success since his own feelings were that he was already a failure at age twenty-one. I jumped up from the table and ran to the bathroom in tears. (This was long before I became perfectly comfortable openly crying in restaurants.) He followed me to the ladies' room, where I sobbed in the stall.

"Busy. Hey. Hey. Come out. I didn't mean it. Of *course* we'll watch you on it. I just— Come on. You know what I meant."

I did. Sort of. But I also had the feeling that there was no way he would be watching me on the show. I felt like even my friends thought this huge job was lame and somehow not good enough.

On the plane to Charlotte, I randomly sat next to Linda Hamilton, the actress from the Terminator movies. She was going to visit family in North Carolina. I felt like it was a good sign that she was my seatmate. She said "bon appétit" to me when our meals arrived, and I was impressed with how fancy she was and wondered if I would ever be that fancy.

Chad Michael Murray and Ken Marino were both on my flight too. Years ago, I got a lot of shit for saying on a Paley Center panel that I thought Chad was a douchebag, but honestly, HE WAS FINE. He didn't do anything wrong—his vibe was just not for me. He was a real MALE ACTOR, and I have a hard time trusting dudes that are that good looking and know it and somehow try to prove to you they're so much more. I sound like an asshole, I know. I'm sorry. He just reminded me of a guy on the football team who carries around a guitar so people think he's deep but really he just knows the G chord. Like how Franco carried Dante's *Inferno* around on set. It's like CALM DOWN

WE GET IT YOU WANT US TO THINK YOU'RE HOT *AND* SMART.

The South is unbearably hot. And I say this as someone who grew up in Arizona, where we would play softball in a 105-degree heat. But North Carolina in the summer is a whole other thing. The heat smacks you in the face like a hot, wet wall. I was *not* prepared for it. We were all put up in this funny little boutique hotel off the main drag of downtown Wilmington. The hotel was "movie" themed, with a little kitchen and rocking chairs on the front porch. My room was *Some Like It Hot*, which apparently was also the room Michael Pitt had stayed in. As we were all checking in to reception, James Van Der Beek popped out of one of the rooms. Obviously I hadn't thought the main cast members were staying there; I'd assumed they'd all gotten homes when they'd relocated to Wilmington. But James was at the hotel for some reason—I think his house was under construction—and it seemed like he'd been waiting for us.

"Hey! I'm James!" he said. "You're Busy, right? Jon Kasdan said we're going to be friends. This is my fiancée, Heather!"

She popped out of their room and I shook her hand. I couldn't help but notice her enormous ring. I was like HOLY SHIT. People *our age* get rings like that when they get married?? He looked past me, over my shoulder.

"Oh, look," he said. *"Michelle!"*

I turned around to where he was looking, and across the street at the mini-mart, Michelle Williams was walking out. I'd been prepped by Jon Kasdan that Michelle and James would be my friends, I guess because Michelle and James were *his* friends, and he and I were friends. Michelle walked over to say hi and introduce herself. She was tiny and adorable, her perfect face makeup-free. She was carrying Fig Newtons and water. She asked if I wanted one, and we walked over to her room and sat in the rocking chairs so I could smoke. We started talking about bands we liked and books we were reading. I liked her immediately: Jon was right, of course. She talked quietly, as if the things she was saying were just for me, but I loved when she would have moments of laughing loudly or shrieking in agreement at something I had said. She was wearing the most beat-up Converse I had ever seen, and I made a mental note to get a pair of Converse and start wearing them in ASAP. She told me that she was going to be moving to the beach in a few days but her house wasn't ready yet because there were still summer vacation renters in it.

"You don't own a house here?" I asked, and she shook her head.

"No. No. I just rent houses. And honestly, I wasn't sure if I was going to come back this season. I sort of asked if maybe I could leave. I was thinking of trying to go to college this year but . . ."

I nodded as she trailed off. "Well. I've *been* to college. Trust me, you're not missing out on much. And I feel like most college students would be super stoked to be on a TV show so . . ."

She laughed. "Yeah. You're probably right. Are you hungry? Want to go get dinner? There's this place that we eat at a lot. It has the best steak."

We all ended up at Deluxe, a super fancy restaurant within

walking distance of the hotel. She was right. The steak was fucking amazing. She and I realized that we had just missed each other the year before when I was in London visiting Colin. She was there shooting a movie and was staying in the same hotel, at the same time. I remember seeing her costar from that movie in the lobby, but somehow I never saw her.

I started work the next day with a wardrobe fitting, and I also met the hair and makeup teams. Wardrobe was really disheartening. The woman looked at my body skeptically.

"Hmmm. I think the trick with you will be to just accentuate your chest and push up your boobs and maybe show your legs, and then just try to hide from here"—she pointed to right under my boobs—"to here." She pointed to right above my knees.

I was confused. There needed to be a trick? My body was a problem? I hadn't realized that yet. I just assumed because I'd gotten the part, they wanted me the way I was. I didn't know there were parts of me that should remain *hidden*. But I would be learning a lot, I guess.

The makeup department was no better. "So, I guess we have to cover all these moles? What have people done in the past about it??"

I looked at the makeup artist in confusion. "What do you mean? No one has ever asked me that."

"Oh, honey, okay. Yeah. I guess the network and producers don't like all these moles on you, so we're supposed to cover them up. Although I've never had to do that, and it seems insane."

It seemed insane to me, too. I called Lorraine, and she agreed to get to the bottom of it. But in the meantime, I needed to just do what they wanted. Which I could do. After all, this was my *job*. But I was so offended. The network and producers don't like my *skin*? I'd gotten the job on *Freaks and Geeks* and was fine the way I was, but *clearly* the message here was a little different.

The hair department was a hilarious mother/daughter team. The daughter, Tracey, seemed like she was only a few years older than me, with a short asymmetrical haircut that was dyed purple. She was smoking when I walked up to the trailer.

"HEEEEYYYYY!" she said. "I'm doing your hair! Wanna smoke?"

I knew right away that we were going to be friends.

I met Katie Holmes my first day on set. She'd been shooting another scene and was coming to the other location to rehearse and shoot my first scene with me. Right away, she jumped out of the transpo van and hugged me. "Jon Kasdan told me you're *wonderful*!"

Thanks, Jon! He really did pave the way for everyone to be extra nice to me. I wished I had more scenes with Michelle, but she and I hung out when we weren't working. We drank a lot of wine and went out to fancy dinners, spending money I hadn't yet started to make, a real *theme* to my life. She told me all the good places to go in town, like the local indie record store, CD Alley, which was owned by an amazing man named Fred, a soft-spoken Southern man in his late thirties who loved indie rock and would sometimes convince bands to take a detour from the real venues in Chapel Hill and play in his loft apartment in Wilmington. I saw a lot of great bands there, and would spend much of my free time hanging out and buying records.

With *Dawson's*, it was immediately clear to me that I wasn't walking into a situation like we had on *Freaks and Geeks*, where everyone hung out all the time. Maybe that was how it had been when the show first started, but by the fifth season, when I showed up, the main cast didn't really hang out together that much and they obviously had some fairly intense dynamics going on. It was clear that Joshua Jackson and James didn't really like each other, and while Katie and Michelle were friendly, it didn't seem like they were very close. Kerr Smith was sort of friendly with everyone. Josh really fancied himself "one of the guys" with the crew. The *Creek's* very own mini George Clooney! He's a good guy and just wanted to be well-liked but I wish I'd known the term "mansplaining" when I met Josh. His ability to turn a conversation into a dissertation was incredible. Katie was very sweet, but we didn't spend that much time together. I knew she worked out a lot. She didn't seem to like to drink very much, and while I knew she'd sneak a cigarette every once in a while, she wasn't really like a hang-out-and-smoke kind of girl. I went over to her house a few times and she showed me some artwork and arts and crafts she was working on, since she knew I did that kind of stuff too, but I had a hard time really connecting with her. She'd been going out with Chris Klein for a while, and he came out to Wilmington and spent a good deal of time there, so she was mostly off with him. I mean, also, look . . . by the time I got there, those kids had already been thrust into a very specific kind of fame—a kind I wasn't used to. And they'd all lived there, with each other and the crew of the show as their only friends, for the majority of the previous four years.

The second weekend I was there, Michelle and I both had a Friday and a Monday off. She told me she was flying back up to New York and that I should come with her. So I did. She was newly friends with a guy I'd done the Oxford School of Drama with (Zach Knighton, later on *Happy Endings*), and he came over and we drank wine and hung out. She took me shopping in SoHo, and I remember seeing the price tags on the vintage Levi's and not being able to imagine spending that much on *jeans*. She had books everywhere in her apartment in TriBeCa. Stacks of them, against each wall. She was never not reading at least three at a time. But it didn't feel forced or pretentious. She was a girl who had been working since she was a child, so she'd missed out on traditional school and had decided that she needed to educate herself beyond what on-set school tutors were capable of.

We met some of her friends in Central Park on one of the days, an artist she knew and Gaby Hoffman, who had just re-turned from backpacking around Europe with friends. She took me to the Guggenheim because there was an exhibit she wanted to see. We met another friend of hers and sat outside at a café in the early afternoon and were served wine, even though Michelle was a month shy of twenty-one. Everyone seemed so worldly. They lived in *New York*. And New York was magical. I had never really spent time there as a grown-up, only doing my Barbie job, which was mostly just work and hotel and work. But those four days I really fell in love. I guess with both the city and Michelle. She's easy to fall in love with; anyone who really knows her will tell you that. And probably some people who barely know her will tell you that, too.

Back in Wilmington, I tried to get my footing on the show. It was clear that what I was used to on *Freaks and Geeks* wasn't how things worked on the *Creek*. There was no room for improv, and I would be corrected if I said one word wrong. On set, it was clear that Katie was the star.

One day I was having an issue getting a fairly long speech out "word perfectly" and the director came over to me. "Listen, yeah, that was terrible but don't worry if you can't get it. We'll just cut to Katie. That's what we mostly do anyway, because . . . I mean. Look at that face!"

He laughed and walked back to the monitors. Katie looked at me sympathetically and reached out to hand me the script. "Here. You want to look at it again?"

"Nope!" I said. "I'm good."

I wasn't good. I was barely okay. I was homesick already and I missed Craig. We talked all the time, but between my work schedule and the time change, it was difficult. Finally, I was able to fly back to Los Angeles for a few days. My friends and I had tickets to see Madonna at the Staples Center and I'd been away for over a month. I was going to miss Michelle's birthday while I was gone, but I got her a cute present and we had plans to go to Deluxe when I was back and celebrate.

But at the end of the trip, on the morning I was supposed to head back to North Carolina, I woke up to my mother calling me super early. "Busy! Busy! Do *not* go to the airport, honey. Something horrible is happening."

Sometimes my mother sounds hysterical even when it's just like, the dog needs new cataract eye drops. So it's difficult to tell when something terrible really *is* happening. But for some reason, that morning, I just knew.

I went into the living room and Emily came out too, fresh from the shower. "My mom says to turn on the TV."

We turned it on and watched in horror with the rest of the world as the events of September 11 unfolded. I yelled for Craig to wake up and come out of my room. Our friend from high school worked in one of the towers, but no one knew which one. Jeff's girlfriend Liz still lived in the city and he obviously couldn't get in touch with her. All the phone lines were jammed. We didn't know what to do. Emily wasn't sure if she should go to work or not, so she got dressed and went in. I called Caleb, the production coordinator on *Dawson's Creek.*

"Hey, darlin'," he said. "You didn't already go to the airport, did you?"

I told him I was at home.

"Yeah, just stay there. I don't want you waiting there all day. It doesn't seem like there will be any flights out today. Maybe tomorrow. I'll call you when I know."

In retrospect it seems so insane, like there would have even been a *possibility* that I would've been able to fly out *later* that *day* or even the next day. No one knew what the fuck was happening. All day, Craig and I watched TV and cried. His brother didn't go to work and came over to my apartment and hung out with us. Around lunchtime, we decided we couldn't cry anymore, so we turned off the TV and walked to a weird sports bar in my neighborhood. We sat there, shell-shocked, and drank beer and hung out with a ton of other people who didn't know what else to do but drink at 11:45 a.m. Emily called and said everyone was going home, so she met us at the bar and we sat there until six or seven, when we decided we probably should eat and we all walked back home.

We found out our high school friend was okay the next day, although he got covered in white soot and debris from when he ran away from the collapse. It's hard to explain to millennials and younger kids what was such a fundamental shift in the world. What it felt like before and then after. I remember asking my mom if she felt that way after JFK was shot.

"Oh, Busy. That was horrible. Just horrible. We were all *so* devastated. But this is different."

I flew to North Carolina the very first day they reopened the airports. Despite the national tragedy, the show literally had to go on. They were able to take one insurance day shutting down production, but after that, we had to keep shooting. So on September 13, I got on a flight from L.A. to Charlotte. There were very few flights going out; they were only for those who *had* to travel. I was panicked and crying and smoking outside when an actor named David Monahan—who was also going to Wilmington to guest star on the show—found me. "Hey," he said. "You must be Busy? Caleb told me I needed to find a crying blond girl and make sure she gets to Wilmington."

He held my hand through security and onto the plane and asked the woman who was sitting next to me to switch so we could be together. Everyone was really quiet. In the airport and on the plane. It was eerie. Like people were concentrating so hard, willing things to be normal and okay. It was a giant plane, like one of the ones you take to Europe, and it was probably only half full. The pilot came out and gave a little speech on the loudspeaker about how things were going to be okay, that he had personally made sure that all the security inspections were done, and then he walked up and down both aisles of the plane and said hi to everyone.

We made it to Charlotte, where production had hired a stretch limo to drive us the four hours to Wilmington, since there was only limited airline service and commuter flights were still suspended. I felt so silly at work the next day, dressed in a costume for the Halloween episode. The world was fucking ending and I was trying to get Joey Potter to come to a party with me. I remember there were a lot of pep talks about how this is what we do. We make entertainment for people so that they can escape the real world for forty-three minutes a week. It's not without value or merit. It's important to not just tell stories, but also to remember to entertain. And anyway, *someone's* got to. May as well be us.

And so we did.

Not long after that, I got an apartment downtown; Caleb helped me find it. It was in a big Victorian house that had been cut into four units, two downstairs and two upstairs. I went to a Ross Dress for Less and outfitted it with pillows and blankets and candles to try to make it feel more like home, but I never felt right in the house. I was always kind of creeped out by it. I was sure there was a ghost. A woman. I thought a few times in the middle of the night I heard someone crying outside my door and would open it and find no one. The South is haunted like that, though. There's weird energy flying around.

Also, I was just *so lonely*. Tracey and I would go out most nights, and I would try to get just drunk enough that I would be able to fall asleep before scaring myself. I called the police twice because I was convinced there was someone in my house. I should've moved to the beach and been closer to the rest of the cast, but I thought I wanted to be near the downtown strip so I could walk to bars and restaurants and not worry about driving drunk out to the beach, which seemed *so far*. Plus it was more expensive, and I was responsible for paying my rent in Wilmington since I had been given a "relocation fee," which means they pay you a lump sum and then production is off the hook for your rent and plane tickets. As a rule, relocation fees are never advantageous to the person relocating. I also had to buy a car in Wilmington. So this job was costing me money.

For Halloween, Michelle, Tracey, and I went out together. I dressed as Valentine's Day Barbie with this amazing vintage dress I'd found. Michelle went as Angelina Jolie with a vial of Billy Bob's blood around her neck. I did her makeup and was really proud of myself. Tracey went as Miss Patriotic USA (there were a lot of random patriotic costumes that year, as well as *many* people dressed as the twin towers, which still makes me feel weird). We went first to a party at Katie's house, where she was dressed like Marilyn Monroe and her boyfriend Chris Klein was dressed kind of like a farmer, though his costume was unclear.

I frowned at him. "Wait. What are you?"

"I'm half a scarecrow!" he told me proudly, like that was a thing, "I wanted to be Joe DiMaggio, 'cause, you know, *Marilyn*, but we couldn't find a costume in time, so this is what I am!"

"You could've just been Arthur Miller, I guess? That would have been pretty easy."

He looked at me like I was an idiot. "Ummm. Okay. I'm half a *scarecrow*, Busy."

Got it. Cool.

The three of us went out downtown afterward, and Michelle and I got trashed; then she slept over. It was fun for her, I think, to be in costume and not have people know who she was. She was clearly very famous, and in Wilmington, the college kids who attended UNCW were always seemingly on the lookout for one of the *Dawson's* kids, which is why I think that by season five they'd all retreated to the beach to be left alone. When a group of college kids *would* recognize Michelle, and later me, they'd rudely scream out across the bar, or across the street at us, generally something lame about the show: "HEEEEEYYYYY, GIRL FROM *DAWSON'S CREEK*!!! WHERE'S JOEY????" Or "ISN'T GRAMS GONNA GET MAD AT YOU????"

It wasn't super fun. It was confusing (to me, anyway). I had spent my whole life wanting people to *notice* me, and then all of a sudden it was happening and it felt invasive and rude.

I paid for Craig to fly out to see me. He only wanted to come for a few days, because he didn't want to take too much time off work. I'm not sure what he was doing at the time. I think working at California Pizza Kitchen as a waiter and trying to figure out what he was going to do next. I offered to pay for headshots and he took me up on it. I even asked him to come to Wilmington and live with me. I didn't understand why he wouldn't. I mean, he was just waiting tables in L.A., which he could do anywhere. He obviously thought that was ridiculous and didn't understand why I couldn't see that it was a totally unreasonable request.

I just loved him and wanted us to be together. But more than that, I was lonely. I was used to being around a ton of people I knew. I spent a lot of time on the phone with friends back home and with my high school friends in Arizona. I flew back to L.A. as much as I could, but I was low on the totem pole in terms of scheduling. They would obviously need to make Katie and James and Josh and Michelle happy before me, so getting a Friday *and* a Monday off was rare.

The flights were always empty in those months following September 11, and they would always use those huge planes. I got used to flying coach and having three seats to myself and being able to lie down and sleep the whole five hours. Then when I got to the Charlotte airport, I would buy two Chinese chicken salads from the CPK ASAP and bring them on the commuter flight back to Wilmington for Michelle and me to eat together for dinner. (Michelle usually flew direct to New York, so she didn't go through the Charlotte airport very frequently, and we both loved that salad.)

One morning, as my flight from Charlotte to Wilmington

took off, I looked out to the right side of the plane and saw a ton of smoke on the ground at the airport. When we landed, Caleb was waiting for me and told me the commuter flight that took off right before ours, which was heading to Greenville, South Carolina, had crashed and everyone was killed. CNN hadn't been sure which flight it was that had gone down at first. He handed me his phone and said, "Call your mom." My mother was, as you can imagine, *apoplectic*. But I assured her I was fine and would be fine; after all, my guardian angel told me when I was fifteen that nothing bad would ever happen to me on a plane, remember? "Oh! That's right, Busy. Well, I guess I won't worry then."

In general, I tried to be good at my job. I got used to people staring at me in airports. But it was hard to feel settled or like I had any ownership over my involvement in the show, since I'd been added in the fifth season. Even recently, when I was asked to participate in the reunion for *Entertainment Weekly*, my first reaction was, "Are they sure they want me involved?" Also, even though my friends and Craig had agreed to watch me on the show, I don't think they actually ever did. Truthfully, even I stopped watching after a few episodes.

I settled into the weekly wardrobe humiliations, where I was tucked and pulled and my body looked at with *such disdain* by the woman doing the costumes, all while she would talk about how *Katie can just WEAR ANYTHING, you know? Because she just WORKS SO HARD at it. She LOVES running and SPIN CLASS!* I knew it was pointed. I'm not an idiot, lady. But guess what? I'm depressed and away from my friends and boyfriend and living in a city where I'm basically friends with two people, so *forgive* me that I want to eat turkey burgers and fries and drink vodka cranberries on the regular.

Michelle started dating a guy who lived close by, so she was basically gone all the time. Tracey and I would go out almost every night, especially if I didn't have an early call. But even when I did, I got fairly used to working with a hangover. The only thing that temporarily made me forget my loneliness was drinking—and passing out before the ghosts had a chance to freak me out.

Work was fine. I liked everyone okay and everyone seemed to like me. I was neutral territory, since I had no drama and history with any of them, so I could work with anyone with no problem. One day, the whole cast was sitting around a table filming the Thanksgiving episode, and James looked at me and said, "See? You got lucky. Your show was canceled after the first season."

I was so shocked by his complete lack of perspective, I was speechless. I mean. YOU ALL are the lucky ones, here on SEASON FIVE of your HIT TV SHOW. Your LIVES were changed. No one gave a fuck who I was after my *one* season on *Freaks and Geeks*. So what if they had some personality clashes? They were green-lighting *movies*. James had gotten a *million* dollars for *Varsity Blues*. Katie was working with huge directors.

Sometimes people on TV shows get fooled into thinking that the very thing that made them to begin with is the thing that's now holding them back. It's a weird phenomenon that happens, mostly because I think their reps start telling them, "Just wait. As soon as you're OFF THIS SHOW, the opportunities will be

ENDLESS!" But the opportunities exist *because* of the show. And when you stop being in people's living rooms week after week, the other opportunities start to disappear. Most people learn this the hard way. I felt like I already knew it.

After Christmas break, I somehow convinced my roommate from college, Diana, to come live with me until the end of the season. She had graduated the spring before and was back with her parents in San Diego, looking for work as a graphic designer. It was so much fun living together again. I wasn't lonely, I was sleeping again, and I didn't have to be drunk to fall asleep!

She'd only been there for a few weeks when I heard her on the phone in the living room screaming. I went in to find her pacing and near hysterics. She lit a cigarette. Her best friend from childhood, Sarah, had been in London working as an au pair and she'd been found unconscious and brain dead in her room. She'd been sick for a few weeks. I knew this because just a few days earlier Diana had been on the phone with Sarah while I was leaving for work, and as I walked out, Diana called out to me, "Busy! Tell Sarah to go to the doctor! She's been sick for weeks!!" and I screamed into the phone, "GO TO THE DOC-TOR, SARAH!!!"

She didn't and ended up with meningitis. Her parents had to fly to London and take her off life support and bring her body home. It was truly tragic. I knew Sarah well; she was Diana's Emily. Diana was devastated but I knew what to do. I got a cold washcloth and had her sit down and cry and I made the plans for her to return to San Diego to be with her and Sarah's families.

After Diana left, I was even sadder and lonelier. I started

drinking more. One Friday night, I was shooting a scene with Josh where we were in bed together making out, a classic WB sex scene. He had a new girlfriend who was in town visiting, and he brought her to set that night. I wasn't ever really comfortable with the make-out and sex scenes, partially because I had been made to feel so bad about my body, but also because it's just a really awkward thing to do. But having the other actor's *girlfriend* there, watching me and making weird comments after each take, like how she was going to need him to Listerine his mouth before she kissed him again, was just too humiliating. I felt like shit. *What the fuck was this job? This was the thing that was going to change my career? This was it?*

After I was wrapped for the day, I told Tracey I wanted to go to Deluxe and get some shots. I drank so much. I can't remember the number of drinks, but it was a lot. Too many. Chad Michael Murray was also there, with some other people from the show. It was almost closing time when I started hanging on the side of the bar and sort of swinging back and forth. Suddenly, my left knee gave out and I fell to the ground, knocking down a bunch of barstools. Tracey screamed and ran over to me, laughing. "Biz! Get up!!! What are you doing??"

I knew immediately. I couldn't get up. My knee was dislocated (once again). I was too drunk for it to hurt, so I grabbed her shirt and pulled her down toward me.

"Tracey," I said. " Imma need you to call an ambulance. My knee is FUUUUUCCCKKKKEEEDDD. I have to gotoa-hospital."

"Biz. What the fuck? Get up!"

"Tracey. My knee is dislocated; I have to have an ambulance."

The bartender called an ambulance and Tracey and Chad Michael Murray sat with me while I laughed about what a fucking dumb idiot I was. I tried calling Michelle, but she didn't answer. Tracey wasn't sure if she should call someone from the show. She didn't want me to get in trouble. I was laughing hysterically. How fucking dumb was I? Here I was, on this show and I should be so grateful. And I was *miserable*. I missed my boyfriend. I missed my friends. I missed my home. I wanted to go to sleep without panicking. I wanted someone to tell me I was doing a good job. I wanted someone to tell me I was pretty enough to be on the WB even though I WAS ON THE FUCKING WB. That my body was good enough and didn't need to change or be *hidden*. That my moles were beautiful. That my acting was different than what they were used to but it was fucking refreshing.

BUT GUESS WHAT? No one is going to tell you all the things you want to hear all the time. You have to know them yourself. And if you don't, you end up on the floor of an upscale bar and restaurant in a small town in the South with ambulance sirens screaming toward you to take you to the local hospital, where you'll sit for hours until they determine you're sober enough for them to give you some medicine and pop your knee back in place. And Chad Michael Murray, who you judged as a douchebag, will stay the whole time and hold your fucking hand. And you'll scream and cry when they do it, because it hurts, but also it's not just about the knee, and someday you'll realize that. And when you do, you'll also be glad the internet didn't exist the way it does now, that people didn't have tiny cameras on their phones at the time and that Perez Hilton was years away from gossiping about messy actresses, because it gave you a chance to be messy and gross and get the fuck over it and get your shit together and be an adult and deal with your shit without the world knowing about it.

And when the writers turn your character into an alcoholic for your second season, it will hurt your feelings, but you'll get over it. And when they don't write you into the finale, it will hurt your feelings, but you'll get over that too. Because you understand they probably would have just cut to Katie anyway.

A MOVIE SCRIPT ENDING
(Death Cab for Cutie)

I knew my mom didn't really like Craig. She and my sister had confronted me when we were all in Chicago visiting my grandparents and staying in a hotel room together. They thought he was using me. They didn't care for him and they missed Colin.

It had come out because my sister was dating a guy she met online (this was the early days of online dating), and my mom and I were convinced he was a serial killer. I looked into hiring a PI to make sure he hadn't killed anyone. My mom talked me into saying something about how creepy the guy was to my sister on the trip, at which point Leigh Ann exploded and told me that *everyone* hated Craig, including my mom!

So . . . *my mother* somehow got us to confront one another about what *she* thought of our boyfriends. Meanwhile, she's in the corner asking us not to fight. When I left Chicago, I was still angry with Leigh Ann, even though my mom tried to get us to make peace before we went to bed. It was actually kind of an amazing and manipulative plan on her part. She was always good at stuff like that. And honestly, she wasn't totally wrong about Craig.

At the time, he was working at Starbucks and taking classes at a UC school, trying to get a degree or waste time until something better came along, I guess. He still wanted to be an actor. It was what he'd gone to school for in Chicago, but nothing was really happening for him in L.A. I'd paid for some classes for him at the Groundlings, an improv comedy school, and also his new headshots. I paid for most everything, as you can probably imagine. Like when his car got booted and I covered the eight hundred dollars in back parking tickets. I maybe even paid his rent once. But there was the free Starbucks for me! And plus, I didn't give a fuck about money. Still don't, much to my business manager's horror. If I have it, I'm happy to spend it on people I love. And I loved Craig completely. I was certain we were going to get married. But whenever I'd talk about the future—like the two of us moving in together or getting married—he would get really cagey and say in a weird cartoon voice that he liked to use, "Who knows what the future will bring?"

And then he would sort of shrug his skinny shoulders and change the subject. I thought he probably felt like he wanted things to be on a more even playing field, career-wise, before we moved forward. Not to mention, he and his brother had a fairly intense and impenetrable bond. Jeff and I had recovered from our one-night make-out when I was in high school, and it almost seemed like it had never even happened—like we had been two different people all together.

Most of the time, the three of us hung out together. Jeff wasn't exactly a third wheel, because it kind of seemed like Craig would be just as happy to hang out with his brother without me anywhere to be found. In fact, I felt like I was the third wheel most of the time. I seemed to embarrass Craig when I would try to join in on their jokes or talk about movies with them. He told me I laughed too loud in restaurants, asking if I always needed people to look at me. I knew that maybe he was right and I should try to be quieter, which would in turn make me more lovable to him, so I vowed silently to work on my dumb loud laugh.

In spite of all this, leaving Craig to go back to Wilmington was tough, but we made it through the season. That year, I lived at the beach and got a roommate, a friend of Michelle's boyfriend who was working as a PA on the show. My old friend Oliver Hudson (who I'd been friends with since we spent a summer in Wisconsin when we were nineteen filming a terrible independent movie called *The Smokers*) did a ton of episodes, as did Bianca Kajlich and Jensen Ackles and Hal Ozsan. It was a really great year, with so many people around to hang out with, I wasn't depressed or as lonely as I'd been in season five. Seth Rogen was cast as a guest star on the show and he came out and did an episode with me, which was fun. He and Judd had brought me back to L.A. to do two episodes of *Undeclared*, where I tried my best not to be jealous that I wasn't on that show full-time, since it was so much more my people and sensibility, not to mention what felt like the entire crew of *Freaks and Geeks*.

I missed Craig so much and would always offer to fly him out to be with me. I was insanely jealous of any girls he was hanging out with or would mention while I was out of town and was prone to sulking on the phone, even though he assured me I had nothing to worry about.

When *Dawson's* was over and I'd wrapped the show, Emily and I moved over to the Hancock Park–adjacent area of Los Angeles, into the upper floor of a Spanish duplex, just two streets away from where Rashida Jones had lived when I was on *Freaks and Geeks*. I loved the neighborhood and I was so much closer to Craig, which was great too. I left my longtime manager Lorraine in favor of a large management firm specializing in comedy called 3 Arts. I didn't love my new managers the way I loved Lorraine, but it felt like an adult work decision that *made sense*, so I did it. I spent the summer auditioning for movies. I had done a fairly terrible pilot earlier that season that hadn't gotten picked up.

Craig's brother, Jeff, had pitched me an idea for a TV show for me, about a senior in high school who starts a makeup line, and I pitched it to my new manager, Mark. He liked the idea of me creating a show for myself but he thought I should work with an established TV writer, as opposed to Jeff, and said, "Look, Biz, if you get a show on the air, you can give him a job!"

Mark hooked me up with an "established writer" that 3 Arts represented who liked Jeff's idea but *what if instead* we made it about a girl who's in her twenties and inherits a bar from her estranged father? He actually sold the pitch and wrote the pilot, but it was never picked up or made. Jeff was weird about it, like I had taken his idea without giving him anything for it. I was confused. I *had* pitched his idea to my manager, but it hadn't gone anywhere, which happens all the time. The show that writer sold and wrote was clearly his own idea. Plus, I made no money on any of it, I was just tentatively attached. And I had told Jeff what Mark had said, that if the other show had gotten picked up, we would've given him a job on it. It all seemed reasonable to me, but what did I know? I was twenty-four. But I also understood that Jeff had been waiting for something to happen career-wise and was getting antsy. I tried passing his scripts on to a few writers I knew, to see if anyone had a writer's assistant job open. I also gave some of his specs to my manager. I thought Jeff, like Craig, was really talented and just needed a break. I wanted to help in any way I could.

Earlier that year, I'd switched agents shortly before switching managers, signing with a woman named Lorrie Bartlett at the Gersh Agency, which was still a smaller agency, but Michelle was represented there, so I felt like I was in good company. Lorrie was a badass agent who seemed to really understand me and had a similar sensibility in terms of the kinds of projects we both liked for me. She called me in late July with an audition for a new Wayans brothers movie. I remember I had passed on auditioning for *Scary Movie*, because I thought the audition sides were demeaning—I think I objected to acting out *giving a blow job to a ghost*. And then of course, the movie was so huge and made Anna Faris a star and I felt like an idiot for not understanding the humor in it and just going for it and humiliating myself. WHATEVER IT TAKES, GUYS!

Before I went in for *White Chicks*, I didn't even read the script. I just looked at the sides and gave it my all for the casting director, who brought me back for Keenen Ivory Wayans later that week. When I GOT THE PART, I still hadn't read the script. The truth was, the log line basically told me everything I needed to know. Plus, I had eventually seen *Scary Movie*, so I had a pretty good idea about the kinds of movies they were making. This one was filming in Vancouver, which was a much shorter flight than to Wilmington, so I was happy to go. Plus, the movie would be over in a few months and then I would be back for pilot season. Craig was going to come visit me as much as he could, and I was promised I would be able to go back to L.A. a few times.

I think the first time I really read the script was at the table read in Vancouver. I mean, there are certainly some projects where you want to really dig into the material, but seeing as how there was a stable of writers and joke writers who were punching up the script the entire time, tracking the insanity of the *story* of *White Chicks* seemed less than important. I guess if I *had* read it, I would've seen that my character's description, which had been erased for the audition sides, was that she was the "overweight friend." As a size 8, I was cast as the overweight friend. Maybe the joke is that the girls are so shallow that a size 8 was overweight? I choose to believe that.

I liked working with the Wayans for the most part. I was sometimes leery of the comedy, like the sleepover blow-job scene, but they really tried to make it feel like everyone on set was now part of an extended family. I was especially impressed with Jennifer Carpenter, who was fresh out of Juilliard and starring on Broadway in *The Crucible* with Laura Linney. She was so committed and prepared every day and really went for it in every scene. When we showed up to do the now-infamous scene where we're driving in the car and changing the song from Vanessa Carlton to Biggie Smalls, she had memorized THE ENTIRE RAP SONG. I was astonished—I had just learned the chorus, the part I knew would be used in the movie. She and I ended up spending a lot of time in our trailers watching DVDs of old movies while Shawn and Marlon sat through their four hours of prosthetic makeup every day.

I was so relieved when Craig finally came to visit. We ran around Vancouver together, spending my per diem eating at nice restaurants and getting drunk on wine. We went up into the mountains and hiked. On his last day, we were hanging out in my hotel apartment, watching TV before his car was coming to take him to the airport. The two things that always seemed to be on Canadian TV were *That '70s Show* and ice-skating. That morning, it happened to be ice-skating. We sat there, tangled on the couch together, hungover from the night before and watched as a ridiculous package about one of the skaters played. It seemed like a parody, the story was so dramatic and insane. I looked at Craig and laughed.

"This feels like a Ben Stiller movie," I said. "Doesn't it?"

"*Ha!* Totally or like Will Ferrell!"

"They should do an ice-skating movie! Like the two of them have to skate together for some reason. The first male-male skating team in the Olympics."

Craig sat up and we laughed and talked about the idea for the next thirty minutes before he had to go, hashing out the plot to a ridiculous movie about Will Ferrell and Ben Stiller ice-skating together. Before he left, we agreed we should write it together. It would be so much fun. I loved Craig's ideas, and I always thought I had really good ones, too. I just had never written a script before. Plus, it would be something we could do together. Shooting *White Chicks* had made me want to create my own stuff. My ideas for dumb movies were just as good as *this* dumb idea.

The next morning at work, I pitched the ice-skating movie to Keenen, who had made it known that he was always open to hearing any pitches from anyone. He liked it, but said he didn't think it was for them but that I should for sure work on it. That night, after work, I was excited to talk to Craig. I had come up with more ideas of funny scenes and characters for the movie. He answered on the second ring.

"So, I told Keenen and he doesn't think it's for them," I said, "but I did pitch it to Mark, and he thinks we should just write it as a spec and then take it to those guys, but he was super into it too—"

"Yeah, actually," he said, "that's what I wanted to talk to you about. . . . I told Jeff about the movie idea and he's super excited and . . . *he wants to write it with us too*!!"

At the end of the sentence he slipped into his weird cartoon voice, presumably because it was what he used when he knew what he was about to say would be unpleasant for me. I paused, stung and hurt that he didn't want to just do this with me. Clearly, I wasn't enough; I never was. I didn't know what to say, but I knew I wanted to do it anyway, with or without Jeff.

"Oh. Okay—I guess."

"Here! He wants to talk to you!"

I heard shuffling as Craig handed the phone over to his brother.

"Hey," Jeff said tentatively. "So listen. I know you guys wanted to do this but—I mean this, this is a *really good idea*. I don't think you guys understand *how good*."

I did actually understand how salable the idea was, but I let Jeff continue to mansplain to me how Craig and I weren't prepared to write a feature script since it wasn't something the two of us had ever done, and how since *he had* (albeit unsold spec scripts that weren't getting his foot in any doors), he would be the perfect person to help us in the *very-difficult-to-figure-out script-writing process*. I was resigned immediately. I knew there was no sense arguing that I wanted to do it with just the two of us. Craig wanted his brother involved. They had clearly discussed this. I had no choice but to suck it up.

"Okay. Yeah. That makes sense. Well, I'm home in a week and I have like, almost three weeks off for Christmas so we can all work on it then, in L.A. and in Arizona over the break!"

I did my best to get on board with the idea. I loved Jeff, I really did. He was really smart and talented and I was sure he would be really helpful in structuring the script and fleshing out the story.

I registered the idea with the WGA, something that I had been told was a good idea to do, especially when something is *such a good idea*. I bought an updated version of Final Draft Pro for us, the screenwriting software, since I was the only one who could afford it. I finished up my work on *White Chicks* the next week and headed back to Los Angeles, excited to see my friends and Craig and work on the movie idea. Craig and Jeff wanted to go get beers at our favorite dive bar to celebrate my coming home. We went to a place called St. Nicks on Third Street, a no-frills sports pub where the beers were cheap, and if you got too drunk, the burger wasn't bad. We settled into a booth, the boys sitting across from me. Craig gave me a weird nervous smile and said, "Soooooo. I know we said we'd wait but we just got so excited and—"

At which point, Craig nodded at his brother and Jeff produced, seemingly out of nowhere, a pile of printed-out papers, which were a detailed outline for the entire movie. I closed my eyes and tried to suck back tears. *Was I just kicked out of something that was my idea? Something that was supposed to be fun and something we were all going to do together?* I took the pages and looked over the outline. It was *fine*, but obviously, I had my own ideas about what I thought should be in the movie and how to break the story. Much of what Craig and I had discussed in Vancouver was in there, but still, I hadn't been a part of this outline at all. It was so offensive. I guess why would I think that I was talented enough to be involved? WHY would I possibly have thought that something that was MY IDEA should remain MINE? Obviously, the boys knew better what to do with it. They'd seen every Coen brothers movie. Jeff had an UNDERGRAD DEGREE FROM NYU IN WRITING. *Ugh. Such a dumb girl. You can't be a part of THIS.*

I felt gaslit. I threw a fit. I was so fucking angry. It got really tense, with Craig telling me to stop being so fucking dramatic and to stop overreacting. Jeff tried to backpedal and say it was just a jumping-off point, but it was too late.

"Jumping-off point?! What are you *talking* about?! You guys worked out an *entire* outline without me!"

Why was I always being left out of everything? Because I had a job? We were supposed to do it together, that was clearly the deal. Why couldn't they have just WAITED A WEEK and done it with me? Because they were selfish and desperate and mad that they didn't have their own careers. But I didn't see that. All I saw was that they didn't wait because they didn't think I was worth waiting for. My ideas, my input, weren't worth it. I was crushed. At the end of our drinks, we went home, all of us angry.

The next day, Craig and Jeff called me to tell me that maybe we should put it on hold for a bit and not discuss it and just all go back to Arizona for Christmas. I agreed, but my feelings were still so hurt. While we were in Arizona, Craig and I were walking his dog around his dad's neighborhood one night so I could smoke a cigarette. He said he was sorry about the fact that they'd gotten so excited and that they still really wanted to write the script with me. I said that was fine but that I thought we should start over with a new outline that we wrote together, and that they would have to wait until I was wrapped on the movie to do it. Everyone agreed on the new plan.

In late January, the three of us started working on the movie together, meeting in Craig and Jeff's apartment and coming up with dumb ideas about why the two male skaters would have to skate together for gold. We wrote a love interest part, that obviously I would play in the movie. We were trying to figure out how the coach gets the idea for them to skate, when I suggested that he sees them on TV fighting and it looks like balletic ice-skating moves. I was proud of breaking that part, since the whole dumb movie hinges on getting them to skate together. But more often than not, it was difficult working with the boys. They had their own shared sensibility and I always felt like—you guessed it—a third wheel. It wasn't the fun bonding project I'd thought it would be for me and Craig. Also, I had to start auditioning for pilots again, and that meant a lot of time when I wasn't available to work with them, so we agreed that they could write pages without me and I would go over them and make suggestions. It worked okay, but my relationship with Craig continued to be strained as the months went on.

In early spring, I was up for an NBC pilot called *Foster Hall* that I was really excited about. I loved it. I would be playing Macaulay Culkin's twin sister. I always thought when I was a kid that I looked exactly like Kevin McCallister from *Home Alone*. Mac had done an arc on *Will & Grace*, and NBC seemed invested in the pilot, which was being produced by Conan O'Brien's company. I went in for my network test and read with Mac, and afterward, the casting agents came out and asked the other actresses to leave, but said they'd like me to stay. They led me back into the office where the auditions had been, and the room erupted in applause. I had gotten the part. That was the one and only time that's ever happened to me—to get the part in the room is rare, mostly because the executives need to talk about things and make sure everyone is on the same page. I drove home, so excited. Craig came over and we went out to dinner to celebrate.

The celebration was somewhat short-lived, however. The next day I got a call from my manager: "*Biz!* Everyone is *so* excited! We just got off the phone with NBC and I think the hope is that maybe you can lose some weight before they shoot the pilot."

My heart sank. Of course there had been the costumer on *Dawson's* who always made me feel terrible about my body. And I knew that technically I'd been cast as the overweight friend in *White Chicks*. But really?

"How much weight do they want me to lose?"

"I think the feeling is THEY JUST WANT YOU TO FEEL YOUR BEST."

What a bunch of bullshit. My best feeling is when I'm not depriving my body of the food I want to eat, BUT THAT'S JUST ME!

"I need a number. Of how much to lose. And I think they should pay for a trainer."

Mark hooked me up with trainer to the stars Gunnar Peterson, who was famous at the time for J.Lo's booty. When I say I had never worked out before that, I really hadn't. I'd attempted to run every once in a while, and Emily and I went to cardio boxing for like two months, but I was definitely not in the habit of working out. Gunnar was very sweet and patient with me. He sent me to a spin class in West Hollywood he thought I would like, which I did. He told me what to stay away from (no more key lime pie at CPK). I started a diet meal–delivery service. I didn't think the weight was coming off very fast, probably because my body was like, "FUCK YOU! I'M FINE!" I only had about four weeks, and in the end I think I dropped like ten to twelve pounds. It felt all-consuming, though. The taping of the pilot was super fun. I felt as skinny as I could, and one of the writers bought me an entire CPK key lime pie for after the shoot. When the show didn't get picked up, I was so bummed, but I also knew that *White Chicks* would be coming out soon and hopefully be a huge hit.

In June, we were almost finished with the script for our movie. Jeff had titled it *Blades of Glory*, which we all agreed was a fucking genius title. I had to do press for *White Chicks*, which was coming out right before my birthday, and I was having a hard time meeting up with the boys to write. Plus, they lived together, so it was easy for them to do it when I wasn't around.

I bought Craig a suit for the *White Chicks* premiere. We went to Brooks Brothers and got him a blue-and-white seersucker with a pink shirt underneath. I bought myself a dress from a fancy store on Montana Avenue in Brentwood, which I loved, but ultimately, my hair and makeup were done in a way that I hated, and I ended up not loving my look. The movie was destroyed by critics, and more than that, it wasn't a hit. *DodgeBall* had come out the week before and people were freaking out about it. *White Chicks* felt like a flop, and worse, an embarrassing flop.

But my twenty-fifth birthday—MY GOLDEN BIRTHDAY— was coming up. Twenty-five on the twenty-fifth!! I was so excited and wanted help planning it. Craig wasn't sure he had enough time, so in the end, Emily and I found a restaurant near our house and planned a big dinner with a Moroccan theme.

At this point, Craig and I were almost always in some sort of argument about something. That night, he forgot to take off work, so he and Jeff were late. He also didn't get me a present.

Or a card. And also, he didn't seem to like me that much any-more. We broke up the next day.

As for the movie script, Jeff suggested that maybe they just take it and finish it, and send me the draft when it was done so I could give notes. Also, Jeff had another idea, a parody of chick flicks, and he and Craig thought maybe Jennifer Carpenter and I could write that together?? That was a fair trade, right?? My ice-skating idea and all the work I'd done on it in exchange for an idea that there should be a movie parodying chick flicks. Totally fair.

I was heartbroken. Also, I was in denial. In spite of everything, I didn't think this could be the end for me and Craig. This had been going on since we were seventeen. We loved each other. And we were still talking a bunch. Maybe this was just a break.

They sent me the *Blades of Glory* script in August, when it was finished. I gave some notes, but I thought it was in really good shape. I sent it to my manager, Mark, and my agent, Lorrie, both of whom thought it was okay, but not worth taking out without more work. The brothers gave it to some of our friends from high school, and also my friends from college. A guy whom I'd gone to college with was now a junior manager at an agency rep-ping comedy writers and was apparently into the script, which was great. I was happy that someone would take it out for us.

In the fall, Lorrie and I thought maybe I should audition for some Broadway musical workshops. I'd always loved to sing, and maybe that would be my next act! I flew to New York to do some auditions and stayed with Rachel Davidson from elemen-tary school and her boyfriend Lewis on their pullout couch. I was there only a few days, but by the time I got in the cab for the airport, I was getting sick; I could feel it. I got to the airport and grabbed a salad from a kiosk. My phone rang from an L.A. number I didn't recognize. I picked up.

"Busy! It's Dan!" Dan was the guy I knew from college, the junior manager now handling *Blades of Glory*.

"So LISTEN, SUCH great news for the boys!!! The script is going out tomorrow to a few select places with Red Hour, and I have to tell you, I think it's gonna be SUCH A QUICK SALE for them! And I know we're all on the same page here, because we don't want there to be any issues with this and you know, it is SUCH A BETTER STORY WITH JUST THE BOYS, right? Like BROTHERS who wrote this kick-ass script out of nowhere?! SO, OBVIOUSLY, you understand why we're taking your name off the script, right? We all just want what's best for the boys, RIGHT?"

I could feel my face start to burn. "Dan? What the fuck are you talking about??"

My other line rang, it was Lorrie Bartlett.

"Dan. I'm gonna go."

I started shaking.

"Lorrie?! What the fuck is happening right now?"

"Busy, I am so FUCKING MAD right now. I don't even know WHAT to say. I am SO SORRY. We'll SUE them. That little fucker. They took your name off the script, Busy. It's out and your name isn't on it."

"Lorrie," I said, taking a deep breath, "I have to go. I have to call them. This is a mistake, because they wouldn't do that to me."

I called Craig and he picked up, defensive from his first hello. I could hear Jeff in the background, whispering things to Craig as we talked. I started crying immediately.

"I . . . don't understand. Why are you doing this? I thought—"

"Busy. Don't be so fucking selfish all the time. This isn't *about* you. You didn't really have anything to do with this. We did all the work—"

"Craig. That's not true. That's not true—"

"You stole Jeff's idea for a TV show. And we gave you the chick flick idea—"

"What? That's not even an idea! What are you talking about??"

"Busy. It's done. I'm sorry *you* have a problem with this, but you didn't even really come up with the idea, I did and—"

I tried not to scream at the top of my lungs in the food court at JFK airport.

"WHAT ARE YOU SAYING? WHAT IS HAPPENING RIGHT NOW? I HAVE TO GO I HAVE TO GO!"

"YOU'RE SUCH A FUCKING DRAMA QUEEN, BUSY."

I hung up the phone and called Emily.

"Please tell me, Emily. Please. Tell me. Am I crazy? I think I'm crazy. They say I'm crazy. Did I make this up? Did I do this? What the fuck??"

I was sobbing hysterically, barely even able to get out the story of what had happened. I was digging through a disgusting salad and sobbing into it and calling my best friend to reassure me that I wasn't a crazy selfish bitch, as these boys, who I had loved since I was a teen, were now telling me that I was.

Emily tried to calm me down. "Listen to me. You're not crazy. I don't know why they're doing this to you, but it's not fair. You have to calm down. Get on the plane. Come home."

Suddenly, I screamed. People looked at me. There was a dead bee in my salad. A GIANT DEAD FUCKING BUMBLEBEE.

"I CAN'T," I sobbed into the phone.

"Pup," she said, using her nickname for me, "go see if there are any seats in first class and pay for it. Calm down. Get on the plane. Come home."

I threw the bee salad in the trash and called Lorrie Bartlett back. I told her not to do anything. I didn't care. They could have it. There were no seats in first or business, so I sat in my middle seat in coach, crying the entire flight, trying to figure out what I had done that was so egregious to Craig and Jeff that they wanted to make me feel like I was insane and selfish. I just wanted to love them. I just wanted Craig to love me back. I didn't know what I had done wrong.

When I landed, I called their home and got the machine, so I tried Jeff's cell phone, which he handed over to Craig. They were all at St. Nick's celebrating the impending sale of our movie. I mean, of *their* movie. Again, Craig reiterated that I was the selfish one who didn't have much if *anything* to do with this script. They had done all the work. Anything I thought I had contributed was so small it was *hardly* worth mentioning. How could I stand in the way of their success? Did I really need the attention *that badly*? I hung up and screamed as I drove down La Brea toward my house.

My agent and manager called the next day. They wanted to know what I wanted to do.

"Nothing. They can have it. It's theirs."

I had a hard time recovering. It wasn't the script. It was that I'd been so easily thrown out, like trash. I was in the way of their success, I guess? Collateral damage. And in order for them to do this insanely shitty thing to me, they vilified me and told me I was crazy. The story became that I was the one who had tried to STEAL ideas from them, that I was ALWAYS just looking out for myself. THEY had come up with this AMAZING STORY, and I was the less-than-talented girlfriend trying to glom on to their talent and carve out a piece for myself. A piece that I didn't deserve. I had a hard time figuring out what was real.

A few weeks later, the deal for the script was about wrapped up when my manager got a call from their shitty fucking douche-bag manager saying, "The boys want to do the right thing and put her name back on the script."

Mark asked me what I wanted to do. I said whatever. I'll take whatever credit and whatever money. I don't care. And I didn't. I was too heartbroken. Plus, I didn't think "the *boys*" wanted to do the right thing. I think they felt the exact same way, but that somehow business affairs or some lawyer needed to cover their ass since I had registered the idea with the WGA to begin with. There was obviously some sort of trail that I was involved in, and no one wanted to get sued. I called Craig to thank them. I still wanted to get back together, something that seemed as insane as I currently felt. I know it's hard to understand. Looking back, it's so wild that I continued to hang on to my relationship with Craig when he clearly thought so little of me. But I didn't see that. I was still in love with him and convinced that we would find a way to work it out.

For a while after that, Emily would come home from work and find me on the floor of our kitchen, halfway through making dinner when I would just give up and lie down and sob. I started getting a weird stress-induced aphasia where I would replace words with other words so what I was saying would be nonsensical. For instance, "You wanna take the stairs or the elephant?"

I lost my voice for over a month and had to go to a speech therapist that my ENT Dr. Sugerman sent me to. My auditions for movies were terrible. I had zero confidence. *Why would anyone want to put me in anything?* I had an audition for *Walk the Line*, the part that Ginny Goodwin ended up playing, which was truly one of the worst, most embarrassing auditions I've ever had in my life. If I ever get to speak to James Mangold, I will have to apologize for the atrocity of my performance. By the way, no joke, Ginny went in *right* after me, and not that she wasn't born to play that part, but I am *certain* that my disaster right before made their choice even easier.

I dyed my hair dark red, thinking that if I looked different, maybe I would start to feel different. I went out as much as I could and drank as much as I could. I ran into one of Craig's best friends from college at a party and made out with him in the bathroom, then fell into the street when I was leaving and cut my hand so badly, I still have a scar on my finger. I went on a yoga retreat in Hawaii where I didn't shower for a week and got a heat rash on over ninety percent of my body. I started taking a memoir-writing class where I met a sweet med student who I tried to pretend I was deeply in love with for a month, fucking him up for a while after, I'm sure. Especially when I dumped him out of nowhere.

I got cast in the Broadway workshop for *Cry-Baby* and went to New York for two and a half weeks at the end of January. Craig and I were occasionally talking on the phone, and I felt like maybe we could still be together. I tried to have sex with one of the actors in the workshop, but it ended up just being awkward bad sex in the freezing basement studio apartment he lived in. Craig called and said he was thinking maybe he would fly to New York to see the performance, but then he didn't.

"I would have liked that," I said.

Back in L.A., I met him at a bar called Star Shoes for a drink to catch up. I thought that this was when we would get back together. I don't know why I thought that. I had made it up, I guess. We sat across from each other—I was already three vodka sodas in when he showed up—and I put my hand on his leg and told him that we could work through whatever it was and that I was ready to give it another try. I knew I could be better and more supportive. I would be. He cocked his head to one side and put his hands up, as if to say "Don't shoot." And then he said, "Busy. No. That's *not* happening. Like *EVER*."

I don't remember getting outside—I barely remember getting a taxi. I do remember asking the driver through my sobs if I could smoke in the back seat. How many sad girls in Hollywood did that cabbie let smoke in the back of his cab, I wonder? It's so basic, really. It's barely special. It's the same for everyone. And yet, it feels unique when it's you. And you can't imagine anyone has ever experienced what you're feeling.

The premiere of *Blades of Glory* was two and half years later. I was on *ER* at the time and, humiliatingly, had actually gone in and auditioned for the part we had imagined I would play in the movie when we were working on it. *I auditioned for and didn't get the part I had written for myself.*

Needless to say, I didn't want to go to the premiere. Why would I want to subject myself to that? I'd heard that one of the producers had been saying I was basically a jilted ex-girlfriend who forced my way onto the script for the credit. I should have pointed out, I was the only one who *had* a fucking IMDB page before this movie. I wasn't the one who NEEDED THE CREDIT, dude.

Anyway, my new boyfriend Marc, a successful screenwriter in his own right, basically forced me to go. "You don't know what it's like for writers, Busy. No one is going to care who the fuck those guys are. People are going to see your name and freak out. Trust me." I did trust him. I've never been more nervous on a red carpet. I hate the pictures of myself from that night, only because I can see how tense I am in all of them; I basically have no neck, my shoulders are hunched so far up. But I made it through the movie and even enjoyed parts of it. One of the biggest laughs was something I know I came up with, which also felt great (not that you should be in the habit of keeping score of whose ideas are whose but come on—*they started it*).

At the after-party, Amy Poehler grabbed me. "Girl," she said,

"Seth Meyers told me the story of what those dudes did. FUCK 'EM! You rock and are so talented. Come here! Sit at our table!!" The rest of the night was insanely fun, hanging with Amy and her friends and the cast of *The Office*, who had come to support Jenna Fischer, and all of them were so impressed that I was one of the writers of the movie. At some point, I turned to Marc and said, "Should we go find those guys and just, I don't know, say hi?" So we left our star-studded table and found Craig and Jeff at their own table in the back, lit by one heat lamp, with their dad taking pictures of them. We said hi and I congratulated them, and then Marc and I headed back to where the real party was.

YOUR EX-LOVER IS DEAD
(Stars)

"Busybee! I was *just* going to call you! I have news, too. *Guess what?*"

She didn't have to tell me. I knew.

"Oh my god, M. How many weeks?!"

I had called Michelle to tell her about a part I'd landed in a pilot with Peter Dinklage. Michelle had worked with Peter in the brilliant movie *The Station Agent*, and I was so excited to work with him too.

She was barely pregnant. The kind of pregnant where you only tell your best friend and the father. I started crying. Michelle was living in Australia with her boyfriend, Heath Ledger, whom she'd met while they were filming *Brokeback Mountain*. He was working on a movie there. She said Heath wanted to fly me to Sydney to hang out with her while he was working. She was just doing yoga and eating Australian yogurt, which was all she was craving, and could use a friend.

As soon as I was done with the pilot, I flew to Australia to be with her for a week. Heath introduced us to a show he loved called

Kath & Kim and we started saying, "LOOKATME LOOKATME LOOKATME," which was our favorite line from the show. I had started running in my break-up devastation and since I was so jet-lagged in Australia, I would wake up at dawn and jog from their house in Bondi Beach to Bronte Beach, along the cliffs overlooking the ocean, listening to the Arcade Fire album *Funeral* and feeling like maybe the future would be okay and maybe I could recover from what was certainly the most intense heartbreak I'd ever experienced. Maybe there was more out there for me, even if it wasn't what I thought it was going to be. I wasn't even twenty-six yet.

When I got back to L.A., I started to fill my days with running at the gym with Jennifer Carpenter and our other friend Candi, and meeting Abdi for lunch at Hugo's. I filled my nights with going out to bars and clubs and concerts with other friends. I went out on a non-date with a producer who was very persistent about dating me, but I wasn't into him. Not my type and the date ended with a handshake and a chaste kiss on the cheek. Years later, I would find out he told people he had fucked me, which was annoying, but I didn't particularly care. I mean, if you're so pathetic that you have to lie about sleeping with me, you have bigger issues. It made me really roll my eyes when he came out in such strong support of the #metoo movement last year. Like, okay, dude. Yeah. I guess if you just *lie* about fucking someone, it doesn't count? I tried to get this cute musician who had recently moved to town to date me but he had a longtime girlfriend back in Boston who, while they were technically on a break while he was in L.A., he was obviously deeply committed to. So we agreed to be friends instead.

I would still have to pull my car over occasionally and sob, deep heaving grief cries, which would hit me in waves when I had a second to myself to think or some song would come on the radio. Some days, I truly thought there would never be a time when I wouldn't feel that way.

A week into June, Carpenter and I went to see Pinback, one of my favorite bands at the time, play at a club in Hollywood called Avalon. After the show, she wanted to go home, and after we said goodbye, I pulled out my phone and called my friend Joel, who was always up for a party.

"Oh my God, BABE! Tonight is the OPENING night of the Roosevelt Hotel pool bar! It's Amanda Demme's night! LET'S GO! I'm PICKING YOU UP NOW!"

Ten minutes later, his vintage Mercedes screeched around the corner.

"BABE! GET IN!!!"

We pulled up to the valet at the Roosevelt Hotel, which was teeming with huge black SUVs all jockeying for space, and scantily clad club girls milling about everywhere. Joel took my hand and pulled me through the packed crowd to the velvet ropes at the front. The scene was already feeling insanely overwhelming, but Joel had connections, and I was certain that this was the place to be on this particular Saturday night. He held my hand tightly as he pushed us through the crush to the two huge bouncers guarding the entrance. I saw him lean into the bouncer and say, "I HAVE BUSY PHILIPPS WITH ME."

I wanted to die. *What??* HE wasn't on the list? He was trying to use me to get into the opening? The bouncer gave me the once-over and *no joke*, shrugged his shoulders like he had no idea what Joel was talking about. Just then, Amanda Demme, the *matriarch* of the Hollywood hotspot scene in the early 2000s, came up with her list. The bouncer whispered to her and gestured to us. She looked at me up and down, like you would see in a movie, then turned back to the bouncer and very clearly said, "NO."

This was beyond. I mean. How does one recover from that kind of humiliation?

Joel turned to me. "That *CUNT*. Now I'm mad. We're getting in there!"

"No. Joel, let's just go to the Abbey or something."

"Fuck no!"

With that, he grabbed me and we snuck around to where there was a service entrance, and all of a sudden, we were in. It was shockingly easy to sneak in, which I wish we would've just done from the start so I could have been spared the humiliation of Amanda Demme's withering gaze of rejection. We tried to get a drink at the bar, but it was at least ten deep. I saw Wilmer Valderrama holding court in the back with a gaggle of hot girls hanging on his every word. I gave a head nod to him from across the pool but there was no sense heading over there to say hi. It was almost impossible to move, it was so crowded.

"Joel. I'm just gonna go home. This is lame."

"Yeah, babe. I thought the crowd would be better, but you know, whatever."

We started to slowly make our way out when I turned to take one last look around.

"JOEL! WAIT! That guy! I want to go talk to him! I'm obsessed with him and every time I see him we talk forever but he's never asked me out. Is he gay?"

On the complete opposite end of the party, a pool between us, in a suit jacket and tie, smoking under a perfectly lit palm tree, was a guy I'd run into three or four times in the year since Craig and I had broken up. And every time we saw each other, we would stand outside and smoke and talk, but he never asked for my number or asked me out. *Obviously*, I assumed he was gay.

"Marc Silverstein? No. He's not gay. But if you're into him you'd better get used to Lizzy Caplan and Kate Towne because those bitches are *always* by his side."

"Let's go talk to him."

"Oh! He's with Anna!"

The only thing Joel liked more than whatever current actress he was hanging out with was finding a *more* famous actress to hang out with. Marc Silverstein was standing with Anna Faris. We headed back into the fray, toward their little group.

"HEY!" Marc said, and I smiled at him.

"Hi!"

"We always see each other at real Hollywood hot spots!"

I laughed. "Yeah, I know. It's actually super embarrassing."

"It's funny! I was just thinking about you. I'm having a birthday party soon with Lizzy Caplan. You know her, right? From *Freaks and Geeks*?"

"Yeah. I haven't seen her in a while though."

"Let me have your email, I'll send you the invite!" He pulled out his Sidekick and looked up, dejected. "Oh shit. It's dead. Oh well. Just tell me. I'll remember."

"Oh. My email is long and dumb and you won't remember it now!"

He threw his cigarette to the ground and stomped on it. "Yeah I will!"

I told him my silly AOL address, which I had come up with freshman year of college. BIZZIEBEEFREE@AOL.COM.

"Cool. I'll email you."

Joel and I headed out, back to the valet, where we waited forty minutes for his car to be returned to us. The next day I got an email from Marc Silverstein.

> Good to see you last night. Here's the invite for the party, as prom-
> ised. But maybe we should try to see each other before that? Like on
> purpose.

I walked into the living room where Emily was doing the crossword and petting our dog, Henry. She looked up at me, "What's up, Pup?"

"I'm gonna go out with this guy," I told her, "and we're totally gonna get married."

Marc Silverstein was a grown-up. The most grown-up adult of anyone I had ever known. Emily started calling him my fiancé in the days leading up to our first date. He took me to Islands, in Burbank, as a sort of joke—like we kept running into each other at cool Hollywood bars, so we needed to get down to who we truly were. It was the same chain burger place where Craig had made me run to the bathroom in tears a few years earlier. But I obviously didn't tell that story.

After Islands, we weren't ready for the date to end, so we went to a bar called the Cat & Fiddle and got distracted by what were clearly Russian call girls and their dates and spent most of the time silently listening in on the insane conversations they were having. When we couldn't contain it anymore, we ran outside to smoke, laughing about the insanity of Los Angeles. He drove a car that looked like something a chauffeur would drive, something I'd never seen or heard of before, a Volkswagen Phaeton. Apparently it was a luxury Volkswagen that they tried to launch in the U.S. for one year but it didn't really go over well. I think only Marc and William Shatner had one. (That's true, by the way, that William Shatner drove one. I saw him like twice driving it around town.)

Marc drove me home and we sat in the driveway of my duplex and talked for four hours. We didn't stop. And only when I was almost actually falling asleep did I say I thought I needed to go to bed and he finally leaned over and grabbed my arm and kissed me over the gearshift in the center console. I knew the rules of dating. We were supposed to play it cool. But he called me the next day.

"Hey. I'm leaving for that wedding in Tulum tomorrow," he said, "so any way you'd want to hang out again today? Is that weird?"

It wasn't.

I went over to his house (HE OWNED A HOUSE) and took him to a frozen yogurt place that Abdi and Candi and I were obsessed with called Pinkberry in West Hollywood. He hadn't heard of it yet. Abdi and I had discovered Pinkberry shortly after it opened and we quickly became regulars, even making friends with Shelly (whom we called Shellyberry) and her boyfriend Young (whom we called Youngberry), who owned the place and were the only employees in the early days. I think people sometimes roll their eyes when I'm like, "Ummm. We were into Pinkberry before anyone else." But TRULY. Abdi went there on opening day and evangelized it to us immediately. It became our hangout. I didn't even have to tell them my order. They knew. Shellyberry even came to Abdi's birthday party. We talked about trying to franchise it. HA! I MEAN! IF ONLY WE HAD.

So anyway, I took Marc there and told him what to order. While we were sitting outside eating, he got a call on his Side-kick, which he answered right away and had a furtive conversation, laughing and getting off the phone as soon as he could.

"Sorry."

"No, that's okay."

"It was my writing partner, Abby."

"Oh. Cool. How long have you guys written together?"

"Ummm. Since we met at grad school. Actually, you tested for one of our shows years ago, it was called *Close to Home*?"

Oh my God. The writer with the good taste in music. OF COURSE.

"Wait. Weren't you guys like *married*??"

He laughed and shook his head. "No. But we were engaged and then we called it off before the invitations went out."

I raised my eyebrows. "But you still work together."

"We still work together. But she's engaged now. She's getting married in December."

Oh. Okay. So, this was how grown-ups did things? I could deal with this, I was certain. Marc seemed worth it.

"I'm bummed you're leaving for two weeks. Plus it's my birthday on the twenty-fifth. I'm having a party. I'm trying to make up for last year, which was kind of a disaster—I wish you could come."

"I know! Well, we'll see. Maybe Tulum will be boring and I'll come back early."

We made out on the couch in his professionally decorated home and said goodbye and that we would talk when he got back.

Gabe Sachs said, "If he comes back early from his vacation, you should marry him FOR SURE."

Kate, my BFF from high school, said, "You know, after my first date with Larry, he left town for two weeks and *we* got married. I think this is a good sign."

Emily BB said, "My grandma is gonna be so mad that you're dating a Jewish guy and I'm not."

Abdi said, "I'm *obsessed* with this for you!"

My mom said, "He sounds great, Biz! What has he written?? Anything I would know?? Also, say, have you seen if maybe you could get on *Grey's Anatomy*?? I think you'd be so good on that show!"

Marc called to tell me Tulum was nothing but rain. The wedding had been fun but there was no reason to stay for the rest of the time if it was just going to rain. Plus, Abby was annoyed he was taking such a big vacation since they needed to start thinking about TV pitches for fall. He would come back the day before my birthday.

Yes. I would marry him. It was decided.

The week after my birthday, he took me to a Fourth of July party at his close friend's house. It was everyone he knew, his giant group of extended friends, most of whom I had never met, the exception being Ike Barinholtz and Josh Meyers, who I knew because Carpenter had dated Seth Meyers off and on and another friend of ours had dated Josh. Almost as soon as we got there and he'd introduced me to a few people, he disappeared. I saw Molly, his roommate—who used to be his and Abby's assistant—and her boyfriend and chatted with them for a while. And then I sort of wandered around, trying to figure out who to talk to. I sat and smoked with a guy named Devin, who seemed closest to my age. He knew Molly from college. Everyone else was in their thirties, many of them married with babies, firmly ensconced in adulthood. I saw Marc talking to a blond actress who looked in my direction and then laughed and put her hand on his chest. I felt so self-conscious. I asked Devin who she was.

"Ahhh. Yeah. She's tricky."

I didn't want to seem needy, so I just waited for him to come find me. Which eventually he did.

Here's the thing. When Marc and I were alone, it was great. He was fun and we could talk about anything. We watched *American Idol* and reruns of *Friends* and movies at his house. We woke up late and walked to Toast, the restaurant around the corner from him, and we would eat giant plates of scrambled-egg quesadillas for me and soup for him. It was easy to fall in love with him. He was certainly the smartest man I'd ever dated, just objectively speaking. The fact that he thought *I* was smart, and was always interested in what I had to say, made me fall for him even more. I had spent so long trying to figure out how to make myself LESS ME in order for Craig to fully love me, and then here was this dude, who HAD HIS SHIT TOGETHER, who thought I was wonderful the way I was. He liked my weird loud laugh, especially in restaurants. This is hard to explain fully, but within weeks it seemed like we had been together for years, in the best way possible. We even took to lying to people about how long we'd been dating, because it seemed absurd to say that we had basically just met.

But when we were out with his friends, things were a little bit more complicated for me. And we basically *only* hung out with his friends. More often than not, I would find myself alone, trying to figure out where he had gone and what I was supposed to be doing. I guess just making friends with his friends, which I tried to do. I tried especially hard with Abby, who seemed unsure about me, and who would also call at all hours. Marc would always pick up and talk to her in a quiet, soothing voice, calming her down about whatever pitch or rejection they were facing. He didn't seem super interested in getting to know my friends, aside from Emily, who I would invite everywhere, like my security-blanket friend from childhood. But I figured that that was just the way it was. He had known all of his friends for years and years. It probably just took a while for him to get comfortable with people. Plus, he was nine years older than us, so that was probably part of it too. But my friends didn't really see it that way.

"Marc's a jerk. Like, he totally thinks he's better than us," one of Emily's work friends said one night when we were out.

I didn't know how to respond. I tried to tell her that it wasn't true, but over time, I slowly stopped hanging out with them in favor of Marc and his friends. It was just easier. Marc took me to a super-fancy resort in Cabo in August for the weekend, where we drank tequila and ate chips and salsa and got massages. If this was being an adult, I wanted all of it.

In the fall, I started working on a sitcom for the now-defunct UPN network. ABC didn't pick up the Peter Dinklage show, and in July I'd gotten a call that UPN was looking to recast the lead on a sitcom that had already been picked up called *Love, Inc.* The part was played in the pilot by Shannen Doherty, but they had decided to replace her only *after* they had trotted her out at the up-fronts and used her for publicity, which I thought was a fairly shitty thing to do and made me wary of going in for it. But the showrunners were huge fans and wanted me to come in and at least meet them. The script was actually pretty funny, and one of the showrunners had worked on *Friends* (my favorite show in the world), so it seemed like something I should consider. After I met with them, UPN asked me to do a screen test. I'm not sure if there were other girls up for it or not. In my memory, it was clear I was the first choice of the showrunners but that's not to say UPN didn't ask them to screen-test more than one girl.

The sitcom was super fun. I loved being in front of a live audience and I liked my costars. Holly Robinson Peete was the other lead and she was so fun and such a real TV *veteran*, I loved her instantly. But I had some difficulty with the showrunner from *Friends*. I felt like he would often try to push me in a direction with my acting that was super cheesy, and he was prone to giving me line readings, which I fucking hated. For me, as an actor, line readings are truly the worst. I know that writers sometimes have in their heads *exactly* how they want a joke to sound, or a particular turn of phrase, but I've always believed there's value in how an actor brings a joke to life. Sometimes in TV, though, it doesn't matter how *you* think it would be funniest—you're just there to service the script. Marc came to every single Friday-night taping of the show, even when it overlapped with Lakers games, for which he had season tickets. The only time he missed one was when the show was on the same night as the rehearsal dinner for Abby's wedding in Napa Valley.

As Marc and I had gotten more serious, I tried my best with Abby. But it actually wasn't the easiest thing for me. I would try not to feel jealous of their relationship and late-night calls, but it was hard. Of course, I knew she was already engaged to someone else and was about to get married. But they were older than me, and a lot of times, I would feel like I was this little kid tagging along with them. I had traded one enmeshed relationship that I could never penetrate for another. Well, at least I have a pattern! Not to mention, all their friends were the same friends that he had when he was engaged to Abby. In fact, most of them, he had met *through* her. She and I had a few run-ins where we were *less than kind* to one another. At one of Marc and Abby's friend's bachelorette weekends that I'd been invited to out of obligation, all the girls were drunkenly talking about their respective boob sizes and teasing one another when Abby piped up about her own bra size. I shrieked with laughter across the table, "WHAT?! ABBY! You DO NOT wear a *C*! YOUR BOOBS ARE *SO SMALL*!!!!!"

She glared at me. "You know, Busy, I think you're kind of a bitch."

I got up to smoke outside and cried as I looked out over the sad little winery hills in Temecula. I hadn't meant to be a bitch. I was just trying to join in with all of the friends. Later, at that same dinner, I got Marc's age wrong and she corrected me in front of everyone. I laughed and corrected myself, but as I looked at her I thought, *Well, whatever, you're all so much fucking older than me, what's the fucking difference?* When I got back to Los Angeles, I told Marc I couldn't do this. It was her or me. He looked at me and sweetly kissed me, "Oh, Buddy. You have my heart, I promise. You already know me in a way she never has. *But she's my writing partner, that's how I make a living.* And that's not going to end now."

Abby had a really beautiful destination wedding in Napa Valley in December. Marc and I had been dating for about six months at that point. Since I had to tape *Love, Inc.*, I couldn't go up with everyone on the Friday morning to be there for all the hiking and massages and golf and activities before the rehearsal dinner that night. I had to fly up right after the taping, on the last flight out of LAX to Oakland. I was super nervous about attending the wedding for many reasons. There's the obvious thing that like *half* of the people invited to *this* wedding had also been invited to the wedding Abby had been supposed to have with my now boyfriend. It felt very fraught to me. Emily helped me pick out a new dress to wear—a really tasteful tea-length, light-bluish-green dress with a built-in corset.

By the time I arrived at the hotel that night, Marc was drunk and going on and on about how the rehearsal was the best thing he'd ever been to—all the speeches were incredible, he couldn't believe I missed it, oh MY GOD! The speech Paul gave was the BEST SPEECH ANYONE HAD EVER GIVEN EVER AT ANY WEDDING EVER. So, needless to say, I was feeling a bit left out.

So I guess, maybe I went into the wedding a little hot. Like, I think I had a cocktail in the lobby of the hotel and then we got on buses to take us to the winery and there were those little Sofia Coppola champagne cans and I think I had one of those and then when we got there I had another drink. Really just trying to soothe my nerves and catch up to the fun time everyone had the night before. The ceremony was beautiful. I cried. The vows her new husband, Jason, wrote were perfect.

Afterward, we found we'd been seated at one of those random tables, as happens at weddings, so we weren't with anyone we really knew or any of our friends. I was super bummed. As soon as we sat down, Marc got up and went outside with some of his friends, leaving me alone. The older woman sitting next to me turned to me and smiled. "Bride or groom?"

"Oh well, my boyfriend is Abby's writing partner."

Her eyes went wide and she looked me up and down. "Oh! Oh! OHHHHHHHHH! You're *Marc's* new girlfriend!"

It was the third *oh* that really pushed me over the top. I flagged the waitress over. "I'll have more wine please!"

It was one of those places where the staff is incredibly well trained and there are like ten million waiters so your wineglass never gets below half full and you have no idea how much you've been served. I think if I had to guess, I was served at least two bottles *myself*. But I wasn't uncomfortable anymore! I felt great! Marc is one of those guys who say they don't dance, so I hit the dance floor with a similarly overserved friend of his. We were dancing UP A FUCKING STORM. I mean, this guy Paul was dipping me and twirling me and I started having the best time ever—also I started just, like, pulling moves on my own, spinning and whooping it up. I saw Abby kind of half dancing toward me and I danced back at her like, "YES, girlfriend! You're married now! I won't be threatened by your weird work-but-also-talk-all-the-time relationship with my new boyfriend slash your ex-fiancé!!!!!!"

She danced right up to me and then SHE GENTLY TUCKED MY ENTIRE LEFT BOOB BACK INTO MY DRESS. Apparently, the renegade boob had been out for quite some time. So long, in fact, the wedding photographer had to find her to tell her to come put my boob back in because he was having a hard time shooting around it. I was mortified. I tried to play it cool and stumbled off the dance floor to go find Marc, who was of course nowhere to be found. As soon as I found him, I got so mad at him that he hadn't been there to stop me from getting so drunk and embarrassing myself and then I just got really sad. I desperately didn't want to do the thing—I mean, I couldn't be the ex-fiancé's new girlfriend who first had her boob out and then started crying at the wedding!!! I couldn't DO THAT! But that's what I wanted to do. So I made Marc leave the party with me early and I sobbed the entire way back to the hotel, thinking how much Abby was sure to hate me now. How I had ruined all those amazing dance-floor photos with my stupid left boob. How I shouldn't have even gone in the first place. I didn't belong with a bunch of grown-ups at a million-dollar wedding in Napa Valley. I COULDN'T EVEN KEEP MY FUCKING BOOB IN MY DRESS! He reassured me that everything was going to be fine. That it was actually pretty funny that my boob flew out and that maybe someday I would feel that way too. And that of course I had to come to her wedding because he loved me, and he needed me there.

Which was all true, of course.

Meanwhile, *Love, Inc.* was far from a success, but it was a job and we did an entire season of it. Aside from one scathing horrible review of my performance in particular, I was sure no one knew or cared that I was on it. The exception being Quentin Tarantino. *Brokeback Mountain* had come out in the fall, shortly after the birth of Matilda, my beautiful and perfect goddaughter. Michelle and Heath were invited to every party and both were nominated for every award (well deserved, by the way). Since they were both nominated, they each were able to bring a guest and Michelle asked me to join at every event, which was obviously incredibly thrilling for both of us. That's basically the origin of me joining Michelle at all the ceremonies for all the awards she's been nominated for. It's hard to even describe the insanity and magic of how much fun that time was, with the two of them so in love, in love with each other and life and their work and this new perfect creature that we all were trying to figure out how to take care of.

After the Oscars, for which *Brokeback* ridiculously lost Best Picture to *Crash* (don't come at me, *Crash* sucks), we picked up Marc in our limo and headed out to all the parties starting at *Vanity Fair*'s. We had been there no less than ten minutes when I noticed Quentin Tarantino looking at us and making his way over. I stepped to the side so he could come into our group and congratulate Michelle, as I'd grown so used to doing. A few times, even, it was assumed I was their publicist and people would ask me if it was okay to talk to them. At one party, a well-known actor asked me to go get him a drink before Heath intervened and spared me from being the dude's cocktail waitress.

"Uh. Actually, Busy's our *friend*," he said. "She doesn't work for us."

So, obviously, at the *Vanity Fair* party, I expected Quentin to be coming over to talk to M or Heath, but instead he beelined for me.

"You're Busy Philipps!" he said. "I fucking *love* you, *man*."

Flabbergasted, I laughed nervously, and Michelle smiled and put her arm through mine protectively. "Ummm. Yeah?" I said. "You're Quentin Tarantino, obviously."

"Man, can I just tell you? I'm fucking *obsessed* with you! You're such a badass! I LOVE *Love, Inc.*! I've seen every episode, I had my assistant get them for me on DVD."

I mean. What do you say to that? Except to call bullshit, which is what I did.

"No," I said. "You didn't."

He shook his head. "No! *Really!* I love it! The whole thing with Mike Smith and then the *other* Mike Smith, man? Genius!"

Now he was referencing specific story lines. He *wasn't* fucking with me? I mean, from knowing who he is I probably don't need to tell you that he then went on and talked at great length for some time about *Love, Inc.* and then *Freaks and Geeks*, which he said he found AFTER *Love, Inc.* since I was on that show, as well. He told me about a project he had coming up and that he wanted me to audition for it. I was over the moon. What?! Quentin Tarantino wanted *me* to audition for him?? It seemed crazy but I was beyond flattered and couldn't wait to call Lorrie Bartlett in the morning and tell her the story.

M and Heath basically had to move to L.A. during the awards season, which thrilled me and made Michelle uneasy, since Los Angeles has never been her favorite city. The traffic and paparazzi and perceived superficiality always made her feel unsafe. But being there with her new family and me and being recognized for her talents in a real way for the first time allowed her to be able to have fun. One afternoon, Marc and I were hanging when my phone rang.

"Are you and Marc at his house?" she asked.

"Yeah. What's up?"

"Heath wants to go to this fancy sushi place. We can't bring a five-month-old in there. Can we drop Matilda with you for an hour or so?"

Next thing you know, Heath and Michelle handed us the baby and zipped away to get sushi. Marc and I spent the next two hours playing pretend parents with my sweet little Matilda, making her laugh, giving her a bottle, and swaddling her up in a towel because we didn't have a blanket. I knew she liked to be swaddled—I had watched Michelle and Heath expertly do it a hundred times—but it would be a few years until I would have to perfect my own swaddling.

Even though the show wasn't the greatest sitcom of all time (Quentin Tarantino's review notwithstanding), I was grateful for the weekly paychecks from *Love. Inc.* since I was in the middle of buying my first house. My business managers were attempting to get me to stay under a certain number on the house, but of course I fell in love with a home way out of my price range that I forced them to make happen for me. In retrospect, I should have held off on buying altogether, but I had already started looking when Marc and I began dating, and it seemed silly not to go through with it simply because I had a new boyfriend who owned his own house, even taking into consideration how serious we already were. Plus, I thought I should live alone as an adult before I got married, not that Marc and I were engaged. We weren't, but it seemed like it was heading in that direction. I mean, I had already made the decision and all of his friends were in the middle of friend wedding season—you know, those two years where seemingly every single person in a friend group gets married and every weekend is another wedding. Weddings were in the air for Marc and his crew. But for my close friends, too. Michelle had Matilda, and my best friend from high school, Kate, had been married for a year already.

After *Love, Inc.* was canceled, I decided I'd had enough of my breakup-trauma red hair and slowly started getting it back to blond. My birthday was coming up again, and I thought maybe Marc and Lizzy and I would all just have the party together, since his birthday is a week after mine. He was super weird about including me in their big party that they had at the Chateau Marmont together every year. At first he tried to say that it would add too many people, then he said that it wasn't really even up to him, he'd have to ask Lizzy. And *then* he said, don't you just want your own party?? My feelings were hurt, but what could I say? The joint birthday party predated me, so I didn't really have any right to get mad about it. But I was. Heath and Michelle offered to host a party in their new house in Hollywood for me, with Heath hiring a DJ he liked and a bouncer to keep Hollywood party crashers out.

As promised, Quentin Tarantino called me in for his new movie, titled *Death Proof*. There were very specific instructions that actresses were to come in cutoff jean short shorts, a tank top and flip-flops. Every girl I knew going in for it rolled their eyes at the request but we all obliged, a waiting room full of scantily clad clones, looking like we were ready for a day at the beach. Quentin read all of the parts opposite me, which was a bit eccentric but obviously what he liked to do. After I did the reading, he explained to me that I was *such* a badass but this part wasn't right for me. Because he had written another role with me in mind, the part of Jungle Julia, the African American heroine of the picture.

I scrunched my nose up, confused, "But. I mean, obviously, I can't play that part because . . ."

"I KNOW! THAT'S THE PROBLEM HERE!"

"Well, is there a way we could talk about me getting *this* part??"

"I just don't see that, man. You're Jungle Julia, through and through. Although, you know, like not."

I thanked him for giving me the opportunity to even audition for him and left, hoping that he would think of me for something else. When the Harvey Weinstein stuff started to come out and #metoo picked up steam and then of course Uma Thurman made her statement against Harvey and Quentin, I still felt like Quentin was a weirdo, certainly, and very particular, maybe even a bit creepy, but not a bad dude. Plus, I loved his movies! I was horrified by his spitting on actresses and choking them himself for shots, but I thought his response was thoughtful, and Listen! ALL FOR THE ART, RIGHT, MAN? But a few days later, I read an article on *Jezebel*, which had dug up his Howard Stern interview from 2003 where he defends Roman Polanski's drugging and raping of a thirteen-year-old. I was ill—actually ill—listening to it. This was ingrained misogynistic behavior, something he believed in deeply. That a thirteen-year-old girl "wanted to have it," as he laughed and made light of child rape. Even Howard Stern, the *original* shock jock, seemed shocked. My daughter is ten. I *know* thirteen-year-olds. I couldn't help it. I took to Twitter, angrily, as we all do nowadays, and fired off a series of tweets condemning him and his stupid art and anyone who ever works with him. Fuck that guy. You don't get to exist in this world anymore, dude. But then he DID issue an apology for that interview, which I guess is all he could do. And so he gets to exist for a while longer, I guess. His movie about the Manson murders is about to be filmed. With Brad Pitt and Margot Robbie and other stars. I'm sure it will be mesmerizing. Probably a hit. I'll skip it.

A few weeks after my birthday, I was on the Pilates reformer with Candi—she was getting her certification to be an instructor and I was getting free Pilates in order to be her guinea pig—when my phone rang.

"Hi, Busy, please hold for Mark and Lorrie."

Wait. What? I wasn't up for any jobs. Why were they calling me?

"Hi guys! I'm not up for any jobs, why are you calling me?!"

Lorrie laughed. "Ummm, Biz, why don't you let me tell you? Apparently John Wells is making good on his word. They want you to come do some episodes of *ER*."

A few years earlier, I had auditioned a million times to play a new nurse on *ER*; the part had ended up being played by my friend Linda Cardellini. In fact, since she and I had the same agents, I knew that for a minute it had looked like her deal wasn't going to work out and that it would come to me next. But obviously, they worked it out and I was fairly bummed about it, buoyed only by the amazing John Wells reaching out to say that he would find a place for me on one of his shows and that

we would work together someday. I guessed, on the Pilates reformer, that day was today. I was offered the part of a new med
student named Dr. Hope Bobeck, and I would be joining on a
recurring basis, since they liked to try people out to see how they
were able to handle the medical jargon and action. I had watched
ER with my mom when I was a kid; in fact, I *distinctly* remember watching the pilot with her. My mother was excited about
a show that took place in Chicago and could finally replace *Hill
Street Blues* as her favorite.

My first day on set was in the first episode of season 12. I was
excited to work with Linda again and to meet John Stamos, who
was joining the cast as a new regular. My very first day I had a
trauma scene, in which Mekhi Phifer, Scott Grimes, Goran Vis-
njic, and I are trying to save someone's life, walking down a hall
with a gurney and yelling out orders at one another. It was a long
tracking shot, all done on Steadicam and if one person fucks up,
you have to start all over. Keep in mind this is *season 12*, so most
of the cast had been on the show for no less than five years. We
did the first take and on my line I froze.

"Fuck! Sorry!!!"

That had never happened to me before but THIS WAS *ER*.
THE *ER*. Goran was really nice but also fairly intimidating. We
went again. This time I got the line, but the medical consultant
said I didn't pronounce one of the words correctly, so we had to
go back and do it again. They were about to call action when
Goran looked at me over the gurney and said, "You get it right
this time, right?"

I didn't think he was being a dick. He was just telling me that I was either going to get it right on the next take or my days on *ER* were numbered.

Not only did I nail it, I remember the line to this day, "Succinylcholine as a paralytic and etomidate for sedation."

I was living in my new house in Hollywood, a house that felt like it had been handed down from actress to actress, because it actually had been. I bought the house from Rachel Bilson, who had bought it from Rose McGowan. I loved my little house, which wasn't so little, but felt right for me. Marc and I split our nights between our two houses. Mine was much closer to Warner Brothers, so on days I was working, we would stay there. We had started to really talk about getting married, like sooner rather than later, because what would be the point of waiting? But we were having a hard time figuring out what kind of wedding we wanted and where. We had been to a bunch of destination weddings, which were fun but didn't really feel like us. Marc and Abby had planned to get married at a big wedding venue in downtown L.A., and before they called it off, they had done all of the typical wedding things, like engagement showers and bachelor/bachelorette parties, and he didn't think he particularly wanted to go through all of that again. Not to mention, we had two houses full of shit already; I didn't need another mixer.

"I wish there was a way we could just throw a huge party and get married without any of the other bullshit," Marc said to me one day as we were lying in his bed. I sat up, excited.

"OH MY GOD! Marc! When I was little, my aunt's best

friend threw this really beautiful croquet party in the summer in Lake Geneva and in the middle of the party, she disappeared and when she came back, she was wearing this wedding dress and she and her longtime boyfriend got married right then, in front of everyone! NO ONE EVEN KNEW THEY WERE ENGAGED. It was just a big surprise. And it was so fun!"

He looked at me. "That's what we should do. Let's do that. We won't tell anyone. Maybe our parents. And we'll just have a party and get married. A surprise wedding."

I loved the idea, so of course I told Emily and Michelle immediately, and Marc told Abby, who was pregnant with a baby girl. I met the two of them for lunch one afternoon when I was off of work. Abby had a lot of questions: "*So*, what about a ring? What about a dress? Where?"

I hadn't thought about any of it really. Except I probably didn't want a diamond. Not for me, I thought! After lunch, the three of us wandered down Larchmont, the street we were eating on, and stopped in at an antique jewelry store to browse and maybe get an idea of the kinds of rings I *would* like, even though we agreed I wouldn't wear it until the wedding day. We wanted it to be a full surprise, and for our friends to not even know we were engaged. The man working there pulled out a beautiful old diamond ring, a mine-cut diamond from 1910 that they'd just gotten in. Marc took the ring to look at it.

"Oh. It won't fit me," I said. "My hands are like weird giant hands. Antique rings never fit."

No sooner had I gotten the words out than Marc had slipped it perfectly on my finger. I looked at the beautiful ring. *Wait. WHO didn't want a diamond? CERTAINLY NOT ME.* Marc laughed and shrugged at the man. "Well, I guess I have to buy it now."

My dress was similarly easy. Abby explained to me that wedding dresses take six months to order and you have to make an appointment to go try them on. But when I called Barneys the girl on the other end said, "Oh. Well, just come in right now. We're not going to be carrying Vera Wang anymore and all the dresses are samples and seventy-five percent off."

Abby went with me to Barneys since Emily couldn't leave work in the middle of the day and I didn't want to go alone. She wasn't exactly who I would have picked for such a momentous occasion, but we'd been getting along much better, and whether I liked it or not, she was going to be in my life. I figured I might as well get used to it. We walked into the bridal salon, which only had a few women browsing, since they hadn't advertised the sale. I pulled a giant Vera Wang couture dress off the rack that looked exactly like the one picture I had torn from a magazine. The saleswoman looked at me approvingly. "You're only the second person to try this dress on."

I put it on and she zipped it up. It fit me perfectly. It needed no alterations.

"I think it's your dress!" Abby said with a smile.

We decided we could fool our friends by having Marc Evite them to a surprise birthday party that he was throwing for me and then when I arrived, I would be in my wedding gown. I googled "COOL DOWNTOWN LOS ANGELES LOFTS PARTY VENUE" and when I saw the Marvimon House, I was certain it was it. It looked perfect. It was a place that was mostly used for parties and art openings and secret restaurants, so it didn't feel "wedding-ish" at all. I called and spoke to Sherri, who owned the place and strangely, they had one weekend open that summer, June 16. It wasn't my birthday weekend, but it was believable that he would be throwing me a surprise party the weekend before. I booked it. On Abby's suggestion, we hired Jo Gartin—who was a wedding planner to the stars but also happened to be a friend of ours—to help us.

Keeping a secret is almost impossible for me, but I liked that we were going to surprise all of our friends with this, so I was committed. But still, I wanted to talk about it and there was only so much talking Emily and Michelle wanted to do. Which is why I would sometimes tell random people that I was getting married in a surprise wedding in the summer. Which is how I found myself telling one of the writers on *ER*, sitting on set one day. I told her all about our plan and how excited I was and how our friends had no idea. A month later, I got a script in which my character was supposed to THROW A SURPRISE WEDDING FOR LUCA AND ABBY. I was so fucking pissed. Look, this is something writers do all the time, *especially* TV writers. They have so many stories to fill that when they're in the writers' room, they throw out pitches from everywhere, including the actors' own personal lives (see also: Audrey's drinking problem, Laurie from *Cougar Town*'s cake-decorating business). It's something I've gotten used to over the years, but this was outrageous. First off, it was my fucking *wedding*. Second, the episode would air *before* my own surprise wedding, so it was weirdly going to look like I stole the idea from the TV show I was currently recurring on!

BULLSHIT! It was my idea! I tried saying something to the writer who I had confided in and she shrugged it off. "No. It *so* didn't come from you! It's a coincidence."

It so *did* come from me, and it was *not* a coincidence, but I had no power to get them to change it.

Abby gave birth to a little girl named Phoebe in February, and Marc and I started going over there at night, bringing Abby and Jason food. I would help Abby, who seemed overwhelmed by the baby and was having a terrible time breastfeeding. I loved Phoebe instantly. She would let me hold her and sing to her and rock her. She was colicky and I could get her to burp and calm down and she would fall asleep in my arms while we were all sitting in the living room with takeout. We started calling her PheBones and then Bonesy for short. Even Marc, who had a hard time with babies and had even expressed that he was "on the fence" about having kids of his own, was no match for baby Phoebe. She adored Marc and would coo and smile and blow bubbles when he took her. It was because of Phoebe that I knew Marc would become an amazing father and was no longer on the fence. It was because of Phoebe that every last bit of weirdness I had lingering toward Abby melted away. And it was because of Phoebe that I realized sometimes, family presents itself in ways you aren't expecting.

One day, I met Colin for lunch. I wanted to tell him I was getting married. We hadn't spoken much in the few years before. Understandably, it took some time for him to want to see me or hang out. We met at Kings Road Cafe and after I told him my news he congratulated me and said, "I just actually started dating someone. I really, really like her. Like, I don't know. . . . This feels different."

Her name was Samantha and, two years later, they would end up getting married, too. I promised that the four of us would get dinner soon.

I had auditioned for a movie that would be shooting right before my wedding called *Made of Honor* that Patrick Dempsey was attached to star in. I had always loved him. His movies from when I was a kid were some of my favorites. And I liked the part, but I auditioned for the movie not particularly caring whether or not I got cast, since I was getting married and that seemed like a much bigger deal to me. My lack of caring is probably *exactly* why I got the part. The schedule for the film was moving around, and a large part of the movie was to be filmed in the U.K., which I was actually really excited about, but I had to tell Lorrie and Mark about the surprise wedding so they could make sure I would be cleared and in Los Angeles on those dates.

"Oh yeah, Busy, you should be finished by then."

But of course, as often happens with movies, the whole schedule shifted around, and as it turned out, I was needed in THE ISLE OF SKYE, SCOTLAND, to shoot the week of my wedding. The production and producers felt terrible, so they arranged for me to have a car waiting when I wrapped on Thursday night to drive me the almost six hours to Glasgow, where I would have to catch a 6 a.m. flight Friday morning to London in order to make the 10 a.m. flight to Los Angeles, landing me in Los Angeles around 3 p.m. Friday, roughly twenty-seven hours

BEFORE MY OWN FUCKING WEDDING. If I missed any of my flights, or if any part was delayed, I would possibly miss my own wedding. I was so stressed out about it before I left for Scotland that I tried on my wedding dress and it FELL OFF OF ME. I knew I had been losing weight, but this was ridiculous. Also, I am *not* generally someone who loses weight from stress but this was different. I took the dress in to a tailor to get it taken in. I would have to land and go straight there and try it on again the day before the wedding.

The Isle of Skye was beautiful, and because of jet lag and nerves from the fact that I was getting married in five days, I barely slept. Whitney Cummings and I had become fast friends in the three weeks of shooting leading up to our trip to Scotland. She and I would wake up super early and run five miles through sheep fields before our work day began. On the Thursday morning I was to leave, there was a mysterious note on the call sheet: "MIDGES EXPECTED TODAY. BE PREPARED AND COVER YOURSELF AND CAMERA EQUIPMENT PROPERLY." Midges, as it turns out, are horrible little bugs that swarm and bite. They're tiny, like gnats, except when they descend on a place it looks like a gray cloud has covered the area. I had spent hundreds of dollars in the months leading up to my wedding to ensure my skin was clear and beautiful. I wasn't about to get bit on the face by a *midge*! Whitney and I covered ourselves in netting, removing it only when we had to film.

The day was almost over and the car was waiting to speed through the Scottish countryside to take me to get married when all of a sudden I felt a sting on my chin.

"NOOOOOOOOOOOOOOOOOOOOOOOOOOOOOO!" I screamed.

Whitney ran over and looked at my face, "It's fine. It's fine. You're going to be *fine*." She paused. "Maybe you call your dermatologist when you land and get a cortisone shot??"

I had no time to be upset; I had to make the twenty-hour journey back to L.A. When I landed and got through customs, I called Dr. Lancer, who had been my dermatologist since I was eighteen. I frantically explained the situation to one of his nurses.

"He's supposed to leave here in a half hour today, Busy," she said. "Can you come in tomorrow morning?"

"NO! I'm getting MARRIED TOMORROW! It's my wedding!!"

He agreed to stay late to see me.

When I got there, the nurse smiled wide at me, "You're getting married tomorrow? Ali Larter was in here when you called! She was so excited!"

WHAT?! ALI LARTER WAS DATING ONE OF MARC'S GOOD FRIENDS. ALI AND HAYES WERE INVITED TO MY "SURPRISE BIRTHDAY PARTY"!!! Oh my God. Had that fucking *midge* not only ruined my perfect skin but also just ruined the *surprise* of my surprise wedding!?! I panicked and called Marc, who panicked and told me I had to call Ali and tell her they'd misunderstood but that I *had* found out about the birthday party but not to tell anyone because I wanted Marc to still think he really surprised me. It was the best I could do. To this day, I'm not sure if she bought it or not, but she assured me she wouldn't say anything to anyone else, even Hayes.

That night, we ate at Hamburger Hamlet in a private room and Marc's parents and my parents met for the first time. My mother and Marc's dad instantly hit it off. "Well, Arnie is just *fantastic*, isn't he?! Pat is great, too! They both are!" My mom was right: in terms of in-laws, I really won the lottery. We had arranged it so that our families would stay hidden for the actual surprise, since we thought their presence would cause suspicion. We had told a few people who lived far away about the wedding, since we didn't expect them to fly cross-country for my surprise birthday party. Marc's friends from high school came in, as did Rachel Davidson and Kate and her husband, and obviously, Michelle was there. Heath was just beginning to work on *The Dark Knight* so he didn't come. I had actually seen Heath the month before, though, when we were both in Chicago. He was shooting a sequence for *The Dark Knight* and I was shooting exteriors for *ER*. We had lunch at his hotel and he showed me some of his journals he was working on for the movie. I told him I hoped he would make it in for the wedding, but he didn't think it would be possible and I understood.

Marc stayed at his own house that night, because I thought it would be fun for him to see me for the first time at my surprise entrance. In the morning, I woke up and checked my face. No sign of the midge bite: Dr. Lancer had worked a miracle. Emily and Leigh Ann and Michelle helped me get ready at the Standard Hotel downtown, close to the space where the party was. Leigh Ann and Emily went over to the venue early. When Michelle and I got the call from Marc that everyone was there, we went down to my waiting car and headed over. I kept breathing really hard, deep long breaths to steady myself. We had photographers as well as someone shooting the wedding on Super 8 film, and in the video you can see me breathing in and out so deliberately.

The ruse that everyone was told was that I thought Michelle was taking me to an art opening but really it was my own surprise birthday party. But of course, the surprise would turn out to be on all of our friends. Marc and I had planned a perfect party, with our favorite restaurant catering and cucumber martinis and so many colorful flowers, including marigolds, my favorite since childhood when my mom would plant them in the front yard of our Chicago home.

Marc was the best person I had ever met; of course I wanted to spend the rest of my life with him. We had written our vows together and he had sweetly put them in Final Draft, the script software, so that I could read them like a script. But I didn't need to act the part. I was ready for the next chapter of my life. I was ready to start my own family. I couldn't wait to say those vows and to hear them said to me. I was a girl who had always wanted to get married, had always thought about what her wedding would be like. And here it was, finally. About to happen.

We pulled up, and as planned, Michelle ran in ahead of me, through a giant curtain. It was totally silent and for a second I was alone. I took one last deep breath and then I walked through the curtain to Marc, who was waiting for me on the other side.

WHILE YOU WAIT FOR THE OTHERS
(Grizzly Bear)

We realized in August that we had actually forgotten to sign and submit our wedding license, so we had lunch at the Chateau with Phil Pavel, who married us, and Emily and Abby as our witnesses, and signed it there. Weirdly, Heath was having lunch there, too, at the table next to ours, and we laughed that he had somehow managed to make it to our wedding anyway. He and Michelle were in the process of separating at that point, and I felt sad for both of them but weirdly like something would be figured out and it wasn't the end of the story for them. They were so young and that baby was the light of both of their lives. They were just working all the time and it was complicated. Shit is always complicated. Especially when you're twenty-eight. And movie stars. With a baby.

I had decided not to return to *ER* for the full season, since we felt like with the work I was doing, I should be made a regular and paid as such. They didn't agree and were paying me less than half of my television quote. I'd worked hard to get my TV quote and I didn't think it was fair to go under it.

Soon it was clear that there was about to be a writers' strike. A writers' strike meant that all production on TV would effectively stop, including the pilot season for that coming year. There would be a truncated one, for things that were commenced or written before the strike. It also meant there would be fewer movies shot.

One night, I turned to him. "Should I have a baby?"

He looked over at me.

"I mean. Maybe?"

"Have you ever gotten someone pregnant on accident?"

"No. I don't even know if it all works. Why don't you just go off the pill and we can see what happens?"

Exactly one month later, I sat straight up in bed at three in the morning, because it felt like there was a lightning rod shooting through my stomach.

"HOLY SHIT!"

Marc rolled over groggily. "Whaa? Are you okay??"

"Yeah. Go back to bed. I just got pregnant."

I had to wait a few weeks to take a test, but those two little lines showed up before I had even stopped peeing. Marc and Abby had started walking the picket lines with other writers, showing up every day as if it truly was their job. We joked that if the baby was a boy, we should name him Strike. Strike Silverstein is a badass name.

There were some projects hiring despite the strike, so I was still auditioning for movies, mostly while trying to keep my expanding belly hidden under swingy dresses. I auditioned for a movie and they wanted me for a part in it, but when they found out I was pregnant, they said they wouldn't be able to insure me and offered the part to someone else. I was super bummed. I also was cast in a big animated movie, which I was *very* excited about, but then was replaced with someone far more famous than I was after I did a day of work on it.

Things weren't really going my way work-wise, but it was okay, since I was pregnant. Marc had sold his house right after we got married, but now we found ourselves in a bit of a situation, house-wise. My house was great for a single actress living alone but not necessarily the greatest place for a baby. We decided to start looking for a new place, something that we had planned to do anyway at some point. That point was now sooner rather than later. Just like that, we had a looming deadline and needed to figure it out fast. We listed my house. The housing market was taking a little dip, which wasn't a huge deal and was certainly in our favor as buyers, but our Realtors told us that selling my current house could be a little tricky, especially since I owed so much on it—I had bought it at the peak of the market. We found an amazing house and put in an offer, along with nine other prospective buyers. I wrote an impassioned letter about how much I needed this house, how I wanted to raise my children in this house, how this was absolutely OUR HOUSE, and our offer was accepted. Being the daughter of a Realtor paid off! And it was a very sparkly letter.

Marc and I had lunch plans with Colin. I wanted them to meet each other and also to tell Colin the news that I was pregnant. We met at Le Pain on Melrose; it was a really beautiful day. I was nervous for them to meet, but I knew they would hit it off. They were both people that everyone seemed to like a lot, so why wouldn't they like each other? We ate a leisurely lunch and chatted about Colin's new girlfriend and the movie he was about to do. They were thinking of moving to New York together, which I thought sounded like a good idea for him.

During lunch, I noticed that Marc kept pulling his phone out of his pocket and looking at it, without trying to be rude. Finally, right as we were paying the check, he excused himself and took a call. I assumed it was from Abby, some work crisis or her wondering when he would be around to work that day. We hugged Colin goodbye and started across the street when Marc grabbed my arm, "Buddy. I need to tell you something. And I need you to remember that you're pregnant, okay? You have a baby inside you and I need you to remember that."

His voice was weirdly shaky. I was confused.

"Okay?"

We were at his car. He opened the passenger door and sat me in the seat and looked at me. "Heath is dead. He's dead. They found him in New York."

I could not process what he was saying to me. I had talked to Heath on the phone a few months earlier, on Michelle's birthday, when they were really breaking up, and it had been awful.

I didn't know what to do. Michelle was in Sweden shooting a movie and her phone never works when she's out of the country. I called our friend Ben Lee, who answered and told me everything he knew. Then I called Michelle's agent, I think, who gave me her Swedish cell phone number. I sat there, trying to breathe through my sobs, and then I called Michelle, who answered immediately. I don't know who called her to tell her. She already knew. I told her I loved her. I told her it would be okay. I told her

I would fly to New York and meet her there. I told her I loved her. I told her Matilda would be okay. I told her I was sorry. I told her I loved her and I would see her in the morning. She could barely speak.

Marc booked a red-eye for me. I sat by the window, and on the seat back of what felt like every seat, CNN played nonstop footage of Heath's death. I felt like I was in an actual nightmare. I sobbed and sobbed and the girl sitting next to me looked over and put her hand on my arm and quietly said, "You knew him, huh?"

I didn't have the energy to lie, so I just nodded and then she shut off her TV. I coordinated with Michelle's mom, who was flying from San Diego and landing around the same time as I was. Colin somehow arranged for a driver to pick us up at the airport. We had to get keys from Michelle's longtime friend Dan when we landed, which was a little tricky since it was so early. We pulled up just before 6 a.m. and there were already paparazzi camped out. Michelle and Matilda arrived two hours later.

I have snapshots in my head from that time, those first few awful weeks. Things that will stay with me forever. Every person I loved in my twenties lost someone they loved most. Even Marc, although this happened before I knew him. I don't know why. But I was there. To be there and sit with them, I guess. To be a friend. To cry with them and get them cold washcloths for their eyes and calm them down. And to make plans when they couldn't and make a joke when we needed to laugh.

I understand the public's fascination with Heath's death, with him in general, as a cultural icon or as the greatest actor of a generation or whatever. But you know, for me it was really simple. He was my best friend's love and the father of her child. My beautiful magical goddaughter. A child we all love so dearly, who has so much of him in her, without even trying. He was my friend and I loved him.

My prenatal yoga teacher told me to talk to my baby and reassure her that my grief was about something else and that everyone was so excited for her to be born. I did it every day, talking to my little belly and reassuring my unknown child that my tears were for another reason, not her.

As I got bigger and bigger, I couldn't imagine ever working again. I was gaining so much weight, but my baby was healthy and I guess so was I—I didn't have gestational diabetes or anything. What I did have was a craving for fresh strawberry milkshakes and donuts, so I think that probably had something to do with the weight gain.

We still couldn't sell my house, which started to feel like maybe it was a problem since there was a writers' strike, I wasn't working, and now we had two mortgages, but Marc was fairly chill about things, so I tried to be as well. My old friend Josh Friedman called me up and asked if I would be interested in doing a few episodes of his TV show, *Terminator: The Sarah Connor Chronicles* even though I would be hugely pregnant. I thought why the fuck not, it would be something to do and might be fun to be on TV hugely pregnant. My first day on set, Thomas Dekker, who I think was maybe a teenager still, looked at my giant belly and laughed. "Oh my God! Normally our prosthetic dudes are really good, but that looks insane! They overdid it!!!"

His little face fell when I told him that it was real.

"Oh *shit*! I'm so sorry! I've just never seen a pregnant belly that big!"

I couldn't blame him. It *did* look fake. I shot my last scene a week before I gave birth. I am convinced to this day that I am maybe the most pregnant person to ever act on a TV show.

We had moved into our new house when I was eight months pregnant and were settling in. All of my friends came over and helped unpack us. Jennifer Carpenter and Candi unloaded all my books and put them on the shelves, Emily and my mom tackled the kitchen, and I waddled around and pointed a lot. Marc and I were sitting in our new living room, watching TV one night, when he turned to me and rubbed my giant belly, "You know, this really feels like home. I think we did it."

No sooner were the words out of his mouth than we heard a commotion coming up our front steps. Marc jumped up and ran to our front door, which is a huge glass door. On the other side was a man, in his late thirties probably, with a woman who was pulling her hair in front of her face. The man was screaming profanities through the glass at Marc and yelling that he was going to kill him. It was all so chaotic, I got up and waddled into the foyer forcibly saying, "NO! NO! THIS IS NOT HAPPENING! GET THE FUCK OUT OF HERE!"

The man looked at me, taking in my sizable figure, and shouted, "My beef isn't with you, pregnant lady! My beef is with the BEARD!"

I grabbed Marc to pull him away from the glass door. Marc was legitimately trying to figure out what the man was upset about, but it was clear to me that they were cracked out on drugs.

They had somehow made it up into the hills from Hollywood and were looking to fuck some shit up and saw our lights on. I was not about to be murdered while eight months pregnant, or worse, have my husband murdered in front of me, leaving our unborn child fatherless before her birth. I called the police on my home phone as the man started pounding on our glass door, screaming that we needed to give him back his car (the most we could *ever* figure out was that he had parked a stolen car across from our house and it had been towed, which was not our doing, anyway).

"I'm on the phone with the police!" I yelled. "They're on their way!!!"

"Yeah! You call the police!"

He screamed back at me defiantly as he banged on the door a few more times. I was terrified the glass was going to shatter, but then there was silence. He and the woman were gone. My cell phone rang. I handed the home phone to Marc to stay on the line with dispatch as I picked up my cell phone. It was my neighbor across the street, Johnny.

"Shit! Busy! What's going on!? Are you guys okay??"

"Yeah. Yeah," I told him. "Some fucking crazy dude is trying to kill us maybe? Can you see over your fence?"

Just then there was a crazy commotion and screaming from the street.

"HOLY SHIT! Busy! Are the police coming— HOLY SHIT! Oh my God. I'm gonna call you back!"

The lady from dispatch was asking what was happening, but we couldn't see down to the street from our house.

"MARC!" I said. "Do *not* go outside!!!"

But of course he did. Because men are dumb. (I'm sorry, that's a generalization. They're not all dumb. Just when it comes to things like this.) Eventually, I saw the red-and-blue lights on the street and felt like it was relatively safe to waddle down the steps and talk to the police. I wasn't really prepared for what I saw in the street: a yellow cab with the seats and center consoles *ripped out*. There was money and change everywhere and also lots of blood. There was an older man, the driver of the cab, holding a rag to his horribly beaten face, talking frantically to the police in a heavy Russian accent, trying to explain what had happened. I had never actually seen someone who'd been beaten up that badly in person. It was truly horrifying. Another police car pulled up, along with several cabs, who apparently the driver had reached out to and were coming to check on their friend. It was chaos and the two perpetrators were nowhere to be found. After a few minutes, the two cabs sped off, followed shortly by one of the cop cars. The other officers stayed to take statements from all of us and then told us to try to go to bed and not worry about it. And to obviously call 911 if they came back. And to HAVE A GOOD NIGHT!

Even with our house alarm set, I barely slept. Marc took a giant kitchen knife and put it next to the bed, but then I made him return it to the kitchen because I was afraid that somehow one of us would end up accidentally stabbed. I tossed and turned all night, sure that the two perps would come back for vengeance against the beard and the pregnant lady. Here I was, my life was just beginning, and I would be murdered in my sleep over a stolen car. A few days later, I got a call from a detective who was assigned to the case.

"Hey! You must have seen the news! Yeah. Those two went on quite a spree. Seems like it started at your house! We may need you to testify, but honestly, them threatening you is the least of their problems, so we may actually get away with just playing your 911 call. The prosecutor will reach out eventually. You sound really distressed on the call."

We hadn't seen the news but then we looked it up. They had indeed gone on quite a spree, beating up several more people and eventually successfully stealing a cab that, after a high speed chase, they then crashed into a restaurant, which was thankfully closed, with no one inside. And thankfully, they ended up behind bars, so they didn't come back to kill us. Yet.

As the summer wore on, I tried to remain cool, both physically and mentally. I was *huge*. And it was *hot*. I was roughly the size of a house and had taken to getting on the scale at my doctor's office backward so I didn't have to see the number. What I do know is that I was hovering around 140/145 when I *got* pregnant, and two weeks *after* the baby was born, when I was brave enough to weigh myself, I was 212. So that's sixty-seven pounds right there and I'll bet it's possible I had lost a solid fifteen to twenty in those first two weeks. It's always fucking amazing to me what people say to you when you're pregnant. I mean, the number of people who asked if it was twins, or would say knowingly, "Any day now?" and I was like five months pregnant. One time I was hiking with Candi when I was about six months along and a woman sidled up to us and cut in, "Are you trying to put yourself in labor?! You look like you're about to pop!"

Nope. Just trying to stay healthy, lady! The *worst* was a

THIS WILL ONLY HURT A LITTLE

woman at Rachel Davidson's wedding who insisted there must be something "wrong" with me because of how big I was. It was so humiliating. She was an older woman, so I didn't tell her to fuck off, but seriously, the exchange was insane.

"I can tell you're ready to go!" she said, beaming at me. "Any day now?"

"Oh no . . . I'm just seven months—the baby is due in August!"

"NO! That can't be right!! Is there something wrong with you? It's not normal to look that big at seven months!!!"

"Nope. Nothing wrong with me. Okay. Nice to see you. Enjoy the paella! 'BYE."

So around, eight and a half, nine months, I was ready to get this baby girl out of me. Let me say this: I'm a big believer in choice. All across the board. I mean, the choice to have a baby, certainly. But then beyond that, *how* you choose to have your baby is totally up to you: if you want to breastfeed or not, save the cord blood, give birth in a pool of dolphins, be knocked completely out, whatever. I couldn't care less. But I have always felt really strongly that I *personally* would not get an epidural. There are a couple mitigating factors in me feeling really strongly about this. I mean, the least of which is that when I decide to feel really strongly about something, it's hard for me to *stop* feeling really strongly about something. I remember watching a *20/20* when I was in middle school with my mom that was about hypnobirthing (which is a natural and drug-free way to give birth, basically involving meditation and deep breathing and visualization), and I declared after the segment that *that* was how I would have a baby someday. My mother rolled her eyes and said, "Sure, Biz" (I feel like that was her response to me for most of my teen years.)

My two closest friends who'd given birth, Michelle and Kate, had both done it without drugs, too. Also, the idea of sticking that *huge* needle into my back, inches from my spinal cord was *way* scarier to me than any trauma my vag was going to go through. Vaginas are meant to birth out babies (I thought!). Needles are *not* supposed to be put inches from my spinal cord! But most everyone I told that I was going to do the birth without drugs said I was crazy or that it would be impossible. Most of Marc's girlfriends would just snort and give a knowing, "Yeah. Okay. Talk to me after . . ."

My due date was officially August 15, but I knew from my hypnobirthing that babies come when they're ready, not some random date based off when you remember your last period starting. I was secretly hoping the baby would show up on August 8 so her birthday could be 8/8/08 but alas, it was not meant to be. Plus, my doctor later told me that the hospital was a total shit show of women getting induced for that very reason. I've always had this picture in my head of women giving birth in the hallways of Cedars-Sinai because they wanted a cool and auspicious birthday for their baby.

In the weeks leading up to the birth, we didn't have much to do. I didn't really feel like going out, although a few times Marc forced me out of the house to go see bands play or to a friend's birthday party, where I was always miserable. Not that he noticed, since I think he was just happy to be out and seeing people. We spent a lot of time watching TV leading up to my labor. It was August 2008. The second season of *Mad Men* was about to start airing on AMC and people were just finding the show and getting into it. THERE WAS A LOT OF HYPE. Marc and I decided we should watch the first season in the two weeks before the second season started so we could jump in and be all caught up. Marc and I watched every episode of *Mad Men* that existed and SOME OF THEM TWICE, which was a lot of *Mad Men* in a little amount of time.

On Monday the eleventh, I went in for a checkup where my doctor was a little concerned that my amniotic fluid was low. We did a stress test on the baby, which is where you sit in a chair with a fetal heart rate monitor on for an hour and they make sure the baby isn't showing any signs of distress. She was fine, so he told me to leave and go drink a ton of water and come back that afternoon. When I went back, my fluid was better, but he still was thinking that the baby could come sooner rather than later. Since he knew and was on board with my vaginal, no-drugs birth plan, he suggested something called "stripping the membranes." (I'm so, so sorry if you haven't had a baby yet and are reading this, because it all sounds disgusting. And I mean, for the most part, it kind of is. But then you get a baby at the end of it all! Yay?) Basically, if you're a few centimeters dilated, your doctor can put on a glove and then (*gross*) stick his fingers up in your cervix and kind of sweep around and *sometimes* this induces labor. But it's way less intense than having a drug like Pitocin.

So! Membranes swept, I went home. We watched some *Mad Men*, took a walk when it cooled down, and waited for me to go into labor. Which didn't happen. I started feeling some contractions for sure, even painful ones (*or so I thought*) but they weren't consistent enough to count. The next morning, Marc and I went back to sweet Dr. Crane (who is totally famous now, because he's the Kardashians' doctor and was on their show, but he was always famous in L.A., because he's seriously the best). Again, my fluid was on the low side, again stress test for baby; she was fine, again with the membrane sweep. Dr. Crane suggested we walk around Beverly Hills for a bit and see if anything started to happen. We did and bought some pool furniture that was on sale (because why not?) and then walked back dejected. Nothing.

Dr. Crane did one final membrane sweep—I mean, at this point, were there any membranes left? It clearly wasn't working, but whatever. I knew that I would probably end up on Pitocin in a day or so and then probably have to get an epidural. I was a little bummed and tried to google the name of some restaurant in the Valley that serves a salad that puts women into labor, but I couldn't find it and it was too hot to drive to the Valley anyway. Marc had to go to work and I decided to go get my hair colored because I felt like after the baby came, it would be a while before I could get my roots touched up. So I did that, and went home and watched some TV, bored and hot and wanting to go into labor. After it got dark, Marc suggested we take a super-long walk, ending with me hiking up the giant hill that leads up to our neighborhood. We must have looked insane. I was a giant inflatable beach ball, and here was my tall skinny husband pushing me up a hill. We watched the last two episodes of *Mad Men* we had left and then went to bed.

Around 11 p.m., I reached over for a glass of water next to the bed and a huge contraction hit and I threw the water all over the place. AND SO IT BEGAN! Real labor! FUN TIMES!!! We called Debbie, a certified midwife who was acting as a doula for my birth. In case you don't know, a doula is a birth coach who comes over and hangs out with you and gives you support and lets you know when she thinks it's time to call the doctor or go to the hospital. I labored at home for many hours. I thought I would want to get in my giant whirlpool tub, but as soon as I got in, it was really unpleasant for me, so I jumped out. I took a lot of hot showers, letting the water pound my lower back. For some reason we still don't know, I was having back labor mostly. Which means I was feeling all of my contractions in my lower back. Most of the time, if you have back labor, the baby is in the wrong position, but my baby was right-side up, causing me extreme back pain. So that was fairly brutal. Around 7:30 a.m., on her way to work, Emily BB came over with a turkey sandwich for me. I had been craving them but hadn't eaten them in my pregnancy because of listeria concerns (no cold lunchmeat!).

But since the baby was clearly coming out that day, I felt fairly safe that I could eat a turkey sandwich without the fear of exposing my unborn daughter to listeria. When I was almost eight centimeters dilated, our doula suggested we head over to Cedars. I called Leigh Ann on the way and she wanted to know if she should come to the hospital immediately. I told her no, I thought it would be a while, it was only eight in the morning. I had already been in real labor for nine hours. We were assigned a private room and a nurse named Tranell who was a true angel. My water still hadn't broken and almost as soon as we got to the hospital, my contractions all but stopped, which is something that happens sometimes when women get to the hospital. Debbie wanted me to walk around, but that sounded terrible to me. I tried my best to relax so I could get back into labor. Eventually, Dr. Crane's colleague came in (he had been delivering a baby down the hall) and he broke my water with what can only be described as a crochet hook. Then my contractions were back and stronger than ever. I was in so much pain. I wanted the drugs. I needed the drugs. This was too much pain.

I looked at Marc. "I need the drugs. I can't do this. I have to have the drugs."

"Okay. I'll get them to get you the drugs. But I want to just say this. If you take them, everyone was right and YOU COULDN'T DO IT ON YOUR OWN."

I looked at him with true fire in my eyes. "FUCK YOU, OF COURSE I CAN DO THIS ON MY OWN."

"I know you can."

"Okay!"

"Okay."

"GET ME SOME ICE CHIPS!"

My labor went on and on. I hadn't slept in over twenty-four hours. I was exhausted, but there was no way I could sleep. The contractions were *so* painful. Some medical students came in to see me, because I guess when you're in a hospital choosing to give birth without an epidural, you're kind of like an exotic animal and they want everyone to be able to have a look. By the time Dr. Crane showed up and I started pushing, I was beyond delirious. There are actually no words for how out of my mind I was. Time didn't exist anymore. The world stopped turning. It was just me and this room that I lived in now, with its view of Jerry's Famous Deli taunting me, the sun setting and turning the hills of West Hollywood purple and pink and beautiful and here I was, with this baby, this huge baby, trying her best, heart rate never dropping on her little fetal monitor, just taking her sweet-ass time making her way into the world the way she wanted to because that is who she is and has always been. I needed a full episiotomy. Again, if you haven't had a child I apologize, but a full episiotomy is where they cut your vagina down to your rectum. It's as fucking awful as it sounds and with no epidural, they just spray some lidocaine on there, numb it up a bit, and cut. Marc was in charge of playing music that made me happy. As it turns out, it was a lot of Whiskeytown and Arcade Fire. Tranell's shift was over and a new nurse came in, but when Tranell came to say goodbye she changed her mind, "No. I have to stay and see this baby be born. I'm not leaving you."

Unable to really speak, I smiled gratefully at her, and she and the other nurse each took a leg to hold back. I would push and then I would pass out until it was time to push again. I was having full-on hallucinations, about surfing and giant waves and bright colors and light taking me and floating on clouds and talking to people. I was almost done. She was almost out. I pushed so hard and lay back. I opened my eyes and I was in the boardroom of Sterling Cooper. Dressed as Peggy. At the end of the table was Don Draper and Pete Campbell.

Pete said, "I don't think she can do it, Don."

And Don took a drag of his cigarette and said, "Oh she's gonna do it, Pete. She's gonna do it."

And then I was back. Marc said I was only out for a few seconds, but when I came to I was saying under my breath, "I can do it, Don. I can do it. I'm gonna do it."

Marc turned on Arcade Fire's "Wake Up" and Dr. Crane got the baby's shoulders out. It is a pain that has no description. It enveloped my body in a radiating white-hot poker of fire—unable to focus, unable to breathe: all-consuming pain.

"Give me your hands. Here. Reach down. You want to pull her out??"

And with the help of Tranell and my other nurse and Debbie and Dr. Crane, I reached down and put my hands under her little armpits and pulled a giant purple and red butterball out of my throbbing, exhausted body and up onto my chest. I looked around to find Marc. He was there next to me.

"Marc. I'm not crying," I said. "Why am I not crying?"

"It's okay. Just give yourself a minute."

She needed to be suctioned out a little, but she was perfect. And giant. Nine pounds, seven ounces and twenty-two inches long. She was on my boob, not crying or eating, but just kind of looking right at me, intense and focused in a way that a newborn typically isn't. I looked at Marc. "She's my Birdie. Our big Bird."

It had taken seventeen hours of hard labor and three hours of pushing, and here she was. I had been waiting for her my whole life.

FREE FALLIN'
(Tom Petty)

Birdie Leigh Silverstein was certainly not the first baby in the world to be born, but it sure felt like it to me. I had hired a baby nurse, on the advice of Abby, to help me in the early weeks of the baby. She proved to be literally no help at all. First of all, she hadn't planned that I would be early, and she was unavailable in the first few days of my homecoming with Birdie, which were the days I really needed someone to try to help calm me down. Then, when she finally showed up to work, I disliked her immediately. I didn't like how bossy I felt she was, and I didn't think she was paying enough attention to Birdie. A few times in the night, when she was supposed to wake the baby up and bring her to me to feed, she slept through it, and I was the one who woke up in a panic that the baby had missed her 3 a.m. feeding! What the fuck?! That was her only *job*! She was supposed to stay for three weeks, but we let her go after a week and half. I was happy to see her go and leave me with my baby. Clearly I was the only one who could take care of her.

I was so overwhelmed and scared and hormonal. My brain

never stopped spinning. I was afraid Birdie wasn't eating enough, that she was sleeping too much or not enough, that the perfume my mother-in-law wore was going to give her asthma, that her belly button was infected, that she was too hot, that she was too cold, that her swaddle was wrong, that my boob was too big, that she wasn't getting enough milk, that she had acid reflux, that she could die at any second.

My one job in this world was to keep Birdie alive, but I actually had to get another job, too. My other house still hadn't sold, and now we were totally underwater on it. The housing market was crashing and taking me with it. I had no income. Marc was trying his best, but he was carrying our new huge mortgage and my credit card debt and his credit card debt and the writers' strike hadn't been the greatest thing for him and Abby, in terms of new jobs. They had taken a big rewrite job that had been lucrative, but we were in a bit of a situation, financially speaking. Which is how I found myself agreeing to go to an audition exactly seven days after giving birth, for a new Ryan Murphy show called *Glee*. I would get to sing! And they were aware I had just given birth and was larger than normal, but they were getting the show going right away, and it seemed like it was being fast-tracked, so it would probably be immediate work. I had to wear my postnatal diaper to the audition. I left Birdie for an hour to go sing "Sweet Child of Mine" for Ryan Murphy. I didn't get the part, *obviously*.

Back home, I tried to be calm, but I had a very hard time. I didn't want anyone holding Birdie except for me and maybe

Leigh Ann. Marc was useless. He didn't even try. I felt like I had to essentially force the baby on him in order for him to hold her, and after a while I didn't even care if he did. He didn't do anything right, anyway. I did the nighttime routine alone, just me and Birdie. I put her to bed, I woke up with her all night, I fed her, I changed her, I wore her, I took her to my postnatal yoga class with my friend Jennah and her new baby, Killian. When Birdie was two months old, we had to go to an engagement party. We left Birdie at home with my sister. I could only be gone for two or three hours tops, since she would need to be breastfed. Marc immediately left me when we got to the party and when I found him smoking with Lizzy Caplan and some guy friends of his, he was in the middle of saying, "Yeah. It's amazing. She's such a good baby and really our lives haven't changed at all!"

I almost threw up. *His* life hadn't changed, sure. I was a fucking wreck. Marc was still going to his Lakers games and to watch football with his friends on Sundays. He even took a guys' trip to *Las Vegas* when Birdie was three months old, leaving me alone with her. I woke up in the middle of the night and looked out of our upstairs bedroom window to see three men sitting on my steps, smoking blunts. Seriously. I called the cops, but the dudes wandered off before they got there. I swore that as soon as we had money, I was getting a gate installed. I swore that as soon as I had money, I was leaving Marc.

I filled my days mostly with new-mom stuff, hanging out with the moms I had met in prenatal yoga, and we would go to the zoo or the Grove (an outdoor mall in L.A.) or a baby gym class and lay the babies on the ground and talk until it was time to head home for nap time. I tried to surround myself with as many people as I could, but I somehow always felt alone and scared. Even going to the grocery store was too overwhelming for me. In a Ralphs parking lot, I tried in vain to strap Birdie on in her Baby Bjorn by myself for fifteen minutes until I finally just gave up and returned home alone in tears, unable to complete even the simplest task, getting food for the week.

I finally broke down and told Marc one night that if he didn't start doing *something* I was going to officially lose my mind, more than I already felt I had lost it. He agreed and committed to waking up early on Sundays and taking Birdie out of the house with milk I had pumped so I could sleep in. I looked forward to Sunday mornings, waiting all week with the knowledge that at least I would be able to sleep a little and maybe get my brain under control. We hired a babysitter for a few days week whom I really liked, but she got pregnant a few weeks after she started working for us and had that horrible debilitating morning sickness, so she had to quit, which I took as a further sign that I was the only person who was capable of taking care of my little precious Bird. No one else was to be trusted.

But for all of my crazy spinning thoughts and constant tears, Birdie was a sweet and unflappable baby. I mean, I barely would put her down, so she had no reason to cry but she was a baby who was so generally happy that strangers would comment that she was like a little Buddha or call her an indigo child. My biggest regret with Birdie is that I wasn't able to enjoy her babyhood as

much as I should have. I was so in my own head I couldn't enjoy
it at all.

My constant panic about Birdie wasn't helped by our financial
situation. My agents knew I needed a job, badly. My business
managers didn't know what to do about the house. The market
was swallowing people whole. My house wasn't worth what I
owed on it, and no one in their right mind would pay it now. In a
few short months, my investment had become a trash heap. We
couldn't rent it out, we couldn't sell it. I fundamentally didn't
want to default on it, but I had no money. If I let it go to foreclosure, the banks would come after Marc and the house we were
currently living in with our newborn daughter. We couldn't lose
that house. In order to try doing a short sale, I had to stop paying
my mortgage for at least two months, which I did. I spent all my
free time taking calls from different bank representatives, and
trying to figure out who the fuck could buy this house from me.
(The mortgage was two loans—I really don't even understand
why, but it was.) I *personally* found an actress to buy the house
for what I owed on the first, and somehow we convinced the
second to roll into an unsecured loan that I would pay off until
it was gone. It wasn't even a stupid short sale. Everyone ended
up getting paid. But on Christmas Eve, my phone rang. It was
the bank. They told me that it was too late and they were putting the house into foreclosure. I had done all this work, trying
to figure out how *not* to have this happen. We had a signed con-

tract approved by everyone and *now* they were foreclosing on the house? ON CHRISTMAS EVE?? I screamed at the woman on the phone and gave her all the paperwork and all the people who I had spoken to and *all* the approvals that had been given. I went into some sort of fugue state. And I just kept screaming, "ON CHRISTMAS EVE??!!!"

They ended up calling back the next morning. There had been a mistake. The sale was approved, after all. They wished me a Merry Christmas. I told them to go fuck themselves. Not really. But in my head I did. In reality I just mumbled a half-hearted "Merry Christmas to you." Then I hung up the phone and sobbed.

I had been called into an audition for a show that was picked up straight to series by creator Rob Thomas called *Party Down*. I knew one of the stars already cast Adam Scott from the NBC table read years ago and I had become friendly with him and his wife socially. I thought the part was perfect for me. They agreed. I had lost a considerable amount of the baby weight but still had more to go, but I actually liked the idea for the character, you know? It's superrealistic for girls who move from the Midwest where they did sketch comedy to Los Angeles and within a year they've lost like twenty-five pounds and gotten a nose job. I thought it would be a really interesting added layer to the character. Rob and Adam agreed, and I was their first choice for the part. I was so excited. I loved the show and thought it would be so good to get back to work. I could probably even hire a nanny! I would have to! Lorrie was so excited about it, as was my new manager Steven (I had cut ties with Mark; his bro personality didn't work for me). But no one was more excited than I was. I was going to work again!! On something really great!

I was rocking Birdie in her glider when Lorrie Bartlett called. "Hey, Biz, how ya doing?"

"Good, just sitting here with the little Bird."

"Hey. So, there's no good way of saying this so I'm just gonna say it. Biz, it's not gonna go our way. The network."

My heart sank as she paused, because my agent was about to tell me something really fucked up, and I knew what she was about to say, "They . . . really don't feel that physically they can give you the part. It's the network. Not Rob Thomas or Adam. Honey, they just feel like the weight is an issue."

I didn't even try to stop myself. I just started crying, tears rolling onto my baby girl's perfect little head. "Oh . . . I understand. Yeah. It was dumb of me to gain so much weight anyway."

"I'm so sorry, honey. Rob Thomas has an email he'd like to send you. Is it okay if I pass along your address?"

"Sure. Bye, Lor."

I hung up and rocked Birdie and sobbed. What a fucking dumb, bad actress I was. So broke. So miserable. So scared. So fat. The heads of a third-rate cable network thought I was too fat to play a waiter in a show about struggling comedic actors trying to make it in Hollywood. This is the same network that HIRED an executive AFTER another network had fired him for PUBLICLY ASSAULTING his girlfriend! Hollywood is the fucking most disgusting, most vile place on earth. But I couldn't do anything else. *I had* to act. I had no other skills. I hadn't even graduated from *college*. I had tried to write a movie, and we know how that turned out. I had tried to write a book, and the literary agent I gave it to thought no one would care about my "pregnancy-scare and date-rape stories."

"From you, I think people would want to know more about, like, Katie Holmes," she had said. Her dismissal of my past legitimately almost discouraged me from ever writing again.

And now here I was: the only thing I had to do was keep this perfect child alive, and could I even be tasked with that? My husband sucked. I was exhausted. I couldn't stop my brain from thinking that all of the worst things ever were seconds away from happening *all the time*. And I was too fucking fat to work as an actress. The email came. It was kind.

Busy,

I want to let you know that you're everyone's first choice on the *Party Down* team. All the producers'. Adam Scott's. The casting director's.

I loved your audition.

I've also been a huge fan since *Freaks & Geeks*.

The cancellation of that show hit me harder than the cancellation of my own show, *Cupid*, a year earlier. I knew that "small story" television died along with *F&G*, and I'm a writer who likes small stories. I got my start teaching high school, then writing Young Adult novels. I'd always wanted to do a pure-character, non-soapy teen show, and once *F&G* went away, I realized I wouldn't be fulfilling that goal, so I tried to sneak a teen character study into *Veronica Mars*. I gave them "big story," and I got to wedge in a story about a counter culture teen girl. But back on topic—

The slow arc friendship between Kim Kelly and Lindsay Weir is one of the most-earned, most-rewarding friendships I've ever seen executed in the medium. It's the sort of thing television should be really good at, but no one has the patience for it. By the time Kim and Lindsay get on that micro bus to go follow the Dead, tears were streaming down my face. I was so pleased when I met the woman who would become my wife, because she'd never seen the show, and I got to watch the entire season over with her. (Yes, I purchased the special exclusive collector's edition with the yearbook, and everything.)

In the case of Kim Kelly, I went to school with several. I have a cousin who is a Kim Kelly. You absolutely nailed that type. It was a phenomenal performance. You gave so much soul to a role that in -lesser- hands could have been a stock antagonist.

So that's how I feel about you and about your audition and our desire to work with you.

The bad news, I'm afraid, is that the network doesn't see it that way.

Our thoughts regarding the pregnancy weight were virtually identical to yours. We could embrace it. (My son just turned five months; I've got a real visual appreciation about the weight-loss speed we're probably talking about.)

The network is unwilling to go down that path.

If you saw the list of actresses the network wanted us to consider, you'd understand what we're dealing with.

In the past few years, I've either worked with or met several of your F&G castmates: Samm, Seth, Jason. I picketed for a few days with Paul Feig, and I had a bizarre email exchange with Judd Apatow. With each, I've just gushed like a complete fanboy. So now it's your turn. Your agent passed along your email. He may have intended to pull your email address off of it, but he didn't, so it may be slightly out of line my addressing you directly, but I wanted you to know that, at the very least, you had our entire team in your corner.

I genuinely hope we get to work together someday.

Congratulations on the new baby.

Rob

I cried for five days and then Marc told me that he had talked to Lizzy and she was going to do the part, but not until after another actress friend of ours had *also* been rejected by the network for not being "fuckable" enough. I never could figure out which was more insulting—being deemed too fat or not fuckable.

I took it as a challenge to lose most of the weight before pilot season started. Lorrie Bartlett had me come into ICM and talk to the TV agents about what I was looking for. I was not fucking around: "I want to do a single-camera, half-hour comedy where I can be number two or three on the call sheet. A show with a big-name star that will do most of the press and a show that *for sure* is going to get picked up to series."

I read the script for *Cougar Town* and told Marc that it was the show I was going to do. He told me to calm down. That night, we went to a restaurant for dinner and ran into our old friend Kate Walsh, who was having dinner with Steve McPherson, who was the (then) president of ABC. I turned to Marc as we left. "See? It's a sign. I'm getting that part."

"Buddy? You have to audition first."

DETAILS.

I wore two sets of Spanx under my most flattering green DVF

dress that had little white polka dots on it. I belted the waist as tight as I could and went to my audition. I still didn't have a nanny or help, but sometimes our cleaning lady could watch the baby for a few hours while I ran out. I knew Bill Lawrence, who had cowritten the pilot with his wife, Christa Miller, a little through a mutual friend of Marc's. Christa was so intimidating, and mostly what I knew of them was they were super fucking fancy (they had flown private to our friend's wedding!) and they were really well-liked and Bill made hit shows. I auditioned for the role of Laurie Keller in front of the casting directors, Courteney Cox (MONICA!), Bill Lawrence, and his cowriter Kevin Biegel.

I went to dinner with Abby and Phoebe and Marc and Birdie that night and got a call from my wedding planner, Jo Gartin. "Busy! Courteney just called me! They *love* you for that part and she wanted to ask me how it was working with you for the wedding—you know she and I are really close!"

I didn't know that, and I was grateful that I had been a very easygoing bride and that Jo liked me. It was funny getting that information from my wedding planner before even talking to my agents, but that's what happened. I was asked to test and told by my agents that it seemed like everyone really loved me for the part. It certainly felt like I was the favorite. I wondered to Lorrie if I should talk to them about the additional ten or fifteen pounds I still had to lose or if we should just let it go. What I didn't know was that Bill had initially written the part for the actress Eliza Coupe, who had been on the final few seasons of *Scrubs*. At my studio test, there were about five actresses but that afternoon, for the network test, it was me and Eliza, whom

I had just met that day but instantly liked. Bill is an incredibly magnanimous person and wants the best for everyone, truly. He is also married to an actress and understands the pressures and annoyance of testing and jumping through hoops. So when I tell you what he did right before the test, which was hands down one of the weirder things I've ever experienced at a test, know that it came from a place of trying to ease tensions for both of us, even though it came off a little weird.

Eliza and I were sitting together, having just witnessed a young child actress being told she *wasn't* getting a part and having a literal breakdown in the ABC lobby, when Bill approached us. "Hey, guys, how are you feeling? So listen, here's what's gonna happen. We still need to go through with this, because this is the bullshit of how things are done. But Busy, you're getting this part, and Eliza, you have that network test in an hour for the superhero pilot, and you're getting that part. I talked to those guys and you already have it so, yeah! You both have jobs! Yay! See you in there!"

And then he turned and walked off, leaving Eliza and me to sort through the craziness of being told before going in that I had gotten the part and she hadn't but that she was getting another pilot.

She turned to me. "Ummm. That was weird, but congratulations?"

I laughed. "Yeah. You too? How fucking weird. So we still have to go do this, I guess?"

"Yeah."

"What's the show you got??"

"Oh. It's fine. It's some show that's never getting picked up."

We sat there in silence and then were called upstairs for our test, knowing it didn't matter. It had already been decided.

I still had no nanny and didn't know how to work out my breastfeeding schedule and pumping on the pilot. Birdie was only seven months old. The woman who had been cleaning my house once a week agreed to come with me and Birdie to set on the days I had to work. Marc couldn't watch her because he and Abby were on a deadline for some movie.

Christa wasn't very kind to me about not having a full-time nanny. "Well, *that's* not going to work at *all*. No. You need to hire someone immediately."

I was too embarrassed to tell her there was no way we could afford to hire a full-time nanny at the moment. I had lost all my money in my stupid house and had barely worked in over a year.

I hardly remember shooting the pilot, but I loved Courteney and Dan Byrd immediately. I liked working with Bill, and while I thought she was super funny, I was afraid of Christa, which seemed to be the consensus of most of the crew, who had worked with her on *Scrubs*. They liked her and were also terrified of her.

After we shot the pilot, I got an email from our old next-door neighbor Penelope/Stephanie telling me that her cousin was looking to share their longtime nanny with someone. She had worked for them for almost eight years and now the kids were in elementary school and it didn't make much sense for the nanny to continue full-time. Would I want to meet her? I wrote Penelope's cousin an email and she put me in touch with Iliana.

Iliana came over to meet me and the baby and as soon as she

walked into my house and took Birdie from my arms, I knew things would be okay. She asked if she could wash and put away my clothes as well, and I told her that wasn't necessary, but all of a sudden my laundry was done and put away. She helped me make all of Birdie's baby food from scratch, something I had already started doing. She dressed Birdie in her cutest outfits, outfits I never had the time to look for or put together, and would walk her around the house, singing to her in Spanish and calling her "Municita" and "Mama." Birdie adored her, as did I. She worked part-time, a few days a week, which I could afford now that my *Cougar Town* pilot check had cleared. But she would stay late if we needed and encouraged me to go out and have fun and would reassure me that I was, in fact, doing everything right.

"You're such a good mother. You *are*, Busy, *you are*," Iliana would say as she rubbed my back in circles, the same way she would rub Birdie's back when she put her down for her naps. My kitchen was suddenly always clean. My baby was happy. I could breathe and go to the gym and meet friends for lunch without disrupting Birdie's nap schedule. I started to feel a little like myself again.

The show was picked up and I was about to turn thirty. I decided to throw myself a big party in Palm Springs. I had fucking made it. It was all happening. I had almost lost all of my baby weight, no easy feat for me, especially considering I was still breastfeeding. And since Iliana had started working for us, I was feeling like maybe I didn't have to divorce Marc after all.

We started shooting the series the week of Birdie's first birthday. The show was fun and the crew was great. Aside from Christa whispering to Courteney on set, which always made me feel like she was talking about me in the first few months, I liked working. Iliana—who was with us full-time now—would bring Birdie to set to visit and stroll her around the lot. Once the show was officially picked up for a whole season, we were all given dressing rooms and not trailers, so I set up my room as a little playroom for Birdie. I went to Ross Dress for Less and bought a bunch of toys and things that she didn't have at home so she would look forward to visiting me.

Birdie was incredibly bright and verbal. By the time she was one, she had over fifty words that she would use in little two- and three-word sentences. I remember talking to the pediatrician about it, who told me that I needed to know that if we had another child, he or she would probably not be the same as Birdie. I told her not to worry, we were ONE AND DONE. I was NOT HAVING ANOTHER BABY. Birdie's verbal acuity was actually abnormal. But it made sense. In the first many months of Birdie's life, I talked to her nonstop, partially out of daily loneliness on my part and partially because I had read a baby book that said the more you can talk to your child, the calmer they will be. That you should try to explain to them everything you're doing and everything that's happening around them. But just in your regular voice, not in a baby voice. Which is what I had done.

"I'm putting a new diaper on you, so I have to move your legs a little. Excuse me! Here. This is a wipe. It might feel cold on your tush and vagina, I'm sorry. But it'll be over really quickly and I need to make sure you're clean. We always wipe from front to back. That's a good lesson to know as a woman. Always go front to back."

or

"I'm sorry I couldn't get you into the baby carrier. Sometimes I don't know what I'm doing. I've never had a baby before. You're my first. I really want to make sure you're happy and like me. I think you do. Do you even know that I'm your mom? Don't answer that. I'm going to put on some music while we drive. Want to listen to weird yoga music or Arcade Fire? Or should we just call my mom on speakerphone?"

or

"I didn't get that job. They thought I was too fat. It's okay, though, because I have you and you were worth it. But that's the thing about what I do—it can be really confusing sometimes. It's a great job when it's great, but when it's not, it's literally the worst. I'll try to explain it more when you know what TV and movies are. So that's why I'm crying. It has nothing to do with you, just so you know. You are perfect, my little Bird."

A few weeks into shooting, Courteney and I were having lunch at our new favorite place in Culver City, walking distance from the stages where we shot. From day one, Courteney would get a group together to go to lunch and eat something good and have a glass of wine. Her feeling was that work should be fun, and she wasn't wrong. It was super fun. She was asking me about Birdie and Marc—we were all still pretty much getting to know each other. Then she asked me if I had been to therapy recently, since Birdie was born, or if anyone had talked to me about medication. I think it was clear to her that I was in a postpartum fog of anxiety and she could just tell that I needed more help than I was currently getting.

A few weeks later, I was actually at a Grizzly Bear concert when I met a woman who was the mother of one of the lead singer, Ed's, friends. Ed and I had met through MySpace, when he had sent me a message that he was a fan of *Freaks and Geeks*, and then we became friends in real life, traveling together and having dinner parties whenever he was in town with the band. Now he's one of my best friends and is even Cricket's god-father, and she gets very excited when Grizzly Bear is played on SiriusXM.

Anyway, the woman at the concert and I got to talking, and it turned out she was a therapist. She gave me her number and I promised to call. But I didn't, and then a week later, I ran into her again at the valet line at the Grove. I decided that it was a sign and I set up an appointment with her.

One of the problems with struggling with mental illness, I think, is that actually getting help sometimes seems so difficult. Like, *UGH. I have to FIND someone and then go TALK to them and EXPLAIN all the things I'm thinking and feeling? No, that's okay, I'll just stay here in my brain that won't stop turning, and cry in the bathroom when I think people are being mean to me even though they probably aren't and I'm just super sensitive and maybe taking things the wrong way because this fog in my brain won't let me see things clearly. Does anyone see things clearly? Did I ever see things clearly? What did I do before I had a baby? What was I like? Was I fun? What did I do before I was married? What did I do before I had a house? What did I do before I was on TV? Was I happy in high school? Was I*

*happy as a child? Was I ever really happy? Was I ever happy? Have I
ever been happy? Has anyone? Is anyone happy?*

I stayed on Lexapro for over a year and a half. It helped calm
me down and get out of my own way a little. I stopped crying so
much. Or panicking about Birdie. She seemed like she was okay.
I started really enjoying all my work on *Cougar Town*. I liked everyone in the cast, with the exception of Brian Van Holt, who
personally annoyed me because I felt like he was such a weird ag-
gressive bro who thought he was way smarter than he really was.
Sorry, that's mean. But it's true. I could hang with him and not let
his bro-ness get me down, though. Especially since Courteney
thought he was amazing, and she was obviously the clear leader
of our pack. Christa and I slowly became friends and she started
whispering things to me on set, too. The show shifted in tone and
concept from the initial pilot and we started making a show we
all really loved, and the critics started to notice. We were pretty
much flying under the radar, certainly not the immediate huge
hit of *Modern Family*, but we were doing okay and making pretty
funny shows. We were given a second season. The thing I heard
most from people in Hollywood was this, "Oh yeah! *Cougar Town*!
I've never seen it. But you're supposed to be really good on it!"

Which was true. I was really good on it. I loved playing daffy
Laurie Keller with her weird wardrobe and over-the-top hair
and makeup and crazy one-liners and huge speeches that I would
give as fast as I could, as sort of a challenge to myself. The television critics ended up loving *Cougar Town*, a show they had all
been lukewarm about based on the pilot. There was talk about
changing the title to be more reflective of what the show was,

but it seemed almost impossible to get everyone on board with it, so they just left it and let Kevin Biegel do weird title cards that said something funny in the opening.

Toward the end of the second season, the very first Television Critics' Choice Award nominations were announced and Courteney and I were both nominated. I was beside myself. I was a little deflated when Bill gave a speech about how awards are bullshit and don't mean anything, but I was still excited and thought maybe he was just annoyed that he and the show hadn't been nominated. I asked my publicist at the time if we should be doing anything, like getting me press for it in the hopes that maybe I could be nominated for an Emmy and his response was a bit disheartening as well. "Darling, no. I don't really see you having a chance with this."

I didn't have a stylist, so my new friend Irene Neuwirth introduced me to a designer she knew who made me a dress to wear to the event, which I had to buy. It was a daytime award ceremony, held in the basement ballroom at the Beverly Hills Hotel. It wouldn't be televised. I wrote a thank-you letter to each of the critics for my nomination, not because I was trying to win particularly (I mean, I didn't think it could *hurt*) but more because I felt like I had been acting for fifteen years and this acknowledgment really did mean something to me. Awards may be bullshit, but it's nice to feel seen.

A few weeks before the event, my doctor put me on a new drug, a mood stabilizer that he thought would help even me out a little more, since I still was struggling with my moods and spinning thoughts. I started getting really bad canker sores in my mouth and down my throat. I went to Dr. Sugerman, who gave me a rinse to gargle with but had no idea what was causing it. A few nights later, as I was taking the new drug, Marc stopped me.

"Wait. Did you look up side effects from that?"

After a very brief Google search, we found out that one possible side effect of taking this drug was something terrible called Stevens-Johnson syndrome, which basically is a horrible allergic reaction that can end in death. I called all my doctors, and my general practitioner told me to go to the emergency room, which I did. They looked at my throat and mouth and skin and gave me some medicine and told me not to take the other drug anymore and sent me home. I guess because I was so freaked out about that, I decided to stop taking all of my antidepressants. I didn't think the Lexapro was really worth it anyway. I stepped down off the drug but was still having weird brain zaps and feeling really strange and woozy. So that was my state of mind as we walked into the Beverly Hills Hotel.

There was a short press line, and I was sweating profusely, maybe because of the weather (it was June, almost my birthday), maybe because of the drugs, or maybe because I was nervous. Who knows? I wiped off almost all of my makeup with a towel and had a hard time even giving interviews because I was so sweaty. My publicist came up to me, and said, "I weirdly have a good feeling about this!"

We went into the ballroom, where I talked to some of my actor friends and started to calm down. Marc and I found our seats at a table with Courteney and Guillermo from *Jimmy Kimmel*. Jimmy was nominated but didn't come and sent Guillermo in his place in case he won. All the shows that were nominated had big tables; there was one each for *Big Bang* and *Modern Family* and *Community* and all the shows' creators and showrunners were there, but we were at a weird aggregate table, not dissimilar to Abby's wedding. My award was up pretty early. I think Johnny Galecki presented it, maybe? He read out the nominees, "Julie Bowen, *Modern Family*; Jane Krakowski, *30 Rock*; Jane Lynch, *Glee*; Eden Sher, *The Middle*; Busy Philipps, *Cougar Town*; Sofía Vergara, *Modern Family*."

All of those actresses were going to be nominated for an Emmy, for sure. Most of them had already been in years past. Three of them had already won Emmys. And here I was, with my brain zaps from my antidepressants, my mouth and throat still sore from an allergic reaction that could have killed me, makeup totally sweated off, and pit stains growing on the dress I'd bought for the event.

When he announced my name, I couldn't quite understand what I was supposed to do. I didn't see where the steps were, so I kind of just climbed up on the stage awkwardly. As soon as I got up there I looked out at the crowd, and I had the thought that these people didn't want to hear from me! I should get off this stage as quickly as I could! I'd *never* had that thought before, but here I was, dying to get offstage. I remembered to thank Courteney, since she was in the room. I thanked the critics. And then I bolted.

After I had returned to our table, a few friends came over to congratulate me. Courteney was so excited for me. Then the creator and showrunner for *Modern Family*, Steve Levitan, came by our table on his way back from the bathroom. He barely looked at me. "Hey, Courtney! How are you?"

"Good," she said. "I'm good!"

"Yeah, this event is so lame. We're all over there at our table like, 'What even are these awards? I mean, are they even *real*?' "

I glanced at the award I had just won sitting in front of me and then looked up at him. "Well, I mean, it feels real to me since I'm holding one?"

He laughed. "Ha. I guess. All right . . . Well, 'bye Courteney. Tell Bill I said hi."

As soon as he walked away, Marc turned to me. "What a fucking dick thing to say. Fuck that guy. He's just mad because you won and the two actresses from his show didn't."

"That was weird, right? Like a fucking lame thing to do to me, right? I'm not being oversensitive, because I just came off these drugs and I feel crazy, am I?"

"No babe," he said. "That was fucked."

Even Courteney, who tends to be very levelheaded and tries her best to see things from everyone's point of view, thought it was weird. I tried to shake it and not let it bring me down, but it actually really hurt my feelings. It felt like he did it on purpose. Just to be a bully. Here was this guy, this fucking multimillionaire who was set for life because of his TV show, and for no reason, without even thinking, just shit on a thing that I was really proud of. Their show won, by the way (because OF COURSE IT DID) and you know, he acted like it was "real" when *he* was onstage, accepting his award.

I've told this story for years, in the hopes that it would somehow get back to him, I think. I always wanted him to know that you can have all the money and success in the world, but when you're a fucking asshole, you're a fucking asshole and that's all there is to it. A year ago, at an Emmy after-party, Marc and I were standing at a table. I was a little tipsy from tequila when Steve Levitan and his girlfriend came up and set their drinks down at the same table. I've seen Steve many times over the years, occasionally saying hi but mostly just shooting daggers that he's completely unaware of in his direction. Such is the joy of being an oblivious super-successful white man in this business. This was a few short months before all the shit hit the fan in terms of #metoo and the Harvey Weinstein articles, but I was already over holding things in to protect myself for future work. Besides, he had already created *Modern Family*. He wasn't going to create another one. He couldn't do anything to me or for me, so fuck it. I looked at Marc. "I'm gonna tell him."

Marc's eyes went wide as I turned my attention back to Steve.

"Hey, Steve," I said brightly. "How are you?"

He barely looked up from his phone. "Oh. Hey, Busy. How are you?"

He introduced me to his girlfriend, who seemed young and sweet. "Oh my God!" she said. "Hi! I LOOOOOVE YOU!"

"Oh, thanks, that's really nice!" I said, then turned back to him. "So listen, Steve! I'm writing a book—I have a book deal, actually. Like a real book! And you're gonna be in it. Well, there's a story with you in it, I should say."

He looked up, finally interested. "Really? Why?"

"You probably don't remember this. I mean, I'm sure it was so inconsequential in your life, but you were a real fucking dick to me when I won the Critics' Choice Award, and it's always really bugged me. You could have just congratulated me, but you didn't. You came up to talk to Courteney and then said that everyone from your show didn't even think the awards were real even though I had just won one, against Julie and Sofía."

"Oh shit. Did I say that?"

"Yeah. And it sucked. Because it was a really big deal to me, and I enjoyed the moment for like five minutes before you came over and made me feel like an idiot."

"Oh, man, I'm sorry. I'm sure it was all about me. I bet I was just insecure or something."

"Yeah, Steve, that's kind of how being a dick works. I know it wasn't about *me*. But it still sucked. Look, you have your show and your millions of dollars and *all* the fucking awards. I have one. That one. And you made me feel shitty about it. That's all. I just think you could have done better. As a person."

"Well . . . I'm really sorry."

"Okay. I'm really not looking for an apology. I just wanted you to know." I turned to his girlfriend, whose mouth was agape, and dare I say, she looked like she was kind of enjoying it. "It was nice to meet you, honey, have a good night."

And with that, I grabbed my clutch and walked away, with Marc following close behind whispering excitedly, "You are such a fucking badass, Busy. *Such* a fucking badass."

GOOD INTENTIONS PAVING COMPANY
(Joanna Newsom)

Birdie was about to turn four. All of a sudden, I had to have another baby. I know I had said "one and done." I know I had told anyone who would listen that there was no way I was having another baby. But now I had a *kid*. And I wanted a baby. I had a job, and if we timed it right, I wouldn't even have to miss an episode. As an actress, you don't really get maternity leave. Depending on your show, you either miss episodes and they don't pay you, or they make you come to work no matter how old your newborn is. Marc emphatically did not want another child. Our adjustment to Birdie had been *rough*, to say the least. He was finally feeling like we had gotten a handle on parenting and then we were going to throw another wrench into it? The wrench being another human child, obviously.

"She wants a baby," I said. "Ask her. She wants someone else."

Marc looked at me skeptically, "She's three. She doesn't know anything."

"She's smart. She told me it's boring because it's just her and grown-ups. She wants a baby. I want a baby."

"Birdie! Come here. Do you want Mommy to have another baby?"

"Yeah. It's boring for me. It's just me and you guys."

We were in Anguilla, on vacation before I had to return to *Cougar Town* for the fifth season. I looked at Marc. *I told you so.*

"We'll see, Buddy." Birdie jumped back into the shallow water and Marc looked at me seriously. "If we do this, it's all on you. You have to hire all the help you need. I'll take care of Birdie, but seriously, I don't think this is the best idea. I just want to say that."

I nodded and threw away my pills that day. I had figured out the timing. I needed to be pregnant by the end of October in order to not miss any episodes, and it would put me back at work with a four- or five-week-old baby. I could do that. Also, my friend Ashlee had the best baby nurse for me: I would be fine. I would eat placenta pills and make sure I didn't have post-partum anxiety again, and if I did I would get medication as soon as I could, even if I had to stop breastfeeding. I would be chill. I could do this. People have more than one kid all the time! We can do this!

As soon as I found out I was pregnant, I panicked. What the fuck? We couldn't do this. Birdie was a handful, already start-ing with her terrible temper tantrums and refusing to sleep in her bed at night. Marc didn't want this baby. Most days, I didn't think Marc particularly wanted to be married to me. Jesus. What a fucking mistake. At least I had the job. I cried and cried all through my pregnancy. I had terrible panic that the baby was dead inside me. I had to get an at-home fetal heart rate monitor just to make sure. I had terrible panic that I was about to die too. Also, I was going to have to push this baby out? Oh fuck. I really hadn't thought it through.

I spent no time talking to my unborn child, reassuring her that my tears weren't about her, because of course they were and she was no fucking idiot. She knew perfectly well why I was upset. I half-heartedly made a list of names, most of them repeats from the list for Birdie. Some days I tried to be excited. My friend Jennah told me to try going to prenatal yoga, where we'd met and formed such a close bond with Birdie and her son Killian. I went to one class and the model Amber Rose was there with her non-pregnant assistant. The vibe just wasn't the same.

I hired the baby nurse and made sure she knew that I was probably going to be early so she should be available. I took Birdie to New York to see some theater with Abby and Phoebe, and Birdie was a nightmare, throwing horrible tantrums and screaming at me in Central Park. I couldn't calm her down. Marc was at Coachella with his friends. "What do you want me to do, Busy? I'm four thousand miles away!"

I had several friends all due around the same time, including Colin's now-wife, Samantha, whom I had become close with. One by one, all the babies came, even Kim Kardashian's, who I didn't know personally, but I was tracking her pregnancy like a hawk since our babies were due around the same time and I knew from the show that Dr. Crane was her ob-gyn. I would *not* be okay if he ditched me in the delivery room for a more famous baby.

Finally, on Marc's birthday, I went to see Dr. Crane by myself.

My due date was July 4, but Dr. Crane thought maybe the baby was just about ready. He did a membrane sweep. Marc came to meet me in Beverly Hills and we walked over to one of the nondescript Italian places and had dinner for his birthday as my contractions were starting. We drove home and hid outside by the pool so that Iliana would put Birdie to bed and we wouldn't have to. I thought maybe the baby would come fast and be born on his birthday, but she didn't. We went to the hospital at 3 a.m. and she arrived around seven in the morning. She was a little blue and having trouble breathing, so she needed to be sucked out and given oxygen. But then she was fine. And beautiful. Smaller than Birdie by a pound. Eight pounds, seven ounces. Twenty-one inches. She had no name. I called her "the baby." The name I had liked most seemed ridiculous. She wasn't a "Ginger Silverstein." Ugh. Certainly not.

Birdie came to visit after her day camp and lay down on the bed and covered the baby with kisses and pushed into my stomach and laughed at how big it still was.

"Why, Mama? The baby's out. Why're you still so fluffy??"

"Just my body, baby."

The baby was so sweet and smiley almost immediately. She literally sparkled. She was tough, unflappable. You could tell. And she liked to rub her little baby newborn legs together inside her swaddle. She ate right away with no trouble and slept soundly and burped with no issues. She seemed like magic. Loretta, my baby nurse, said she was one of the best babies she'd ever seen. We didn't know what to call her. Marc and Birdie had tried to get me to agree to Cricket but I thought for *sure* people would be mean about it. "THOSE ACTRESSES NAME THEIR KIDS THE DUMBEST THINGS."

But Marc wasn't having any of that. "No! Cricket is the *best* name! Cricket is like, the coolest girl at summer camp!!"

After five days, the hospital called and told us we would have to come name her or it was going to be a huge pain for us. They had let us go, because the holiday weekend was coming up, but now the Fourth of July had come and gone and we had to name this baby ASAP.

I sighed, resigned. "Fine. Name her Cricket. Cricket Ann."

Marc left for the hospital to turn in the paperwork and I called my mom. "Busy. No. Not Cricket. No! What about Dorothy? You *love* that name."

But she wasn't a Dorothy. Or she could be? I didn't know. Also. This was coming from a woman who'd called her own child Busy.

I hung up the phone, crying, and called Marc. "Cricket Ann sounds weird. I don't like it."

"Okay. What should I do?" He sounded exasperated.

"I don't know! Ummm. Can we name her Cricket Pearl? That way if I really hate Cricket, I can call her Pearl?"

"Sure, Buddy. But you're not gonna hate it! She's our Cricket. Trust me!"

He was right. She was our Cricket and she was the fucking best. What wasn't the best, however, was going back to work four weeks after she was born. Bill had left in order to run his new show and had left Blake McCormick in charge, a writer who seemed fine. I had sent him an email before Cricket was born, letting him know that if they wanted to address my weight gain in any way, they could, like how it had been done on *Will & Grace* or *Frasier*. But that ultimately not to worry, I would be coming back to work immediately and would figure out all my baby stuff with the ADs, all of whom were like family by that point.

A week before I had to start shooting, I went in for my wardrobe fitting with my beloved costume department, who had taken such good care of me since day one. Heidi had all kinds of Spanx ready for me and even told me how she had once sewn together three different pairs of Spanx for an actress and that she could do the same for me. We tried on clothes, and while I certainly wasn't close to being back to my original weight—I probably still needed to lose twenty or thirty pounds—I felt like it was okay and I could deal with it. That is, until she said, "And what do you want to do about this stupid hot-tub scene? Or the shower-sex scene with Dan??"

Wait. WHAT THE FUCK? I hadn't gotten any scripts yet. So they wanted me to get into a hot tub *and* have a sex scene in a shower *four* weeks after giving birth??? Motherfucker.

I marched up to the writers' room and busted in. "Hi guys! What the fuck? I'm not getting in a fucking hot tub. You're not even allowed to take a bath for *six weeks* after giving vaginal birth, because your cervix isn't closed up all the way and bacteria can get up in there! So *that's* not fucking happening."

Blake mumbled, "Yeah. I mean. We kind of thought for the hot tub you could just, you know, be up to your boob level? I didn't know that about baths after giving birth. The . . . bacteria or whatever."

"Yeah. Well, maybe someone should have checked. And I'm not doing a fucking sex shower scene next week with Dan Byrd."

"Yeah. It's just that Courteney broke her wrist and we have to explain it, so that's what we came up with."

"Oh, cool. Well, we can shoot it in two months, when I'm not bleeding from my fucking vagina and unable to wear a tampon."

Poor Blake. I don't think he really had considered that dealing with a hormonal new mother would be a part of his big new job promotion. Also, I truly prided myself on being generally very easygoing as an actress, but I couldn't just be chill about this. A few weeks into shooting I saw Brian Van Holt walking around with the AD for the following week's episode. Ian Gomez told me that Brian was prepping an episode as the *director*. And that Josh was going to do one later in the season.

"Ugh, dudes get to do everything," I lamented to Marc later that night. "Why do they get to direct? They don't have any idea what the fuck they're doing."

"If you want to direct an episode," he said, "just ask. I'm sure they'll let you. I mean, I feel like they would have to."

I didn't particularly want to, but I didn't like that the guys on the show were doing it and I wasn't. In fact, in my many years as an actress working in TV, I had been directed by many, many former television actors who had turned to directing once their acting careers dried up. In all my years, I had only been directed by *one* actress who had done the same. Actresses just weren't given the shot. But why? I asked my friend Sarah Chalke, who had been on *Scrubs*. All the male actors had directed episodes—why hadn't she or Judy Reyes?

"I don't know," she said. "I never asked. I also wanted to make sure if I directed that I really, really knew what I was doing."

But she had been on television for twenty years. Didn't that count? I understood what she was saying, though. I don't ever want to do anything unless I'm certain I'm going to be the best at it. Aside from my film 101 class at LMU, I hadn't gone to film school or anything. I didn't know the names of camera lenses or shots. But this was one of those situations where I thought I needed to just do it and then if it sucked, I wouldn't need to do it again. Besides, it wasn't like the men were waiting until they were experts. They just did it. So I would too.

Courteney was directing almost half of the *Cougar Towns* at that point, so I asked her first. She told me that of course I should direct an episode if the show was picked up for another season. Since we were already shooting, the directors were hired and scheduled for the current season. Plus, as much as I wanted to do it on the principle of the thing, I *did* just have a baby and there was no way I needed to take on a whole new project, something I'd never done before. Bill Lawrence agreed to ask Disney and they approved it. If the show got picked up, I could direct an episode. I felt triumphant in my quest for equal rights.

As we were gearing up to shoot the last and final season of *Cougar Town* I sent an email reminding everyone that I would be directing an episode. THEY HAD PROMISED. I was put on the schedule. I called my friend Jason Winer, who had directed the pilot of *Modern Family* among other things. He gave me some advice, but he basically said I would be fine. I knew what I was doing. I knew where the story was, where the jokes were, how to talk to actors and writers and keep it all together. And he was right. Marc told me I should make a shot list, which I did. The thing is, of course directing is something I'm good at. I love making decisions and my episode was actually really fun to direct. There was a whole caper subplot that I got to shoot like one of the *Ocean's Eleven* movies. Our DP Sylvan never made me feel like an idiot for asking what kind of lens we were on and was able to give me exactly what I had asked for. Overall, it was a really fun and exhausting and invigorating week. One of the grips waved me down at the end of the episode. "Hey. Just so you know, we all think you were the best at this, of all the actors. Other than Courteney, of course. No one was sure what to expect this week, but you killed it, girl."

That's all I ever want to hear. That I'm the fucking best. I thanked him and drove home, windows open and music blasting. After that, I told my agents that I for sure wanted to be put up for more directing jobs, especially since *Cougar Town* was ending. I had one meeting with a lower-level executive at Fox who basically told me it would be nearly impossible for me to get hired on any other shows. Cool. Cool. But at least I'd done one.

As *Cougar Town* was ending, I had no idea what I was supposed to do next. I *could* jump on some new network TV comedy pilot, but that didn't seem quite right. I wasn't sure what was to come for me, honestly, which can always be a little unsettling.

One day, in SoulCycle, as I was sitting on my bike, my favorite trainer Angela started in about being grateful in the waiting room. "I'm not saying you haven't been in the waiting room before!" she yelled at us as we peddled away, "I'm not saying that you don't deserve to skip the waiting room altogether. But here you are! And you need to be GRATEFUL in that WAITING ROOM! BECAUSE THAT DOOR IS ABOUT TO OPEN AND IF YOU ARE NOT SITTING THERE IN GRACE, YOUR NAME WILL NOT BE CALLED! BE GRATEFUL IN THAT WAITING ROOM!!!"

Not long after that, I got a call from my agent about a new show called *Vice Principals*. Even though I was "offer only" for television at this point, I told them of course I'd audition for those guys. I had no idea what the part was or how big it would be. But I went in, and I thanked them for seeing me and told them how excited I was to be there, how grateful I was for the opportunity.

And then I read the part.

And of course I fucking got it.

SHOULD HAVE KNOWN BETTER
(Sufjan Stevens)

About a month before the 2016 presidential election, we had some friends over for dinner.

"I bet you *ten thousand dollars* he wins," said my friend's husband. "You know why? Because people are *fucking idiots*, that's why. He's going to win, guys. Sorry."

I shook my head. He didn't know anything. He just liked to agitate people, that's all.

"There's no fucking way, Ben! You don't know what you're talking about. *You* aren't even *from here*."

He shrugged. "Yeah, but I know *people*, man. And you don't know how many people *hate her*. You live in your bubble and think there's no way, but I bet you more people hate *her* than *him*. And also, I think you're underestimating how many people just hate *women* in general." He sat back in his chair with a grim look. "He's winning. I'm telling you. Watch."

I shook my head and glanced at Marc as he stood up to clear the plates. No. There was no way. No *way*. I didn't live in *such* a bubble. I'm *from* Arizona, after all. My sister is married to a

Republican. I knew people didn't like Hillary. I knew what they thought about the dynasty or oligarchy or whatever the fuck word they used when they talked about the Clintons. Plus, a lot of my friends were hard-core Berners. But surely *they* would turn out for Hillary. If for no other reason than to keep this other man—this horrible, dishonest, unqualified bully—out of the White House. It was *insane* to even consider the possibility that he might end up winning. After all, the Billy Bush tapes had just been released: *moved on her like a bitch; when you're famous you can do anything; grab 'em by the pussy.*

No one in their right mind would vote for someone who bragged about sexually assaulting women . . . right?

Since I had done surrogate work for Hillary, we were invited to the Javits Center for election night. Hillary's party. I thought we should go. I wanted to be there when that glass ceiling shattered. I wanted to be in the room when history was made.

While writing my stump speech for the campaign, I'd talked to my mom about what it was like for her as a young woman in order to draw a comparison, to get a sense of how far we've come.

"Well, honey, let's see," she said. "Obviously before *Roe v. Wade* it was just *awful*. You young people will *never* understand what *that* was like for a woman. Oh, and here's something! You know I couldn't open my own credit card account, right? Your dad had to be a cosigner on it. That was for *years*. Also, after my mom and dad didn't let me go to New York to act, I thought maybe I wanted to work in advertising. So when I graduated from college, my dad set me up on a job interview with some man he was friends with who ran an agency in Chicago, and I was *so* excited! I wore my favorite tweed two-piece outfit. Oh, I wish I would've kept it; you would've loved it. I looked really *sharp*. Anyway, after I told this man why I wanted to work there and how I thought it would be the right fit for me, he came around the desk and put his hand on my knee and said, 'A pretty girl like you would be wasted at a desk. Don't you think you should focus on getting married and starting a family?' And I was just *so* . . ."

She paused, her voice cracking,

". . . *HUMILIATED*. Mostly that I had even *thought* it was a real interview."

"Oh, Jesus, Mom. That's so awful. I'm sorry."

"Well, thank you, it *was* sort of awful, Busy. But that's what it was like. And you know, then I married your dad and well, I don't know, *life* kind of happened. But it all worked out because I had you guys! And now you're doing this work for Hillary and I am just *so proud* of you, honey. Of *both* my girls! I don't know how I got so lucky."

"Thanks, Mama," I said. "I love you."

Marc and I flew to New York separately, not because we're superstitious about flying together without the kids, but because we were using miles to go, since money was getting tight again. We were only going for the night, less than twenty-four hours. We met friends for dinner and then all headed over to the Javits Center together. The Comey letter had been a fucking bummer the week before, but it wasn't going to change the fact that *Hillary Clinton* was about to become the first woman president!

The energy (and security) getting into Javits was overwhelming. People were already celebrating. We were escorted up to a room where other celebrity surrogates for Hillary were hanging out. The level of star power in that room was insane, and we immediately felt out of place. I took a seat on one of the couches and started to watch as the results came in. Marc tried to sit next to me but the woman on the end of the sofa put her hand down.

"I'm sorry," she said. "I'm saving this seat for *Jennifer.*"

Marc rolled his eyes at me and took an awkward seat on the floor. A few minutes later, Jennifer Lopez—looking as if she had a permanent Instagram filter attached to her face and body—scooted in and said a soft hi to me before turning her attention to the returns. It wasn't good. I mean, it wasn't good for *me* or anyone sitting in that room. Obviously it was good for others around the country, the ones who had decided that hate speech and misogyny and literal nonsense were better than Hillary Clinton.

When I started to cry, Lady Gaga pointed at me from across the room. "NO! WE NEED POSITIVITY!!!!!! NO TEARS! THIS ISN'T OVER!"

But it was. And we knew it. My friends and Marc and I left, stunned and deflated. For a long time, we wandered around the city, which felt broken somehow. Eventually, we went back to our hotel and fell asleep for a few hours, and when I woke up the next morning, it was official.

I couldn't stop crying. For my mom, for my daughters, for

me. I felt betrayed by my fellow Americans. I felt like I truly didn't understand anything anymore. It just about wrecked me.

"I know," Marc said, trying to comfort me. "It's terrible. But it'll be fine, Busy. No one's gonna let him fuck up the *world*."

He didn't understand. How could he?

It was hard to imagine living in a world where women are so truly reviled that a man can brag about abusing them and still get elected president.

But I did live in that world. Clearly.

A month later, I told Marc I wanted a divorce. I was done. I couldn't do it anymore.

For a while now, things hadn't been great between us. In fact, a few years earlier, I had almost asked him not to come to Charleston while I shot *Vice Principals*. But once he got there, everyone loved him and we ended up having a great summer with the kids.

Lately, though, there was a disconnect again. He didn't let me talk when we were out with friends. Or worse, when it was just us, he didn't speak to me at all. I'd started to do a test when we were alone in the car together, where I wouldn't say anything until *he* did, just to see how long it would take him to talk to me. Some days we rode the whole way in silence.

All those years of feeling so alone had started to add up. I'd just assumed that was what marriage was: two people being mildly miserable next to one another. When I would ask Marc to work with me on something, he never wanted to, which made me feel like an inconvenience to him, a thing that he put up with. Sometimes he talked to me like I was an idiot. (I'm not an idiot.) (Am I an idiot?)

Disdain. That's the word.

About nine months earlier, I'd decided I was done for good. I'd been falling all the time and thought maybe there was something wrong with me neurologically. I'd be walking and then would just fall. *Hard.* I fell holding Cricket. *Twice.* I split my knee open another time at a concert and had to walk around with blood running down my leg. Actually, I fell twice at that concert. I wasn't drinking. Not as punk rock as it seems.

"HOLY SHIT!" my friend Rishi said as he helped me up. "Are you okay??"

"Yeah. Yeah. I fall all the time."

He looked shocked.

As it turned out, there was nothing wrong with me neurologically. I was simply waiting for Marc to notice me. My body was subconsciously propelling me to the ground for attention. But it didn't work. I was still invisible. I started to have panic attacks again. Bad ones.

Then Trump won. And also. Also. Also. There was a man I was friends with, another dad. We'd been having lunch and stuff. Texting. Talking on the phone a lot. Honestly, I had a crush on him. I liked him. Maybe I even loved him? He clearly liked me too. And I thought, "Well, why is everyone just resigned to being miserable for the rest of their lives? No decision is permanent! The world may end tomorrow from some war with North Korea, so may as well BE HAPPY, right?" Right.

So I told Marc I was leaving him. And I told him why, though I left out the part about the other man. He was shocked. But he didn't want to get divorced. He wanted a chance to change. He said I owed our family that.

Emily said, "Whatever you want, Pup. I'm there for you."

Michelle said, "It would be really awful for two years and then you would find a new normal but honestly, if you can keep your family intact, I think you should do it."

My therapist said, "Listen. Divorce fucks up children. It just *does*."

I didn't want to fuck up my kids. I just didn't want to be miserable. I know. This is a lot. I'm sorry. But I am. I am a lot. Marc and I started going to therapy again. We had tried it a few times in the past, but it never stuck or made a difference. This time, Marc got his own therapist. And we started to work through it. But I also kept talking to my emotional boyfriend (for lack of a better term). I know. That part is so shitty. I'm sorry. I really am. I really truly am.

It's not an easy road. Marriage. Kids. Life. Any of it. But weirdly, the more I felt like shit was breaking down in my house, the clearer things became for me work-wise. I guess, if I'm being honest, I wasn't totally truthful about Instagram either. The reason I started the stories—it was because I was lonely. Marc and I weren't talking. I needed to talk to someone. It's who I am. And so I started talking to all of you.

Publicly, people had never been more interested in me and my personal life. Or whatever version of my personal life I was showing. But when they'd comment about how *real* I was, how *relatable*, how *authentic*, I would cringe. I was leaving this whole other side of myself offscreen. Which is okay, of course. Obviously, I know that. *Obviously*. But still.

Meanwhile, as Donald Trump became president, and my personal life started to fall apart, I did a pilot called *The Sackett Sisters*. Tina Fey produced it, and I starred in it with Casey Wilson and Bradley Whitford. It was a no-brainer. *Of course* it was going to get picked up; how could it not? Around the same time, the movie Marc and Abby had written for themselves to direct got financing, and then in a whirlwind, Amy Schumer became attached, and just like that, it was a go for the summer.

We were doing well in therapy together too. In his own sessions, Marc had recently had what I guess is called a breakthrough, and when I finally came clean about the other dude, he was weirdly understanding about it. He really just wanted me to know that he loved me and was sorry I'd felt so alone for so many years and wanted to support me in whatever I needed. He wanted to be a different partner and a different dad, and he was delivering on that. It's hard to explain it exactly, but he broke open in a way and totally changed the way he related to *everyone*, not just me. It wasn't exactly overnight, but it was happening, and I could recognize the change—everyone we knew could see it. For a long time, Birdie had also talked to me like I was an idiot, and I figured that was just what girls did with their moms. It was certainly how I talked to my mom growing up. But once Marc changed, so did she. I sobbed in therapy that I had allowed it for so long: of course my daughter treated me the way her dad treated me. I'd just never made the connection.

We were starting to mend, all of us.

That spring, my mom and dad were celebrating their fiftieth wedding anniversary. *Fifty years.* As a treat for all of us, they wanted to take me and my sister and our families on a DISNEY CRUISE. Marc and I looked at each other skeptically: "A 'treat'?"

We were being such jerks about it, so snobby. Like, *HOW COULD A DISNEY CRUISE POSSIBLY BE ANY FUN FOR US?* Obviously the kids were going to love it, but Marc and I were resigned to being miserable for a week in the Caribbean. Our idea of a vacation wasn't being stuck *on a boat* with a bunch of strangers and my family, eating cruise food and trying to avoid norovirus! But a week or so before we were to leave, I had an epiphany. We were so lucky. People would do anything to go on a trip like this with their families. Why couldn't we just be grateful? Maybe we could go and be open to having a really great time. All of us. I thought of it like a character I was going to play. I went though my closet and built the perfect Disney cruise wardrobe for myself, making sure each of my outfits would work with my Minnie Mouse ears headband, which I would wear the entire cruise. I also decided I would try to deal with my family in a different way so that it wouldn't be so hard on me. Marc was really supportive in helping me navigate the dynamics, which made a big difference.

And then the craziest thing happened. We had *the best time*. To our surprise, Marc and I maybe had more fun than anyone else on the ship. We went to all the events and shows and hit the spa every day. Birdie was thrilled at all the freedom she had and made friends with a little girl from Florida, and Cricket had Iliana and her cousin to play with, so she was having the time of her life too. Marc and I made friends with some of the performers on the ship, plus our favorite bartender, who made me about a thousand skinny margaritas. I Instagram-storied the entire thing with the hashtag #ipaidforthis, because I didn't want people to think I was doing an #AD for @disney. The truth is, they should have fucking paid me. Or at least reimbursed me for my THREE-THOUSAND-DOLLAR INTERNET CHARGE. When I realized how much money I had spent on the high-seas internet, Marc and I dissolved in a fit of giggles. It was *so* much money! But also, weirdly worth it? And *so me* to not know I was spending so much money. We reasoned that since the trip was free thanks to my parents, it was okay. Basically, I just spent three grand documenting a super-fun vacation.

While I was on the boat, I found out that *The Sackett Sisters* probably wasn't getting picked up. I was devastated. It had felt like a sure thing, so sure I had already lived the next year of my life in my head. What was I supposed to do now? I'd started making money from branded deals on my Instagram, or from doing one-off "press days" for brands, so that wasn't the issue. It was the fact that I had been doing this job (*acting*) professionally for twenty years and the rejection has *never gotten easier* for me. I don't know why I kept expecting it to, or kept hoping it would. But I did. I kept thinking maybe one day, I would wake up and it wouldn't break my fucking heart when I wasn't cast in *Bridesmaids*. One day, I wouldn't even flinch when I was asked to lose weight. One day, I wouldn't cry for a week straight when my pilot didn't get picked up. One day. One day. One day.

I love acting. I love it more than I can articulate. I actually just started to tear up writing those words. It's impossible to overstate what being an actor has meant to me. How it's saved me again and again. A favorite question in interviews has often been, "If you weren't an actor, what would you do?" And I always draw a blank. Nothing. There's nothing else I want to do. Nothing else I can do as well. Nothing else I should be doing. This is it. This is what I do. It's who I am, right? But when *The Sackett Sisters* didn't get picked up, I knew somehow that I was done. Done auditioning. Done trying to convince people they should give me a shot, give me the part, put me on TV, make me the star. Done. DONE.

(Probably.)

Not long after that, my manager got a call from *The New Yorker*. It turned out they wanted to profile me about my Instagram stories. *THE NEW YORKER*. I sat down with the reporter, Marisa Meltzer, over lunch while we were in New York shooting Marc and Abby's movie. I have to admit, I was a little confused. I asked her why she wanted to talk to me. I was worried she was trolling me. But she promised she wasn't. She explained that she found my stories infinitely watchable and said that every social media platform has an early adopter who defines what it is and how it should be done.

I stared at her. "And you think that's me??"

She told me the article would be out in a few months and I thanked her, but secretly I was terrified of it. I liked Marisa a lot; she seemed like someone I would be friends with IRL. But I couldn't help worrying the article would somehow be mean or dismissive or worse, make me sound dumb. I still didn't really understand what everyone else was seeing and responding to. But as the summer wore on, I began to notice people's reactions to me in public. I couldn't *not*. It was getting overwhelming.

"Oh my God, I LOVE YOU!"

"BUSY!!! HIIIIIIIII!"

"Oh my God, I'm going to *die*. My best friend and I call ourselves *Busy and Michelle*!!! Can I PLEASE take a picture with you?!"

"Girl! You are KILLING it. Seriously. Just everything is GOALS."

Apparently, I was killing it by just being me . . . only online.

Over the summer, I'd gotten an email from Eric Gurian, who works with Tina Fey. He explained that he and Tina and Robert Carlock had been talking, and they were all thinking we should find something else to work on together, maybe even to develop for me. I was flattered, of course, but when I met with Eric back in L.A., I told him the truth. I didn't know what the fuck I wanted to do, but developing a show sounded potentially painful. Even under the auspices of Tina Fey and Robert Carlock. I'd just been burned too many times at this point. He understood, and as I left the meeting, he said we should keep in touch. "At the very least," he said, "it seems insane that you're giving away all this great content for free."

The article came out and it was so nice. I read it twice in order to make sure I wasn't missing some hidden snark. I was in disbelief. I didn't sound stupid at all. In fact, I sounded pretty smart. Me! In *THE NEW YORKER*!

The following weekend, my manager Julie was having a big birthday party in Palm Springs at the Merv Griffin estate. Marc and I went with the girls and stayed at La Quinta. I love being in the desert because it reminds me of growing up in Scottsdale, but without having to actually be back in Scottsdale. I especially love when the sun sets, turning the mountains purple and the sky pink. The party was super fun, with plenty of wine, and then after dinner and speeches, as everyone else started dancing, Marc and I walked over to sit at the edge of the pool. I got a little stoned as I looked up at the endless desert sky and stars. We sat in silence for a few minutes, just enjoying being together in all that stillness.

Suddenly it hit me.

"Marc," I said, turning to him. "I know what I'm supposed to do."

He looked at me, confused. "What? For what? Right now??"

"No! For my career! My life! I'm supposed to be a late-night talk-show host! I'm supposed to be the first woman host of *The Tonight Show*."

He laughed. "I think Jimmy Fallon probably has something to say about that."

"NO!" I said, shaking my head. "Not like *tomorrow*. But it's mine. I'm going to do it. I need a late-night show. This is what I'm supposed to do, Marc. I'm telling you. The ghost of Merv Griffin is sending me a sign."

He put his arm around me and kissed me sweetly on the forehead. "Okay, Buddy. If that's what you want to do, I'm sure you can do it."

Of course I can. I'm Busy Philipps. Have we met? I say I'm going to do something, and then I go, and I fucking do it. I wanted to go for a walk around the block when I was two. And I went. I wanted to get out of Arizona. And I did. I wanted to be in TV shows and movies. And I was. I wanted this life. And I got it. And now I wanted a late-night talk show. And here we are. Here I am.

I've tried in this book, but I still don't know exactly how to explain how all this has happened for me. My career. This life. Except to say that I willed it to be so. There are so many times when it could have gone in a different direction. There are more than a few sliding doors in my past. And who's to say what could've been better or worse, what might or might not have been?

All I know for sure is . . .

THIS IS WHO I AM NOW.

ACKNOWLEDGMENTS

I would like to thank all of my friends, both past and present, real-life and internet. My editor, Lauren Spiegel, for knowing instinctually that I had a book in me and not making me try to prove it. My longtime badass agent, Lorrie Bartlett. My new literary agent, Kristyn Keene. Julie Darmody, for knowing I was more than just an actress for hire. Steven Levy, Mark Schulman, and Lorraine Berglund, all of whom have managed me at one time or another (as much as I can be managed). Jennifer E. Smith for her literary guidance. Geoff McFetridge and Autumn de Wilde for elevating my book with their art. Molly Kloss for her design expertise. Coffee Commissary, Go Get Em Tiger, Andante, and Le Pain Quotidien in Los Angeles, California, and Black Tap and Collective Coffee Co in Charleston, South Carolina, for providing good light and strong coffee. My iPhone and earbuds and all the music I listened to. Iliana Tojin for her unwavering love of my family, which allows me to be able to work. Everyone in my family for understanding, even though it's hard. My daughters for sharing me. Marc, for loving me so completely and wholly—good and bad, better and worse, rich and poor, crazy and sane, chubby and thin, panicked and strong, drunk and sober, in love and out and back again, and for showing the fuck up when he needed to. And Oprah.

ABOUT THE AUTHOR

Busy Philipps is an actress best known for roles in cult TV classics like *Freaks and Geeks*, *Dawson's Creek*, *Cougar Town*, *ER*, and, most recently, HBO's *Vice Principals*. She has appeared in fan-favorite films such as *Made of Honor*, *I Don't Know How She Does It*, *He's Just Not That Into You*, *White Chicks*, and *The Gift*. She also was one of the writers of the hit film *Blades of Glory*. Busy lives in Los Angeles with her husband and their two daughters.